INDEX TO ONE ACT PLAYS

FOURTH SUPPLEMENT

1948 — 1957

AN INDEX TO

ONE-ACT PLAYS

for Stage, Radio, and Television

FOURTH SUPPLEMENT 1948-1957

By

HANNAH LOGASA

AUTHOR - BOOK SELECTION HANDBOOK

BOSTON

F. W. FAXON COMPANY, INC.

1 9 5 8

TABLE OF CONTENTS

PREFACE

Over two thousand plays are included in this supplement, in addition to the great number of duplicates that appear in more than one volume.

The number of one-act play collections available was disappointing. It would seem as though that medium of literary expression does not attract the number of writers it formerly did. However, we are fortunate that some of the earlier classic writers in the field have been reprinted in collections with a later copyright date, and are included in this supplement.

In the past, many one-act plays were written by outstanding authors as well as good craftsmen. The form was right for the unities of time, place and mood. The very shortness of the material as it treats a single incident or event lent itself to that unity. Such plays as "The Riders to the Sea", and many others provided a rich emotional experience.

Not many of the very recent plays observe the unities. They are influenced by television and the movie. Scenes are shifted from one place to another with rapidity, with little dialogue in each. This scene shifting takes away from the impression as a whole.

As always, there is a preponderence of plays for children. These are mostly on the subjects of Christmas, fairies, holidays, and the great characters in American history. Recently more plays have been written for the junior level. The subjects treated are mostly those also written for children with the addition of a few concerned with the special interests of the teen-agers. For both children and young people there are now a great number of plays that can be performed without royalty.

Scenes from well-known three-act plays have been made into one-act plays. The selection of a scene may not answer the criteria of a one-act play, but since they do so in form and content, they were included.

There are also a number of adaptations of novels. Scenes have been made into one-act plays. In this, it is much like what happened to the three-act plays. Since outstanding books were used, they enrich the field, and add variety to it.

Foreign writers are represented in this supplement. Here also, there are fewer one-act plays than formerly. The question may be asked whether the seeming lack of interest is not a general trend.

Play Magazine has contributed a great number of plays to this supplement. These are for children, and young people. Some of them have appeared before in collections, or as separates.

Both for radio, and television, there is a dearth of one-act plays that can be identified as such. This is especially true of television where one might expect to find a wealth of material in a relatively new field. However, this is not the case. Such plays as are available have been influenced by the screen technique, and are, in form not one-act plays. No matter how broad the basis for selection might be — few could be included.

A survey of the field of the one-act play would indicate that it is not as prolific as formerly. Few collections were published then in a comparable period.

I wish to thank the Library of Congress, and the Public Libraries in various cities for the opportunity of examining their drama collection, and for providing the facilities for me to analyze the material I found suitable for this purpose.

August 1, 1957.   Hannah Logasa.

HOW TO USE THIS INDEX

The Key is the bibliographical identification of a play. Key letters refer to the book in which the play may be found; if a pamphlet separate, to the publisher responsible for its publication; to the magazine in which the play appeared.

The Title Index contains full information about each individual play, whether it is a radio, or television play; author; number and kind of characters; setting or background, — suitability for elementary, or high school pupils — followed by the key letters which show where the play is to be found.

Refer to the title index from the author, subject, and collections sections.

ABBREVIATIONS

Adapt.	Adaptor, adaptation
Ann.	Announcer
b.	Boy character
c.	Suitable for children
Char.	Characters
com.	Comedy
Comp.	Compiler
ed.	Edited
ext.	Extras
g.	Girl character
Int.	Interior
J.	Juvenile
m.	Men characters
Nar.	Narrator
n.d.	No date
n-r.	Non royalty
r.	Radio
rm.	Room
Sc.	Scene
t.	Television
V.	Voices
w.	Women characters

AN INDEX TO ONE-ACT PLAYS

KEY

A

ARL	Arlett, Vera I. and others. Mixed bill. Seven varied one-act plays. Lond. Muller, 1948.
ARM	t Armer, A. & Grauman, W. E. Twenty tested television playlets. N. Y. French, 1955.

B

BAK	Baker, Walter H. Co., Bost. Separate pamphlet plays.
BAL	Baldwin, Martin T. George Washington and other one-act plays. N. Y. Exposition, 1952.
BAN	Banner Pub. Co., San Francisco. Separate pamphlet plays.
BANN	Bannister, Winifred. comp. North Light. Ten one-act plays from the North. Glasgow, Scotland, 1947.
BAR	Barrows, Marjorie. Quintessense of beauty and romance. Chic. Spencer, 1945.
BE	Bentley, Eric. ed. From the modern repertoire. Ser 1. Bloomington, Uni. of Indiana, 1949.
BF	Bentley, Eric. ed. From the modern repertoire. Ser. 2. Bloomington, Uni. of Indiana, 1952.
BRE	Brewton, J. E. and others. English and Continental literature. Chic. Laidlaw, 1950.
BREW	Brewton, J. E. and others. Excursions in fact & fancy. Book 1. Chic. Laidlaw, 1949.
BRI	Bridie, James. Tedious and brief. Lond. Constable, 1944.
BRIN	Brings, L. M. ed. Golden book of church plays. Minneapolis, Denison, 1955.
BRIO	Brings, L. M. ed. Modern treasury of Christmas plays. Minneapolis, Denison, 1955.
BRU	Bufano, Reno. Book of puppetry. N. Y. Macmillan, 1950.
BU	Burack, A. S. ed. Christmas plays for young people. Bost. Plays, 1950.
BUF	Burack, A. S. ed. One-hundred plays for children. An anthology of non-royalty one-act plays. Bost. Plays, 1949.
BUR	Burger, Isabel B. Creative play acting. Learning through drama. N. Y. Barnes, 1950.
BUS	Bussell, Jan. ed. Plays for puppets. Lond. Faber 1951.

C

CAR	Carlson, Bernice W. Act it out. Nashville, Abingdon, 1956.
CARP	Carpenter, Frank. Six animal plays. Lond. Methuen, 1954.

CARV   Carver, Charles. ed. New one-act plays. Waco, Texas, Baylor Uni. 1948.

CER   Cerf, B. A. & Cartmell, V. H. ed. Thirty famous one-act plays. N. Y. Modern Library, 1949.

CHA   Chamberlain, R. W. ed. Beacon lights of literature. Bk. 7. Syracuse, N. Y. Iroquois, 1949.

CHAM   Chamberlain, R. W. ed. Tales and trails. Bk. 8. Syracuse, N. Y. Iroquois, 1949.

CHAO   Chamberlain, R. W. ed. True and otherwise. Syracuse, N. Y. Iroquois, 1949.

CLA   Clark, Jean. Jolly Junior Assembly plays. Chic. Denison, 1947.

COL   Collins, Freda. Put on the armour of light. Lond. National Soc. S.P.C.K., 1955.

COO   Cook, Luella B. & others. Adventures in appreciation. 3rd. ed. N. Y. Harcourt, 1947.

COOK   Cook, Luella B. & others. Adventures in appreciation. Mercury ed. N. Y. Harcourt, 1952.

COW   r Cowgill, Rome. Fundamentals of writing for radio. N. Y. Rinehart, 1949.

CRO   Cross, E. A. ed. Literature-Heritage of British literature. Rev. ed. N. Y. Macmillan, 1954.

CROP   Cross, T. P. & others. American writers. Rev. ed. Bost. Ginn, 1946.

CROS   Cross, T. P. & others. English writers. Rev. ed. Bost. Ginn, 1951.

CUN   Cunningham, G. F. Unjust steward and other plays. Edinburgh. Oliver & Boyd, 1951.

D

DAV   Davis, E. C. ed. Eight popular plays for amateurs in prompt book style. N. Y. Greenberg, 1948.

DEN   Denison, T. S. Co. Minneapolis. Separate pamphlet plays.

DIA   Dias, E. J. Melodramas and farces for young actors. Bost. Plays, 1956.

DUB   DU Bois, Graham. Plays for great occasions. Collection of royality-free one-act holiday plays. Bost. Plays, 1951.

DUN   Duncan, Marion. ed. & trans. Harvest festival dramas of Tibet. Hong Kong, China. Orient Pub. Co. 1955.

E

EI   Eisenberg, Helen & Eisenberg, Larry. Skits and stunts. N. Y. Association Press, 1953.

EM   Emurian, E. K. More plays and pageants for many occasions. Bost. Wilde, 1954.

EMU   Emurian, E. K. Plays and pageants for many occasions. Bost. Wilde, 1953.

F

FA   Fagan, J. B. & others. Modern one-act plays. N. Y. Penguin books. 1942.

FI	Fisher, Aileen. Health and safety plays and programs. Bost. Plays, 1953.
FIS	Fisher, Aileen & Rabe, O. United Nations plays and programs. Bost. Plays, 1954.
FIV	r ——— Five radio plays. Lond. V. X. Mundi. 1948.
FLE	Fletcher, Lucile. Sorry, wrong number. N. Y. Dramatic Play Service, 1952.
FO	t Foote, Horton. Philco Television Playhouse. N. Y. Dramatist Play Service, (date?)
FR	French, Samuel, Pub. N. Y. Separate pamphlet plays.

G

GAS	Gassner, John. ed. Twenty-five best plays of the modern American theatre. Early series. N. Y. Crown, 1949.
GOL	Goldschmidt, Walter. Ways of mankind. Bost. Beacon Press, 1954.
GR	Griffith, F. J. & Mersand, J. ed. Modern one-act plays. N. Y. Harcourt, 1950.
GRO	Gross, Edwin & Gross, Nathalie. Teen theatre. N. Y. McGraw,, 1953.

H

HA	r Hackett, Walter. Radio plays for young people. Fifteen great stories adapted for royalty-free performance. Bost. Plays, 1950.
HAC	r Hackett, Walter. Radio plays from history and literature. Bost. Baker, 1952.
HAL	Halpin, Rev. L. F. & others. Adventures in English. Cardinal Newman ed. N. Y. Harcourt, 1954.
HAM	Hamilton, Hamish. Anthology of 21 years of publishing. Lond. Hamish Hamilton, 1952.
HAN	Haney, Germaine. Showers for all occasions. Minneapolis, Denison, 1954.
HAR	Hark, Mildred & McQueen, Noel. Junior plays for all occasions. A collection of royalty-free one-act plays for children. Bost. Plays, 1955.
HAS	Hark, Mildred & McQueen, Noel. Modern comedies for young players. A collection of non-royalty one-act plays. Bost. Plays, 1951.
HAT	Hark, Mildred & McQueen, Noel. Twenty-five plays for holidays. A collection of non-royalty one-act plays. Bost. Plays, 1952.
HAU	r Hatton, C. Radio plays and how to write them. Southend-on-Sea Essex, England, 1948.
HE	t Heath, Eric. Writing for television. Los Angeles, Research Pub. 1950.
HO	Howard, Vernon L. Short plays for all boy casts. Thirty royalty free comedies and skits. Bost. Plays, 1954.
HU	Huber, Louis J. Easy arena plays. Minneapolis, Northwestern, 1951.
HUB	t Huber, Louis J. Easy television plays. Minneapolis, Northwestern, 1952.

I

IN   Inglis, R. B. & others. Adventures in English literature. N. Y. Harcourt, 1949.

J

JA   James, Thelma G. & others. World neighbors. N. Y. Harper, 1950.

JOH   Johnson, Crane. Past sixty. San Francisco. International Theatre Press, 1953.

JON   Jones, E. M. ed. Canadian school plays. ser. 1. Toronto, Ryerson, 1948.

K

KA   Kamerman, Sylvia E. ed. Blue-ribbon plays for girls. A collection of royalty free . . . all girls casts. Bost. Plays, 1955.

KAM   Kamerman, Sylvia E. Little plays for little players. Fifty non-royalty plays for children. Bost. Plays, 1952.

KAT   t Kaufman, W. I. ed. Best television plays. vol. 3. N. Y. W. I. Kaufman, 1954.

KAV   t Kaufman, W. I. ed. Best television plays of the year. N. Y. Merlin, 1950.

KE   Keating, E. H. Dramas for boys. Lond. French, n.d.

KEL   Kelley, Mary ed. Group play-making. Lond. Harrap, 1948.

KI   r Kissen, Fan. Bag of fire and other tales. Bost. Houghton, 1949.

KIC   r Kissen, Fan. Crowded house and other tales. Bost. Houghton, 1950.

KIS   r Kissen, Fan. Straw ox and other tales. Bost. Houghton, 1948.

KN   Knickerbocher, E. Van B. Short plays. Rev. N. Y. Holt, 1949.

KO   Koppe, Richard & others. comp. Treasury of college humor. N. Y. Penn, 1950.

L

LA   Laurie, Joe Jr. Vaudeville from honky-tonks to the Palace. N. Y. 1953.

LE   Lehmann, Adolph. Vignettes. N. Y. Pageant Press, 1952.

M

MAC   McCaslins Nellie. More legends in action. Ten plays of ten lands. Evansville, Ill. Row Peterson, 1950.

MAG   McGraw, Charles. Acting is believing. N. Y. Rinehart, 1955.

MAK   r Mackey, D. R. Drama on the air. N. Y. Prentice-Hall, 1951.

MAL   Malone, Dumas, ed. Jeffersonian heritage. Bost. Beacon Press, 1953.

MAR   March, Olave. Actor's theatre plays. Lond. Favil Press, 1945.

MARC   March, Olave, comp. London actor's theatre. vol. 1. Lond. Favil, 1945.

MARO   Marriott, J. W. comp. Best one-act plays of 1942-3. Lond. Harrap. 1944.

MARP   Marriott, J. W. comp. Best one-act plays of 1944-5. Lond. Harrap, 1946.

MARQ   Marriott, J. W. comp. Best one-act plays of 1948-9. Lond. Harrap, 1950.

MARS   Marsh, W. A. Plays and patterns for puppets. Lond. Harrap, 1955.

MAU   Maughan, W. S. Encore. Original stories and screen plays. N. Y. Doubleday, 1952.

MAUG   Maughfling, Mabel. Five mime plays. Original ballad mimes. Lond. French, 1948.

MAUR   r Maurois, Andre. Art of being happily married. Tr. fr. the French. N. Y. Harper, 1953.

MAYH   Mayorga, Margaret. ed. Best one-act plays. 1950-1. N. Y. Dodd, 1949.

MAYJ   Mayorga, Margaret. ed. Best one-act plays. 1949-50. N. Y. Dodd, 1950.

MAYK   Mayorga, Margaret. Best one-act plays. 1950-1. N. Y. Dodd, 1951.

MAYL   Mayorga, Margaret. ed. Best one-act plays. 1951-2. N. Y. Dodd, 1952.

MAYN   Mayorga, Margaret. ed. Best short plays of 1952-3. N. Y. Dodd, 1953.

MAYO   Mayorga, Margaret. ed. Best short plays of 1953-4. N. Y. Dodd, 1954.

MAYP   Mayorga, Margaret. ed. Best short plays of 1954-5. N. Y. Dodd. 1955.

MAYR   Mayorga, Margaret. ed. Best short plays 1955-6. Bost. Beacon Press, 1956.

ME   Mercedes, Sister Anna & others. Adventures in reading. N. Y. Harcourt, 1954.

MIC   rt Mickel, Joseph. Radio and television drama. N. Y. Exposition, 1953.

MIL   Miles, D. H. & Keck, C. M. Literature and life. Bk. 1. Chic. Scott Foresman, 1947.

MILL   Miller, Madge. Minature plays. vol. 1. Cloverlot Anchorage, Ky. Children's Theatre Press, 1954.

MIM   Miller, Helen L. Holiday plays for teen-agers. Collection of one-act royalty free plays. Bost. Plays, 1952.

MIN   Miller, Helen L. Plays for living and learning. Bost. Plays, 1955.

MIO   Miller, Helen L. Prize plays for teen-agers. Bost. Plays, 1956.

MIR   Millett, F. B. ed. Reading drama. N. Y. Harper, 1950.

MO   Molnar, Ferenc. Romantic comedies. N. Y. Crown, 1952.

MOL   Molnar, Ferenc. Stories for two. N. Y. Horizon Press, 1950.

MU   Murray, John. Mystery plays for young people. Royalty free. Bost. Plays, 1956.

N

NE   r Nehr, Jack & Pratt, Dallas. Hi, Neighbor!. Ten radio plays on mental health. Phil. Nat'l. Mental Health Found. 1950.

NEF   Nelson's theatre craft plays. Bk. 3. Plays for Women. Lond. Nelson, 1940.

NEG   Nelson's theatre craft plays. ser. 4. Plays for women. Lond. Nelson, 1941.

NEV   Neville, M. A. & Payne, L. W. Jr. comp. Broadening horizons. Chic. Rand McNally, 1949.

NEVI   Neville, M. A. & Payne, L. W. Jr. comp. Exploring new fields. Chic. Rand McNally, 1949.

NEW   New World Writing. Fourth Mentor selection. N. Y. New American Library, 1953.

NEWA   New World Writing. Sixth Mentor selection. N. Y. New American Library, 1954.

NEWB   New World Writing. Eighth Mentor selection. N. Y. New American Library, 1955.

NY   Nygaard, N. E. Bible comes alive. Biblical sermons in costume. Bost. Baker, 1947.

O

OF   Olfson, Lewy. adapt. Radio plays of famous stories. Bost. Plays, 1956.

ON   ———— One-act plays for stage and study. 10th. ser. N. Y. French, 1949.

P

PA   Paradis, Marjory B. One act plays for all-girl casts. Collection of royalty-free plays. Bost. Plays, 1952.

PARK   t Parker's television plays. Minneapolis, Northwestern Press, 1954.

PH   r Phillips, D. C. & others. Introduction to radio and television. N. Y. Ronald Press, 1954.

PL   Play Club. 551 Fifth Ave., N. Y. Separates.

PLA   Plays. Drama magazine for young people. vol. 7., 1948.

PLB   Plays. Drama magazine for young people. vol. 8., 1949.

PLC   Plays. Drama magazine for young people. vol. 9., 1950.

PLD   Plays. Drama magazine for young people. vol. 10., 1951.

PLE   Plays. Drama magazine for young people. vol. 11., 1952.

PLF   Plays. Drama magazine for young people. vol. 12., 1953.

PLG   Plays. Drama magazine for young people. vol. 13., 1954. (incomplete).

PLH   Plays. Drama magazine for young people. vol. 14., 1955. (incomplete).

PLJ   Plays. Drama magazine for young people. vol. 15., 1956. (incomplete).

PLK   Plays. Drama magazine for young people. vol. 16., 1957. (incomplete).

PLU   Plumb, Beatrice & others. Wedding anniversary. Minneapolis, Denison, 1951.

POL   r Pollock, S. & Grantham, W. Men of God. Lond. Gollancz, 1947.

POT   Potell, Herbert & others. Adventures for today. N. Y. Harcourt, 1955.

PR   Preston, Effa E. Fun with stunts. Minneapolis, Denison, 1956.

R

RE   Rees, Leslie C. ed. Modern short plays. Sydney, Australia, Angus & Robertson, 1951.

RI   Richards, Brother Besilian. & others. Adventures in appreciation. N. Y. Harcourt, 1954.

RIC   Richmond, S. S. Career plays for young people. Non-royalty vocational guidance plays. Bost. Plays, 1949.

RID   Ridge, Antonia. Puppet plays for children. Lond. Faber, 1953.

RO   t Roberts, E. B. Television writing and selling. Bost. Writer, 1954.

ROS   Rose, Kenneth. Georgiana. Seven portraits. Lon. Miller, 1947.

ROW   Row-Peterson & Co. 1911 Ridge Ave., Evanston, Ill. Separate plays.

RU   Russia-Today, Soc. The theatre is our weapon. Lond. Russia-Today Soc. 150 Southhampton, n.d.

S

SC   Scarborough, Rehn. V for victory. Bost. Baker, 1942.

SCH   Schofield, J. A. Jr. & Joudry, R. C. Easter playlets for children and young people. Bost., Wilde, 1955.

SE   t Sebby, S. R. Easter fantasia. Bost. Christopher, 1953.

SEK   Selden, Samuel. ed. First steps in acting. N. Y. Appleton, 1947. (scenes)

SEL   Selden, Samuel. ed. Internationl folk plays. Chapel Hill. Uni- of North Carolina, 1949.

SET   t Settel, Irving. ed. Top TV shows of the year. 1954-5. N. Y. Hastings, 1955.

SH   Shattuck, Marquis E. Gateway to adventure. Bk. 4. Syracuse, N. Y. Iroquois, 1948.

SI   ———— Six one-act plays by South African authors. Pretoria, So. Africa. Van Schack, 1949.

SK   r Skornia, H. J. & others. Creative broadcasting. N. Y. Prentice, 1950.

SP   Sper, Felix. ed. Modern short plays. N. Y. Globe, 1952.

SW   Switz, T. MacL. & Johnston, R. A. Great Christian plays. Greenwich, Conn., Seabury, 1956. (With music score).

T

TE   Teasdale, Verree. Aren't people funny? N. Y. French, 1947.

TH   r Thomas, Dylan. Under milkwood. N. Y. New Directions, 1954.

TO   t Tooley, Howard. Television workshop. Minneapolis, Northwestern, 1953.

W

WA   Wall, L. V. ed. Complete puppet book. N. Y. Crowell, 1951.

WE   r Weaver, Luther. Technique of radio writing. N. Y. Prentice, 1948.

WEI   Weiss, M. J. Guidance through drama. N. Y. Whiteside, 1954.

WF   t Weiss, Margaret R. The TV writer's guide. N. Y. Pellegrini, 1952.

WH   r White, M. R. ed. Children's program for radio broadcast. Minneapolis, Northwestern Press, 1948.

WI   Williams, H. V. Puppets go to school. Chic., Winston, 1955.

WIN   Winn, Georgia G. & others. Action! Beacon lights of literature. Syracuse, N. Y. Iroquis, 1952.

WO   Woolsey, Janette & Sechrist, E. H. It's time to give a play. Phil. Macrae, 1955.

WOO   Woolsey, Janette & Sechrist, E. H. New plays for Red Letter Days. Phil. Macrae, 1953.

Y

YE   Yeats, W. B. Collected plays. London. Macmillan, 1952.

YEA   Yeats, W. B. Collected plays. New ed. N. Y. Macmillan, 1953.

TITLE INDEX

A

J **A B C for safety.** Hark, M. 16 char. Sc. Courtroom. HAR

C **A B C for safety.** Pendleton, E. 10 b. 6g. Sc. Stage. PLD

T **Abbie, the bug boy.** Conkle, E. P. 3m. 2w. Sc. Int. HAYN

C **Abe Lincoln — Champ.** Carlson, B. W. Puppet. 5b. Sc. General Store. CAR

   Abe Lincoln goes to school. Very, A. 5b. 4g. Sc. Cabin. PLK

   Abner Crane from Hayseed Lane. Dias, E. J. 4m. 5w. Sc. Farm. DIA

C **Abe's winkin' eye.** Fisher, A. 4b. 4g. Sc. Cabin. PLE

   Abu Hassan pays his debts. Hadlington, R. 10w. Sc. Baghdad. Farce. NEG

J **Accident of birth.** Fisher, A. 13 char. Sc. Stage. FIS

   According to plan. Parsons, G. 4m. Sc. Barn. RU

   Accounts settled. Morebath Drama Group. 1m. 7w. Market. KEL

   The actor. Weiss, M. J. 2m. 2w. 1c. Sc. Int. WEI

   Actor from Vienne. Molnar, F. 4m. 1 w. Sc. Hunting Lodge. MO

   Actress and the Count. Schnitzler, A. 1m. 1w. Sc. Int. BE

C **Adalmina's pearl.** Asbrand, K. 1b. 3g. Sc. Rm. Fairy. PLA

   Admiral. Molnar, F 2.m. Sc. Row boat. MOL

J **Admiral's daughter.** Paradis, M. B. 6g. Sc. Dormitory, PA PLE

   Adventure after midnight. Huber, L. J. 2m. 2w. Sc. Street. HU

   Adventures of Mr. Bean. Meredith, B. 4m. 1w. Sc. Studio. GR

   Adventures of Tom Sawyer. Mark Twain. 1w. 5b. Sc. Int. & outdoors. NEV PLH

J **Advice Doctor.** Macdonald, D. M. 3b. 3g. Sc. Int. DEN

J **Advice to the lovelorn.** Hark, M. 3b. 2g. Sc. Int. HAS

R **After ten years.** Maurois, A. 2m. 1w. Sc. Int. MAUR

   After the air raid. Thomas, H. Reader, 1m. 1w. Sc. Stage. SC

J **After the day's work.** Preston, E. E. 1m. 1w. Sc. Int. PR

   After the fog lifts. Hackett, W. 5m. 3w. Sc. Int. BAK

J **Afternoon of Oct. Twentieth.** Preston, E. E. 12m. 3w. Sc. Courtroom, Farce. PR

   Afterpiece. ———. 5m. group. Sc. Courtroom. LA

   Aged but not mellowed. Lehmann, A. 2m. 1w. Sc. Int. LE

C R **Aladdin & the wonderful lamp.** White, M. R. Nar. 4b. 1g. Fairy. WH

J **Aladdin, Inc.** Hark, M. 3b. 2g. Sc. Int. HAS

J **Aladdin steps out.** Hark, M. 10b. 4g. Sc. Int. PLK

J **Albright acres.** Richmond, S. S. 4b. 1g. Sc. Office. PLB

   Alfred, dear. Molnar, F. 2w. Sc. Theatre. com. MOL

J **Alice in Puzzleland.** Fisher, A. 11 char. Sc. Woods. FIS

   All aboard. Huber, L. J. 2m. 1w. Sc. R.R. Station. PLU

C **All aboard the "Bookworm Belle."** Ridge, A. 4b. 1g. Sc. Curtains. RLD

    As you like it. Shakespeare. Im. 1w. Sc. Forest. com. SEK

C **Ass & the lap dog.** Bennett, R. 6b. Sc. garden. PLB

R **Astonishing Mrs. O'Shaughnessy.** Johnson, C. 3m. 1w. Sc. Museum. JOH

J **At the cleaners.** Richmond, S. S. 4b. 3g. Sc. counter in store. PLA RIC

    At the Hawk's well. Yeats, W. B. 3m. group of musicians. Sc. Wall. YE YEA

J **Athletes all.** Howard, V. L. 11b. Sc. School Gymnasium. HO

C **Attic treasure.** Gould, J. 4b. 1g. Sc. Attic. PLE

J **Attorney for the defense.** Du Bois, G. 3b. 4g. Sc. Int. 1776. PLA

C **Auction.** Schwartz, M. K. 5b. Sc. Backyard. PLD

J **Awful fate of a fibber.** Balm, C. M. 1b. 3g. Sc. Int. EI

    August heat. Richards, S. 4m. 5w. Sc. Outdoors. Melo. BAN MAYJ

    Aunt Fanny from Chautaugua. Ade, G. 1m. 3w. Sc. Int. ON

    Auntie & the bull. Maughfling, M. 3m. 2w. Sc. Country road. MAUG

J **Author of liberty.** Hark, M. 6b. 2g. Sc. Int. PLE

J **Ay, there's the rub.** Du Bois, G. 8b. 2g. Sc. Int. 1863. PLC

B

    Bab buys a car. Carlton, J. 5m. 4w. Sc. Int. Farce. BAK

C R **Baba Yaga.** Kissen, F. Ann. 9 char. Sc. Farm. KIC

C **Babe of Bethlehem.** Williams, H. V. 6b. 2g. Sc. Stable. WI

    Baby sitter. Macdonald, D. M. 3b. 3g. Sc. Int. DEN

    Back to Boston. Rogers, J. 2w. ext. Sc. Int. 1751. CARV

J **Background for Nancy.** Manning, S. 3b. 4g. Sc. Int. PLA

J **Backward — Jumping frog.** Howard, V. 6b. 6g. Sc. School. PLJ

C R **Bag of fire.** Kissen, F. 4b. 3g. Nar. No sc. KI

    Bailiff's wonderful coat. McCaslin, N. 6m. 5w. Ext. Sc. Rm. in Castle. MAC

J **Bake a cherry pie.** Hark, M. 4b. 3g. Sc. Int. PLF

C **Baker's three daughters.** Marsh, W. A. 2b. 3g. No sc. MARS

    Balcony scene. Elser, D. 4m. 4w. Sc. Church. ROW

R **Bands of love.** Pollock, S. 9m. 3w. No sc. POL

J **Bang goes my stocking.** Marsh, W. A. 3b. 1g. No sc. MARS

C **Banner, Boys.** Clark, J. 10b. Sc. Platform. CLA

C **Barefoot boy.** Peacock, M. 2b. 2g. Sc. Ooutdoors. PLB

    Bargain's a bargain. Johnson, L. E. 3m. 2w. Sc. Int. DEN

C **Bar-none trading post.** Miller, H. L. 7b. 6g. Sc. Trading post. MIN

    Bats in the belfrey. Denbury Drama Club. 3m. 6w. Sc. Kitchen. KEL

    Battle hymn of the Republic. Emurian, E. K. 6m. 2w. Male quartet. Sc. Camp meeting. EMU

T **Battleship Bismark.** Valency, M. 11m. ext. Sc. Sea. KAV

R **Be my ghost.** Murray, J. 5m. 5w. Sc. Int. MU PLH

N–R **Be my "Walentine."** Miller, H. J. 5b. 5g. Sc. Farmhouse. com. MIO PLA

    The beacon. Erskine, J. 2m. 2w. Sc. Holland 1573. MAR MARC

    Beams of our house. Apstein, T. 5m. 2w. Sc. Village. HAYN

c **Black Ivo.** Colson, J. G. 8b. Sc. Outdoors. PLF

Black Piet. Schenkkan, R. 7m. Sc. Top of hill. SEL

t **Black sheep.** Huber, L. J. 3m. Sc. Warden's office. HUB

t **Black star.** Armer, A. 1m. 1w. Sc. Cafe. ARM

j **Blackbird.** Howard, V. J. 5b. Sc. Office. HO

t **Blank check.** Huber, L. J. 3w. Sc. Int. HUB

c **Blue beans.** Ridge, A. 4b. 1g. Sc. Int. Puppet. RID

Blue concerto. Seiger, M. L. 2m. 1w. voice. Sc. Apartment. HAYR

j **Blue serge suit.** Howard, V. L. 6b. Clothing store. HO

c **Blue toadstool.** Bellan, M. 6 char. Sc. Grassy patch. KAM PLC

Blue willow plate. Shand, B. 4b. 2g. ext. Sc. Stage. JON

j **Bobby & the Lincoln speech.** Hark, M. 3b. 3g. Sc. Int. HAR

j **Bobby & the Lincoln speech.** Pendleton, E. 3b. eg. Sc. Int. PLH

R **Bobby soxers' rebellion.** Neher, J. Nar. 2m. 2w. No sc. NE

c **Bob's Armistice parade.** Streacher, L. 8b. ext. Sc. Playground. BUF

j **Body, body, who's got the body?** Preston, E. E. 11m. Sc. Int. Farce. PR

c **Boo-Hoo princess.** Buntain, R. J. 2b. 2g. Sc. Front of castle. PLF

J N–R **Book a day.** Hark, M. 4b. 4g. Sc. Int. HAT PLE

Book of Job. Rogers, M. 7m. Sc. Throne of God. ON

j **Book revue.** Hark, M. 33 char. Sc. Book fair. HAR PLH

j **Books to the rescue.** Hark, M. 4b. 3g. Sc. Int. PLH

Boney. Sangster, A. 11m. Sc. Rude barn in 1804. FA

J R **Bonnie Annie.** Lathers, H. Q. Ann. 3b. 1g. Song play. Sc. stage. PLA

j **Boomerang.** Miller, H. L. 2b. 3g. Sc. Int. MIM PLC PLK

The boor. Chekhov, A. 4m. 1w. Sc. Int. com. CER

c R **Boots & his brothers.** Kissen, F. Ann. 5b. No sc. KIS

j **Born to the soil.** Richmond, S. S. 5b. 1g. Sc. Farm house. RIC

Boston O'Tooles. Casey, F. M. 9m. 5w. Sc. Outdoors. com. FR

Boswell meets Johnson. Rose, K. 3m. Sc. Tavern. ROS

Border, folk. Thomas, M. 4m. 1w. Sc. Cape Colony in 1834. SI

R **Bottle imp.** Stevenson, R. L. Ann. 10m. 2w. no. sc. GR

c **Bow to the Queen.** Colson, J. G. 7b. 1g. Sc. Int. PLE

R **Boy next door.** Murray, J. 2m. 3w. Sc. Int. MU PLH

c **Boy who couldn't tell a lie.** Very, A. 6b. 2g. Sc. Int. KAM

J N–R **Boy who didn't belong.** Miller, H. L. 9b. 4g. Sc. Int. MIM PLB

c **Boys in books.** Miller, H. L. 15b. Sc. School. MIN PLG

Boys will be boys. Molnar, F. 2g. Sc. Int. com. MOL

c **Brave little Indian brave.** Holler, R. M. 6b. 2g. Sc. Stage. PLE

c **Bread & butter shop.** Miller, H. L. 12b. 10g. Sc. Shop. MIN

Brewsie & Willie. Stein, G. 6m. 2w. Sc. Int. MAYP

Bridal boquet. Spence, W. 2m. 2w. Int. com. BAK

Bride's first dinner. Teasdale, V. 1w. Sc. At the telephone. TE

Brigands of the Black forest. Bussell, J. 9m. 1w. ext. Sc. Forest. BUS

c **Bright stream.** Pyle, M. T. 4b. 5g. Sc. Stage. PLE

t **Bright world.** 2m. 1w. Sc. Bench in the park. HUB

j **Bringing up father.** Fisher, A. 3b. 3g. Sc. Int. PLJ

c **Broken doll.** Spamer, C. 12b. 4g. Sc. Stage PLA
   Brome — Abraham & Isaac. Switz, T. MacL. 4m. 1 voice. Sc. Wilderness. SW
c **Broom market day.** Molloy, L. L. 5b. 4g. Sc. Cottage. BUF PLA
J **Broomstick beauty.** Miller, H. L. 2b. 4g. Sc. Office. PLA
c **Broth of Christkindli.** Leuser, E. 5b. 2g. Sc. Cottage. BU PLC
J **Brothers.** Castro, E. 2b. Sc. Street. MAYK
   The brothers. Ratcliffe, N. 6w. Sc. Hills. NEF
   Browning version. Rattigan, T. 5m. 2w. Sc. Int. FR HAM
c **Brushes for Benjy.** Leuser, E. 9b. 2g. Sc. Parlor. PLF
R **Bubble bath.** MacGregor, J. J. Ann. 1m. 1w. Sc. Int. WE
J N-R **Bud for President.** Hark, M. 3b. 2g. Voice. Sc. Int. HAS
c **Bunnie & bonnets.** Miller, H. L. 6b. 9g. Sc. Television station. PLF
   Bunny comes to town. Du Bois, G. 1m. 2b. 2g. Sc. Int. DUB
c **Bunny of the year.** Newman, D. 8b, 2g. Sc. Garden. PLC
c **Bunny picnic.** MacLellan, E. 5 char. Sc. Forest. PLB
c **Bunny who was always late.** Spamer, C. 3b. 1g. Sc. Outdoors. PLC
c **Bunnyland brigade.** Spamer, C. 8 char. Sc. Bunnyland. KAM PLB
c **Buried treasure.** Barr, J. 7b. 3h. Sc. Woods. PLF
   Bury the dead. Shaw, I. 12m. 5w. ext. voice. Sc. Platform. CER
J **Business is business.** Richmond, S. S. 7b. 4g. Sc. Office. RIC
J **Buster picks a winner.** Richmond, S. S. 2b. 3g. Sc. Office. PLD
   But I know what I like. Sinclair, L. Any number of char. Sc. garden. GOL
   But one life to give. Du Bois, G. 4m. 3w. Sc. Tavern. DUB PLB
c **By order of the King.** Fisher, A. 8b, 1g. Sc. Throne rf. FI PLG
   By Christ alone. Smith, W. S. 12m. 3w. Sc. Hillside. BRIN

C

   Cabin by the lake. Walden, R. S. 1m. 1w. Sc. Int. automobile. com. MAYP
   Call it a day. Graham, M. S. 8m. 20w. Sc. Doctor's office. ROW
   Call me Mac. Cox, T. St. J. 4m. 2w. Sc. Int. BAK
c **Callers.** Very, A. 2b. 4g. Sc. 1 Int. PLA
c **Callie goes to camp.** Porter, E. W. 4g. Sc. Summer camp. KA PLC
   Campbell of Kilmhor. Ferguson, J. A. 5m. 1w. Sc. Cottage. RE
R **The camel and I.** Wishengrad, M. Nar. 5m. MAYJ
   Campus bride. Ashton, N. 5m. 4w. Sc. Int. BAK
   "Can die but once?" Dawson, N. 8m. 1w. Sc. Int. PARP
T **Can long endure.** Tazwell, C. 2m. Sc. Int. ON
   Candle in the window. Childs, C. 5b. 6g. Sc. Int. BRIO
J **Candy for your birthday.** Carroll, R. F. 1b. 1g. Sc. Int. FR
c **Candy canes.** Spamer, C. 4b. 1g. Sc. A wood. BU
J R **Canterville ghost.** Wilde, O. Nar. 5m. 3w. No sc. HA PLA
   Canticle of the nativity. Bechet, R. 7m. 3w. 2c. ext. Sc. Curtains ROW
J **Cape of feathers.** Ziegler, E. E. 9b. 4g. Sc. Roof garden. PLG
c **Captain Tall tells all.** Clarke, J. Any number of boys. Sc. Gym. CLA

R **Captains Courageous.** Kipkling, R. 11m. 1w. No sc. OF PLJ

c **Caractacus.** Collins, F. 6b. Sc. Stage. COL

Cardinal's learning. Williamson, H. R. 4m. 1b. 2w. Sc. Inn. MARQ

J **Career for Ralph.** Richmond, S. S. 7b. Sc. Int. RIC

J **Career girl.** Richmond, S. S. 3b. 4g. Sc. Office. PLB RIC

J **Carfare home.** Olds, H. D. 3b. 7g. Sc. Studio. PLA

Carling moth. MacLellan, R. 2m. 2w. Sc. Cottage

Carrier pigeon. Phillpotts, E. 2m. 1w. Sc. Cottage. RE

J **Casanova Jr.** Williams, G. R. 2b. 4g. Sc. Int. DEN

J **Case for books.** Hark, M. 4b. 3g. Sc. Int. PLD

R **Case for Mrs. Hudson.** Murray, J. 3m. 3w. Sc. Parlor. MU PLE

R **Case for two detectives.** Murray, J. 6m. 6w. Sc. Home. MU PLJ

J **Case for Mr. X.** Richmond, S. S. 3b. 3g. Sc. Hospital. PLC

c **Case of the balky bike.** Miller, H. L. 11b. 4g. Sc. Police station. MIN

J N–R **Case of the easter bonnet.** Miller, H. L. 5b. 2g. Sc. Int. MIN PLA

Case of the missing pearls. Dias, E. J. 6m. 4w. Sc. Int. melo. DIA PLK

R **Case of the missing poet.** Murray, J. 5m. 3w. Sc. Hotel. MU PLF

Case of the sea-lion flippers. Sinclair, L. 6m. 1w. Sc. Outdoors. GOL

J N–R **Case of the silent caroler.** Miller, H. L. 4b. 4g. ext. Sc. Int. MIM PLE

Cat & the Kingdom. Bussell, J. 3m. 1w. cat. Sc. Curtains. BUS

Cat & the moon. Yeats, W. B. 2m. Sc. In Ireland. YE YEA

c **Cat for Halloween.** MacLellan, E. 8 char. ext. Sc. Cottage. PLF

R **Catastrophy.** Maurois, A. 2m. 3w. Sc. Bedroom. MAUR

c **Catch as catch can.** Fisher, A. 1m. 6b. 6g. Sc. Throne rm. FI

c **Cats & the cheese.** Barr, J. 3 char. Sc. Kitchen. PLB

Cathleen ni Houlihan. Yeats, W. B. 3m. 4w. ext. Sc. Cottage. MIR YE YEA

c **Caught in the Narrows.** Fisher, A. 3b. 3g. Sc. Kitchen. PLC

Cause for gratitude. Du Bois, G. 2m. 6w. Sc. Puritan home. DUB PLJ

Cause to serve. Du Bois, G. 5m. 4w. Sc. Shepherd's hut. DUB

J **Cavalcade of human rights.** Fisher, A. Nar. large number of char. Pageant. Sc. Int. FIS PLJ

Cavalry. Yeats, W. B. 3m. 3 char. 3 musicians. Sc. Ireland. YE YEA

J **Cecily entertains the enemy.** Waite, H. E. eb. 4g. Sc. Int. PLH

J **Census taker.** Preston, E. E. 1m. 1w. Sc. Int. com. PR

Certain man had two sons. Finch, R. 3m. 2w. Sc. Farm. BRIN

Change for the worse. Bridie, J. 4b. 3w. Sc. Street. BRI

J N–R **Change of heart.** Hark, M. 5b. 5g. Sc. High School. HAT PLB

The changeling. Stephens, P. J. 4m. 2w. Sc. Farmhouse. MAYN

Charge it, please. Knapp, B. 3m. 4w. Sc. Int. BAK

Charge it to George. Rogers, J. A. 10 char. Sc. Int. DEN

J **Charity begins at home.** Preston, E. E. Sc. Int. Farce. PR

J **Charlie's May basket.** Woolsey, J. 3b. 4g. Sc. Int. WOO

Child of destiny. Du Bois, G. 7m. 2w. Sc. Inn in Granada. DUB

Child of her spirit. Du Bois, G. 3m. 3w. Sc. Cabin. DUB

c **Children of Chocolate St.** Kane, E. B. 2b. 3g. Sc. Int. KAM PLD

c **Children of the Calendar.** Hartley, C. 13 char. Sc. Workshop. BUF c   **Children of the sun.** Rittenhouse, C. 23 char. Sc. Schoolroom. BUF

c   **China comes to you.** Asbrand, K. 7b. 6g. Ext. Sc. Home in China. BUF

    China-handled knife. Conkle, E. P. 7m. 2w. Sc. Int. FR

c   **Chinese Rip Van Winkle.** Chandler, A. C. 12 char. ext. Sc. Village. BUF

    Chinese romance. Wall, L. V. 3m. 1w. Sc. Garden. WA

c r   **Christmas angel.** Kissen, F. Ann. nar. 10 char. Sc. Int. KIC

c   **Christmas at the Cratchits.** Newman, D. 4b. 4g. Sc. Int. PLF

c   **Christmas cake.** Fisher, A. 2b. 1g. Sc. Kitchen. PLD

j r   **Christmas carol.** Dickens, C. Nar. 4m. 1b. ext. Sc. Int. HA PLA PLD

j r   **Christmas carol.** Hackett, W. Nar. 4b. 2g. Sc. Int. BU

c   **Christmas carol.** Hare, W. B. 10b. 7g. ext. Sc. Counting house. BRIO

c   **Christmas comes to Hamelin.** Mills, G. E. 2 char. ext. Sc. Town hall. BUF PLJ

j   **Christmas cowboy.** Miller, H. L. 4b. 4g. Sc. Hospital. PLD

c   **Christmas doll's revue.** Preston, E. 20g. Sc. Santa's stockroom. BRIO

j   **Christmas eve letter.** Hark, M. 3b. 4g. Sc. Int. PLA

j   **Christmas eve news.** Hark, M. Any number of char. Sc. Street. HAR PLD

j   **Christmas eve visitor.** Baden, R. Any number of char. Pageant. Sc. Stage. BRIO

r   **Christmas every day.** Howells, W. D. 22 char. Sc. Stage. PLF

    Christmas for Cinderella. Barbee, L. 7w. Sc. Int. BRIO

c   **Christmas house.** Waite, H. E. 4b. 6g. Sc. Int. BUF

    Christmas in her eyes. Crouch, M. 7w. Sc. Int. BRIO

j   **Christmas in the woods.** Hark, M. 4b. 3g. Sc. Forest. HAR

    Christmas lamb. McCaslin, N. Ann. 4m. 4w. Sc. Workroom. MAC

j n–r   **Christmas oboe.** Miller, H. L. 5b. 2g. Sc. Int. com. MIO

    Christmas on Main St. Draper, W. 11m. 5w. Sc. Street. FR

c   **Christmas party.** Hark, M. 12 char. Sc. Apartment store. KAM PLC

j   **Christmas promise.** Miller, H. L. 3b. 3g. Sc. Int. MIM PLF

j   **Christmas recaptured.** Hark, M. 4b. 4g. Sc. Int. PLE

c   **Christmas sampler.** Leuser, E. 6b. 4g. Sc. Kitchen. PLE

j n–r   **Christmas shopping early.** Hark, M. 3b. 3g. Sc. Int. HAT PLB

    Christmas shopping — in June. Teasdale, V. 2m. Sc. Department store. TE

c   **Christmas snowman.** Hark, M. 4b. 3g. Sc. Int. BU PLC

    Christmas star. Posgate. E. D. 4m. 5w. Sc. Curtains. BRIO

c   **Christmas story.** Ashton, L. S. 4b. 3g. Sc. Field. BRIO

    Christmas story. Nygaard, N. E. 8 char. ext. Pageant. Sc. Stage. NY

c   **Christmas train.** Howard, H. L. 10 char. ext. Sc. R.R. track. BU PLB

    Christmas tradition. Emurian, E. K. 3m. 3w. Sc. Int. EMU

c   **Christmas tree surprise.** Newman, D. 3b. 3g. Sc. Stage. PLE

    Church in the wildwood. Emurian, E. K. 8m. 3w. ext. Songs. Sc. Int. EM

c   **Cinderella.** Barr, J. 1b. 4g. ext. Sc. Kitchen. KAM PLB

c   **Cinderella.** Bufano, R. 2b. 5g. Sc. Curtains. Puppets. BRU

c   **Cinderella.** D'Arcy, A. 1b. 4g. ext. Sc. Fireplace. BUF

C R **Cinderella.** Kissen, F. Ann. 2b. 5g. Sc. Int. KI

C R **Cinderella.** White, M. R. Nar. 3b. 4g. No Sc. WH

C **Circus parade.** MacLellan, E. 9b. 4g. Sc. Street. PLE

R **Citizen.** Pollock, S. Nar. 11m. 3w. Sc. Stage. POL

C **Citizens of the garden.** Clark, J. Any number of char. Sc. Garden. CLA

J **Clean-up club.** Fisher, A. 2b. 2g. Ext. Sc. Back yard. PLK

C **Clean up, shine up.** Hark, M. ib. 1g. Sc. Outdoors. PLB

R T **Clever Manka.** Kissen, F. Nar. Ann. 3b. 1g. Sc. Farm. KIC

The climbers. Grant, A. 2m. 3w. Sc. High craggy place. MAR MARC

C **Clock says.** Marsh, W. A. 2 char. Puppet. No sc. MARS

C **Clock's secret.** MacLellan, E. 2b. 4g. Sc. Int. BUF

The clod. Beach, L. 4m. 1w. Sc. Kitchen. CER

Close shave. Brome, R. 3m. 2w. Int. DEN

The closet. Brownell, J. C. 2m. 1w. Sc. Int. DEN

T **Closing time.** Armer, A. 1m. 1w. Sc. Cafe. ARM

J T **Cloud that couldn't rain.** Brewer, F. Nar. 3b. 2g. ext. no. sc. SK

Cloud-burst. Weaver, J. C. 3m. 3w. Sc. Int. ROW

J **Coach scores.** Richmond, S. S. 8b. Sc. Office. PLA RIC

R **Coals to Newcastle.** Monroe, C. S. Ann. 6m. 1w. Sc. Int. WIN

C **Cock & the fox.** Very, A. 3b. 3g. Sc. Cottage. PLA

Colonel, you're wonderful! Teasdale, V. 1m. 2w. Sc. Int. com. TE

Color-conscious conscience. Lockridge, I. 2m. 2w. Sc. Heaven. CARV

Colossal, stupendous! Murray, J. 6m. 3w. Sc. Office. PLK

Columbia, the gem of the ocean. Emurian, E. K. 5m. 2w. Sc. Int. EMU

C **Columbus sails the sea.** Barbee, L. 4b. 1d. ext. Sc. Sea dock. BUF

Come home. Lehmann, A. 1m. 1w. Sc. Int. LE

Come out of it. Kaser, A. L. 4m. 4w. Sc. Int. DEN

Comedy sketch. ———. 1m. 1w. Sc. Kitchen. LA

Common touch. Hammons, R. 3m. 2w. Sc. Farm. CARV

C **Compass for Christopher.** 6b. 4g. Sc. Harbor. PLF

Concert in the park. Elser, D. 3m. 1w. Sc. Park. ROW

The confession. Lehmann, A. 1m. 1w. Sc. Stage. LE

R **Connecticut Yankee in King Arthur's court.** Mark Twain. 6m. ext. Sc. England. OF PLH

The conqueror. Wincelberg, S. 4m. 2w. Sc. Japan. MAYP

T **Conquest of pain.** Poole, L. Nar. voices. Sc. Int. SET

Contest fever. Murray, J. 4m. 4w. Sc. Int. DEN

C **Contrary Mary meets Boy Blue.** 1b. 1g. ext. Sc. Stage. MARS

T **Coral.** Armer, A. 1m. 1w. Sc. Int. ARM

Corfe gate. Foy, H. 7m. 3w. Sc. Lofty hall. MARO

J **Corn but not forgotten.** Eisenberg, H. 2b. Sc. Int. com. EI

Corn meal & poetry. DuBois, G. 2m. 5w. Sc. Int. DUB PLC

J **Corner store.** Richmond, S. S. 7b. 2g. Sc. Store. RIC

J **Cornerstone of freedom.** Asbrand, K. 6b. 5g. Sc. Ancient Rome. PLA

The Counsellor. Loudan, J. 3m. 2w. Sc. Farmhouse. BANN

Count & the prostitute. Schnitzler, A. 1m. 1w. Sc. Int. BE

Countess Cathleen. Yeats, W. B. 5m. 3w. Sc. Ireland. YE YEA

T   **Country cousin.** Armer, A. 1m. 1w. Sc. Hotel. ARM

C   **Courage piece.** Leuser, E. 6b. 3g. Sc. Kitchen. PLB

C   **Court of the Druids.** Collins, F. 6b. 1g. Sc. Stage. COL

J   **"Courtesy."** MacDonald, D. M. 4 char. Sc. Int. com. DEN

Courting of Marie Jenvrin. Pharis, G. 5m. 2w. Sc. Hotel. JON ME SEL

C   **Courting trouble.** Fisher, A. 4b. 3g. Sc. Courtroom. FI

R   **Courtship and conquest.** Maurois, A. 2m. 2w. Sc. Int. MAUR

Cow was in the parlor. Kauffman, S. 4m. 2w. Sc. Int. DEN

Cracked ice. LePelley, G. 3m. 2w. Sc. Weather station. ROW

Cradle in the dust. Miller, J. 2m. 1w. 3c. Sc. Int. SI

J   **The Creeper.** Ruscoll, J. 6m. 2w. voices. Sc. Int. WF

T   **Crime clues.** Beebe, T. 4m. 1w. Sc. Office. HE

J   **Crimson glory rose.** Phillips, M. K. 2b. 5g. Sc. Int. PLF

J   **The crisis.** Richmond, S. S. 6g. Sc. Hospital. RIC

C   **Crisscross streets.** Deming, D. 1b. ext. Sc. Stage. PLD

C   **Crocus.** Spamer, C. 6b. 6g. Sc. Stage. PLA

R   **Cross of gold.** Andersson, D. 9m. 7w. Nar. PLE

C   **Cross Princess.** MacLellan, E. 4b. 6g. Sc. Bedroom. PLF

J   **Crosspatch & cupid.** McGowan, J. 7b. 6g. Sc. Classroom. PLK

J   **Crowded house.** Jacob, E. 6b. 6g. Sc. Cottage. PLK

C R   **Crowded house.** Kissen, F. Nar. Ann. 1b. 1g. Sc. Village. KIC

Crowsnest. Manley, W. F. 6m. Sc. Vessel. DAV

T   **Cry on my shoulder.** Parker, K. T. 5m. 3w. voices. Sc. Stage. PARK

J   **Cry witch.** Miller, M. L. 7b. 7g. Sc. Meeting house. PLD

J   **Crying clown.** Nicholson, M. A. 4b. Sc. Circus. PLH

C   **Crystal flask.** Asbrand, K. 2b. 6g. Sc. Palace. BUF

J   **Cub reporter.** Richmond, S. S. 5b. 1g. Sc. Office. RIC

J   **The cuckoo.** Murdock, M. 7g. Sc. Int. KA

Cup of kindness. Mauermann, W. G. 3m. 3w. Sc. Bookshop. ROW

T   **Cup of tea.** Parker, K. T. 2m. 4w. Sc. Gypsy tea rm. PARK

J   **Cupid & Co.** Callanan, C. C. 2b. 2g. Sc. Office. PLF

Cupid on the loose. 3m. 2w. Sc. Park bench. PLH

Cupid's partner. Paradis, M. B. 2m. 8w. Sc. College campus. PLH

J   **Cupid's postoffice.** Hark, M. 16 char. Sc. Postoffice. HAR

J   **Cupies & hearts.** Hark, M. 3b. 3g. Sc. Int. HAR PLH

C   **Cure for lions.** Ridge, A. 46. 1g. Sc. Int. RID

C   **Curious quest.** Miller, H. L. 6b. 3g. Sc. Int. MIN

R   **The curtain.** Mickel, J. Ann. 4m. 1w. Sc. Int. MIC

R   **Cyrano de Bergerac.** Rostand, E. 5m. 6w. Sc. French int. OF PLJ

D

T   **Dancers.** Foote, H. 3m. 7w. Sc. Int. FO

C   **Dancing children.** Very, A. 10b. 7g. Sc. Forest. PLE

C   **Dancing Princesses.** Cory, C. H. 4b. 15g. Sc. Hill. PLF

R   **Danger of freedom.** Wishengrad, M. Ann. 3m. 1w. Singers. MAL

J **Danger — pixies at work.** Howard, V. M. 7b. Sc. Kitchen. HO PLH

Danger! Women at work. Jeaffreson, M. 9w. Sc. Office. NEF

J **Daniel Boone: patriot.** Mackay, C.D'A. 9b. Sc. Woodland. NEVI

Daring innovation. Molnar, F. 2m. Sc. Int. com. MOL

Dark brown. Johnson, P. 2m. 5w. Sc. Int. MARP

Dark rider. Finch, R. 6m. Sc. Int. ROW

R **Dark tower.** Macneice, L. 16 char. Sc. Curtains. BF

Darkest hour. Du Bois, G. 3m. 3w. 1c. Log hut. DUB

T **Date with Kate.** Huber, L. J. 2m. 3w. Sc. Int. com. HUB

J **Date with Washington.** Hark, M. 3b. 2g. Sc. Int. HAT PLB

J N–R **Date-time.** Gross, E. 3b. 2g. Sc. Int. GRO

J **Daughter of the gods.** Du Bois, G. 3b. 4g. Sc. Int. PLC

C **David & the second Lafayette.** Davis, L. R. 10b. 3g. Sc. School. BUF

R **David Copperfield.** Dickens, C. Nar. 5m. 3w. Sc. Int. OF

Day after forever. Emery, C. im. 4w. Sc. Int. Melodrama. FR

Day before yesterday. Holland, N. 3m. 4w. Sc. Seacoast. MAYJ

C R **Day camper's siesta.** Powell, T. T. Ann. Large number char. Sc. Camp. WE

C **Day of trees.** Hark, M. 5b. 5g. Sc. Woods. PLF HAR

C **Day is bright.** Myrick, M. 6b. 3g. Sc. Studio. BUF

C **Day of good deeds.** Carpenter, F. 7 char. Sc. Woods. CARP

J **Day the shoemaker came.** Pyle, M. T. 5b. 6g. Sc. Int. PLB

J N–R **Day to remember.** Miller, H. L. 4b. 2g. Sc. Kitchen. MIM PLC

R **Day dreams go to school.** Neher, J. Nar. 1m. 3w. 2b. Sc. Int. NE

T **Dead weight.** Ayer, A. 2m. 2w. Sc. Int. ARM

Deadwood. Lee, W. C. 1m. 4w. Sc. Int. BRIN

Dear reparted. Houghton, S. 3m. 3w. 1g. Sc. Int. CER DAV

Dearie, You're a dreamer. Casey, F. M. 1m. 2w. Sc. Int. FR

Death of a hero. Rose, K. 3m. Sc. Cabin on battleship. ROS

C **Death of Boadicea.** Collins, J. 3b. 3g. Sc. Stage. COL

Death of Cuchulain. Yeats, W. B. 5m. 2w. Sc. Stage. YE YEA

R **Death of the average man.** 8m. 2w. Sc. Int. MAK

T **Death of the old man.** Foote, H. 4m. 3w. Sc. Int. FO

Debby's dilemma. Weiss, M. J. 2m. 5w. Sc. Dean's office. WEI

Debt to pay. Nagel, L. 5w. Sc. Int. BAK

C **December gifts.** Duggar, F. 2g. ext. No sc. KA PLF

Decision. Hackett, W. 1m. 3w. Sc. Farm. BAK

Deer of another color. Dias, E. J. 4m. 3w. Sc. Stratford-on-Avon. ROW

J **Defense never rests.** Deming, D. 8b. 5g. Sc. Courtroom. PLC

Deirdre. Yeats, W. B. 5m. 1w. ext. Sc. Guest house. YE YEA

R **Democrat & the Communist.** Geiger, M. 5m. Sc. Int. MAL

Desert soliloquy. Peterson, L. 2m. 2w. Sc. Indian village. GOL

Diamond earring. Paradis, M. B. 4m. 4w. ext. Sc. Int. PLK

Digby — Conversion of St. Paul. Switz, T. MacL. 9m. Ext. voices. Sc. Church. SW

Disconsolate apparition. Bembridge, J. 1m. 3w. Sc. Country house. MAR MARC

Discrimination for everybody. Mabey, E. 20m. 2w. Sc. Auditorium. FR

R **Divided we stand.** Wishengrad, M. 7m. 2w. singers. Stage. MAL

Dixie. Emurian, E. K. 4m. 1w. Sc. Boarding house. EMU

Doctor Faustus lights the lights. Stein, G. 7 char. ext. Ballet. Sc. Door of rm. MAYJ

C **Doctor fox.** Carpenter, F. 5 char. Sc. Cave. CARP

Doctor from Dunmore. 7m. 5w. Sc. Island cottage. GR

R **Dr Heidegger's experiment.** Cowgill, R. 4m. 1w. Sc. Lab. COW

C **Doctor Knowall.** Howard, H. L. 8b, 4g. Sc. Office. PLC

J **Doctor manners.** Hark, M. 3b. 4g. Sc. Office. HAR KAM PLD

Doctor O'Toole. Fagan, J. B. 5m. 3w. Sc. Dispensary. FA

Dr. Paynter. Broadhembury Drama Group. 4m. 3w. Sc. Inn parlour. KRL

C **Dog gone.** Carlson, B. W. 5b. 3g. Sc. Dog pound. CAR

Dog in the manger. Law, W. T. 4m. 2w. Sc. Racing track. BANN

J **Dolls.** Hark, M. 1b. 6g. Sc. Attic. HAR PLA

C **Dolly saves the day.** Miller, H. L. 4b. 3g. Sc. Farmhouse. BUF

C **Domino Family's picnic.** Marsh, W. A. 4b. 3g. Sc. Outdoors. MARS

C **Dominoes have a fire.** Marsh, W. A. 6b. 2g. Sc. Stage. Puppet. MARS

C **Donkey brays loudly.** Marsh, W. A. 2b. 1g. Sc. Stage. Puppet. MARS

Don't forget the baking powder. Grant, A. 4w. Sc. Country house. MAR MARC

J N–R **Dooley & the amateur hour.** Gross, E. 3b. 6g. Sc. Stage. GRO

R **The door.** Murray, J. 1m. 2w. Sc. Cottage. MU PLD

T **The door.** Stuart, J. 7m. 3w. Sc. Street. KAV

Dope, Lee, M. 4m. 2w. ext. Dancers. Sc. In Harlem. MAYN

Double blackface act. ———. 2m. Sc. Stage. LA

Double Dutch act. ———. 2m. Sc. Stage. LA

J **Double exposure.** Hark, M. 3b. 2g. Sc. Int. HAS

T **Double identity.** Parker, K. T. 5m. 3w. ext. Sc. Int. PARK

Double Irish act. ———. 2m. Sc. Stage. LA

T **"Double talk."** Fitzsimmons, E. G. Sc. Office. HE

Double wop act. ———. 2m. Sc. Stage. LA

Dowry. Molnar, F. em. Music. Sc. Int. com. MOL

Drama society meets. Teasdale, V. 1m. 1w. Sc. Rehearsal. TE

Dramatic sketch. ———. 3m. 1w. Sc. Stage. LA

C **Dreadful dragon.** Brydon, M. W. 7b. 8g. Sc. Chinese int. PLD

Dream. Zimmermann, A. L. 6m. 1w. ext. ON

Dreaming of bones. Yeats, W. B. 2m. 1w. ext. Sc. Rm. in Ireland. YE YEA

Dreamlost. Johnson, R. E. 2m. 4w. Sc. Int. ON

J **Drexel.** Howard, V. L. 6b. Sc. Woods. HO

Drovers. Esson, L. 7m. Sc. Campfire. RE

Drowazangmo. Duncan, M. Any number of char. Sc. In Tibet. DUN

Drum head. Stevens, T. W. 6m. 1w. ext. Sc. Palace. ON

C **Drummer boy.** Wall, L. V. 4b. 2g. Sc. Beach. WA

J **Drums in the dusk.** Laure, K. 3b. 2g. Sc. Int. PLD

Drums of Oude. Strong, A. 1m. 1w. Sc. Palace. CER
c **Dulce man.** Blanton, C. 3b. 2g. ext. Sc. Pueblo. com. BUF PLA
Dungeon of thyself. Seaton Drama Group. 1m. 11w. Sc. Gaol. KEL

E

J **Each star a state.** Woolsey, J. 2 Nar. 49 char. Sc. Stage. WOO
Ear of Vincent Van Gogh. 2m. 1w. Sc. Int. BRI
Early start. Hollister, L. D. 3m. 3w. Sc. Int. com. DEN
Easter bonnet. Molnar, F. 2w. Sc. Int. com. MOL
J **Easter egg magic.** Stansbury, M. 6b. 3g. Sc. Stage. PLK
J T **Easter fantasia.** Selby, S. R. Nar. 4b. 2g. Sc. Int. SE
J N–R **Easter hop.** Hark, M. 4b. 3g. Voice. Sc. Int. HAT
c **Easter lily.** King, W. 5b. 2g. Sc. Int. PLA
J **Easter reminders.** Hummell, V. 12 char. Sc. Woodland. PLK
c **Ebenezer Neverspend.** Colson, J. G. 2b. 2g. Sc. Kitchen. PLF
c **Election day in the U.S.A.** Newman, D. 11b. 4g. Sc. Voting place. PLE
Elijah, the firebrand of the Almighty. Nygaard, 8m. 5m. Sc. Church. NY
Elizabeth. Rulon, S. 3m. 5w. Sc. Int. ROW
J T **Elves & the shoemaker.** Kane, E. B. 4b. 3g. Nar. ext. Sc. Int. BU PLA
Emergency call! Teasdale, V. 1w. 1b. telephone operator. Sc. Int. TE
Emergency, stand by! Powers, T. 2m. Sc. Plane. GR
c **Emperor's daughters.** Draper, C. C. 7b. 4g. Sc. Garden. PLD
c **Emperor's new clothes.** 5b. 3g. Sc. Throne rm. PLF
J **Empty bowls.** Ficher, A. 4m. 3w. Sc. Stage. FIS
Empty room. Du Bois, G. 9m. 2w. Sc. Yard of inn. DUB PLA
End of the beginning. O'Casey, S. 2m. 1w. Sc. Kitchen in Ireland. BANN
R **End of the line.** Murray, J. 5m. 3w. Sc. Subway train. MU
R **End of the line.** Stewart, B. 8m. Sc. Army quarters. PH
End of the road. Du Bois, G. 3m. 4w. Sc. Farmhouse. DUB
J **Engineering a bid.** Richmond, S. S. 3b. 1g. Sc. Office. PLC
J **Enter George Washington.** Hark, M. 2b. 3g. Sc. Int. HAR PLA
J **Enter Juliet.** Barbee, L. 3m. 5w. Sc. School auditorium. PLB
Enter the hero. Helburn, T. 1m. 3w. Sc. Int. SP
Epidemic. Mirbeau, O. 6m. ext. Sc. City council. BF
Erna Kemer of Ebenstadt. Bishop, J. 4m. 4m. Sc. Kitchen. RU
Eternal bride. Seller, T. 4m. 2w. Sc. Int. in Switzerland. BAK
R **Ethel & Albert.** Lynch, M. Ann. 1m. 1w. Sc. Int. COW
Eve's delight. Biscombe, M. 5w. Sc. Int. com. NEG
J **Every day is Thanksgiving.** Du Bois, G. 4b. 5g. Sc. Int. PLE
R **Everybody gets into the act.** Neher, J. Nar. 2m. 2w. 2b. Sc. Int. NE
Everyman. Switz, T. MacL. 16 char. Sc. Stage. SW
J **Everything nice.** O'Keffe, A. A. 2b. 5g. Sc. Int. ROW
c **Everywhere Christmas.** Very, A. 25 char. Sc. Stage. BU PLJ
J **Excursions.** Carlson, B. Any number of char. Pantomime. CAR

Exodus. Robinson, M. W. 5m. 3w. Sc. Steamer. MAYJ

J **Experiment.** Richardson, S. S. 5b. 3g. Sc. Int. PLA RIC

R **Experiment of a free press.** Probst, G. 1m. voice. Sc. Stage. MAL

C **Express to Valley Forge.** Dias, E. J. 2b. 4g. Kitchen. PLC

C **Eyes right!** Deming, D. 3b. 4g. Sc. Recreation rm. PLF

F

J **Fabre's little world.** Murray, J. 3b. 3g. Sc. Kitchen. PLE

Face is familiar. Dias, E. J. 9m. 3w. ext. Sc. Dormitory. DIA

Facts of life. Teasdale, V. 1m. 1w. Sc. Int. TE

The failure. Corrie, J. 3m. 2w. Sc. Village. MANN MARP

C **Fairy in the dell marionette.** 2b. 1g. Sc. Wooded dell. CAR

R **Fall of the House of Usher.** Poe, E. A. Nar. 3m. 1w. Sc. Int. HAC

J **Family affair.** Ward, M. 5b. 4g. Sc. Int. PLE

Family heirloom. Williamson, C. H. 4w. ext. c. Sc. Int. BAK

J **Family matter.** Miller, H. L. 3b. 2g. Sc. Int. PLB

Famous fathers. Emurian, E. K. 19m. 1w. Sc. Stage. EM

T **Fan mail.** Huber, L. J. 1m. 4w. Sc. Television studio. HUB

Fantasia on an old familiar theme. 11m. 3w. ext. Sc. Park. MAYJ

Far-distant shore. Finch, R. 3m. 2w. Sc. Int. GR

Farewell appearance. Holland, N. 3m. 5w. Sc. Int. HAYK

Farewell supper. Schnitzler, A. 2m. 1w. Sc. Rertaurant. MIR

J **Farmer in the dell.** Preston, E. E. 3m. Sc. Farm. Farce. PR

Farmer's daughter. Eisenberg, H. Ann. 3m. 4w. Sc. Int. Farce. EI

Farrell case. Cohan, G. M. 6m. 2w. Sc. Law office. ON

C **Fashion show.** Deming, D. 4b. 3g. Sc. School. PLC

The fat woman. Bridie, J. 2m. 5w. Sc. Inn. BRI

J **Father hits the jackpot.** Garver, J. 4b. 6g. Sc. Int. PLJ

Father keeps house. Hark, M. 6b. 4g. Sc. Int. com. HAR PLH

J **Father talks turkey.** Miller, H. L. 3b. 4g. Sc. Int. MIM PLA

J **Father's Easter hat.** Hark, M. 3b. 3g. Sc. Int. HAR

Favour is deceitful. Biscombe, M. 6w. Sc. Int. NEF

C R **Feast of lanterns.** Kissen, F. Ann. 8 char. Nar. Sc. Int. KIC

J **February failure.** Miller, H. L. Ann. 1b. 1g. Sc. Classroom. MIN PLH

J N–R **February frenzy.** Miller, H. L. 4b. 4g. Sc. Int. com. MIO PLG

J **February play.** Werner, S. 13 char. Sc. Stage. PLG

J **Fetters and dreams.** Du Bois, G. 9b. Sc. Prison. PLA

Feudin' fun. Dias, E. J. 5m. 3w. Sc. Cabin. DIA PLJ

J **Field of honor.** Hamilton, G. 4b. 3g. Sc. Int. PLE

J **Fiesta.** McArthur, J. 7b. 10g. Sc. Mexican home. PLK

T **Final curtain.** Armer, A. 1m. 1w. ext. Sc. Back stage. ARM

R **Final curtain.** Murray, J. 1m. 5w. Sc. Theatre. MU

Final edition. MacNaughton, J. A. 5b. 1g. Sc. Newspaper office. JON

J **Final edition.** Sayre, G. W. 8m. Sc. Editorial rm. PLJ

Final word. Albright, H. 5m. 1w. Sc. Stall in Mexico. ON

Finders keepers. Kelly, G. 1m. 2w. Sc. Int. GR WIN

J **Finger in art.** Paradis, M. B. 11g. ext. Sc. Library. PA
Finger of God. Wilde, P. 2m. 1w. Sc. Int. SP
c **Fire in a paper.** Hagey, J. 4g. Sc. Chinese home. KA
J **Fire bug.** Paradis, M. B. 4b. 4g. Sc. Int. PLA PA
c **First aid first.** Deming, D. 2g. 2b. Sc. School playground. KAM PLE
J **First aid to first troop.** Woolsey, J. Ann. 14g. Sc. Curtains. WOO
First and ten. Huber, L. J. 2m. 2w. Sc. Football field. HU
J **First butterfly.** Spamer, C. 9 char. Sc. Meadow. PLK
c **First day of April.** Barbee, L. 5g. Sc. Int. PLB
c **First Easter egg.** Bennett, R. 3b. 5g. Sc. Stage. PLE
c **First flowers.** Wilson, M. L. 14 char. Sc. Forest. KAM
c **First New England Christmas.** 6b. 2g. ext. Sc. Colonial home. BUF PLA
First of the Dandies. Rose, K. 4m. Sc. English Int. ROS
c **First Roman invasion.** Collins, F. 9b. Sc. Stage. COL
J **First Thanksgiving.** Newman, D. 6b. 6g. Sc. Puritan home. PLG
Fishers of men. Nygaard, N. E. 5m. 1w. Sc. Lake shore. NY
R **Fisherman & his wife.** Barr, J. Nar. 3b. 1g. Sc. Int. PLB
Fisherman's luck. Kaser, A. L. 3m. 3w. Sc. Int. DEN
Fit for victory. Stevens, C. 3m. 3w. Sc. Int. DEN
J **Five boys & a Santa.** Howard, V. L. Sc. Int. HO
c **Five brothers.** Leuser, E. 6b. Sc. Int. PLF
R **Five buttons.** Murray, J. 3m. 4w. Ann. Sc. Int. MU
Five days. Zeigler, H. 8m. 1w. Sc. Prison camp. MAYR
J **Five senses.** Hark, M. 7 char. Sc. Garden. HAR PLB
J **Flag the Limited.** Richmond, S. S. 6b. Sc. Railway tower. RIC
c **Flag of the U.S.** Barbee, L. 10b. 4g. ext. Sc. Stage. BUF
J **Flair for fashions.** Phillips, M. K. 6w. Sc. Int. KA PLE
Flash-back. Aklom, M. 3m. 2w. Sc. Cottage. PARK
Flattering word. Kelly, G. 2m. 3w. Sc. Rm. in parsonage. DAV
c r **The flea.** Kissen, F. Ann. 6b. 2g. Sc. Int. KI
Fleas & figs. Seelye, M. A. 2m. 3w. Sc. Courtyard. SEL
c **Flibber turns the tables.** Knight, L. 3b. 1g. Sc. Front yard. KAM PLC
J **Flight completed.** Richmond, S. S. 4b. Sc. Airway office. PLA
c **Floating stone.** Foulk, C. W. 6b. 4g. Sc. King's court. BUF
Flobelle goes shopping. Teasdale, V. 1m. 2w. Sc. Shoe store. TE
Florence unlimited. Carmichael, F. 6w. Sc. Int. Farce. BAK
J **Flowers for mother.** York, M. A. 6b. 10g. Sc. Flower stand. PLG
c **Flowers for Mother's Day.** MacLellan, E. 14g. Sc. Garden. KA PLF
Fly by night. Bussell, J. 2m. 1w. 1cat. Puppets. Sc. Street. BUS
J **Flying high.** Richmond, S. S. 3b. 6g. Sc. Plane. PLB RIC
c r **Flying ship.** Kissen, F. Ann. 10b. 1g. Sc. Plane. KI
Fog on the valley. Powers, V. 3m. 3w. Sc. Cabin. ROW
Folk festival script. Eisenberg, H. Nar. Any number of char. Sc. Stage. EI
Folk life in ancient Greece. ———. Large number of char. Sc. Outdoor bowl. KO
c **Follow the north star.** Sanderlin, O. 7 char. Sc. Mountain top. KAM

Folly of Seithenyn. Etheridge, K. 4m. 2w. ext. Sc. Cottage. HARP

Followers of Christ. Switz, T. MacL. 2 groups. Voice. Sc. Int. SW

J N–R **Football hero.** Miller, H. L. 3b. 3g. Sc. Teen-age Club. MIM PLB

For each man kills. Agoston, G. 4m. Sc. French town. MAYH

For old times sake. Herbert, M. D. 1m. 1w. Sc. Int. FR

For the glory of St. Patrick. Du Bois, G. 2m. 3w. Sc. Int. DUB

R **For the ladies.** Weaver, L. Ann. 3m. Sc. Int. WE

J **For the welfare of all.** Richmond, S. S. 2b. 4g. Sc. Office. PLD

J **Forest of Arden.** Speare, E. G. 4b. 1g. Sc. Globe theatre. PLE

Forever yours. Kaser, A. 4m. 4w. Sc. Int. Burlesque. PLU

Forgotten land. Sheffield, J. 2m. 1w. Sc. Barren land. MAYO

Form 1040. Teasdale, V. 1m. 2w. Sc. Int. com. TE

Fortunata writes a letter. Apstein, T. 2m. 1w. Sc. Int. MAYH

C **Fortunes of Merrylegs & tawny-whiskers.** Molloy, L. L. 11b. Inn. PLA

J **Fountain for a Duke.** Burlingame, C. 3b. 2g. Sc. Int. PLA

C R **Four clever brothers.** Kissen, F. Ann. 6b. 1g. Sc. Int. KI

C R **Fox brings luck.** Kissen, F. Nar. Ann. 6b. Sc. Int. KI

Franklin & the King. Green, P. 8m. 1w. Sc. Audience rm. GR

R **Freedom train.** Hackett, W. Nar. 8b. Sc. Int. PLA

R **Freedom's forge.** ———. Nar. 8m. Many voices. Sc. Stage. SK

R **Freedom's herald.** Mickel, J. Ann. 4m. 1w. Sc. Stage. MIC

R **Freeing the land.** Mindel, J. 8m. 1w. 1 voice. Sc. Int. MAL

J **Fresco for Unesco.** Fisher, A. 8 char. ext. Sc. Stage. FIS

C **Friday foursome packs a box.** Barbee. 7g. Sc. Sunrm. BU KA PLA

C **Friendly advice.** Preston, E. E. 2w. Sc. Int. com. PR

C **Friendly as can be.** Asbrand, K. 4b. 4g. 1dog. Sc. Street. KAM

C **Frolic of the leaves.** Spamer, C. 6b. 5g. Sc. Outdoors. PLA

C **Frightful forest.** Summer, J. N. 2b. 2g. Sc. Witch's novel. PLE

From Paradise to Butte. Finch, R. 4m. Sc. Int. ROW

Full moon in March. Yeats, W. B. 3m. 1w. Sc. Curtains. BE YE YEA

Fumed oak. Coward, N. 1m. 3w. Sc. London home. com. CER

G

J **G. for Gettysburg.** Hark, M. 5b. 5g. Sc. School Auditorium. PLH

Galileo. Brecht, B. 40 char. Large number of sc. Curtains. BF

Game of chess. Goodman, K. S. 4m. Sc. Int. CER KN MU

J **Game of chess.** Murray, J. 2b. 3g. Sc. Int. PLF

J **Game of hearts.** Hark, M. 3b. 2g. Sc. Int. HAS

George Washington. Baldwin, M. T. 1m. 6w. ib. Sc. Summer home. BAL

J **George Washington Carver.** Hark, M. 7b. 3g. Sc. Log cabin. PLB

J **George Washington comes to town.** Leuser, E. 3b. 2g. Sc. Colonial Int. PLG

R **George Washington's chair.** Johnson, C. Ann. 1m. 2w. Sc. Int. JOH

J **General Gage's chowder.** Dias, E. J. 3b. 3g. Sc. Inn. PLA

J **General returns.** McGowan, J. 6b. 4g. Sc. Int. PLA

J **Generous fisherman.** Eisenberg, H. 3m. ext. Sc. Int. EI

Gentle heart. Arlett, V. I. 3m. 2w. Sc. In Italy. ARL

R   **Gentleman from Philadelphia.** 3m. 2w. Nar. 3b. 2g. Sc. Colonial Int. PLD

J   **Get up & bar the door.** Wall, L. V. 3b. 1g. Sc. Kitchen. WA

J   **Getting in line.** Fisher, A. 13 char. Nar. Sc. Int. FIS

J   **Get-together dinner.** Fisher, A. 3b. 2g. Sc. Int. FIS

  Ghost from Genoa. Dias, E. J. 3m. 2w. Sc. Int. Italian. PLJ

J N–R   **Ghost in the house.** Miller, H. L. 4b. 3g. Sc. Int. MIN PLB PLF

C   **Ghost-layers Inc.** Deming, D. 4b. 2g. Sc. Empty rm. PLC

J N–R   **Ghosts in the library.** Hark, M. 13 char. Voice. Sc. Library. HAT

J   **Ghosts in the library.** Pendleton, E. 7b. 6g. Sc. Library. PLC PLF

C   **Ghosts on guard.** Fisher, A. 4b. 3g. Sc. Int. PLC

C   **Ghost walks tonight.** Nicholson, J. 9b. 3g. Sc. Abandoned house. PLE

J   **Gift for the world.** Newman, D. 7b. 11g. Sc. Nursery. PLJ

C   **Gift of forgiveness.** Collins, F. 4b. 4g. Sc. Village. COL

R   **Gift of music.** McCaslin, N. 2Nar. 5m. 2w. 2c. ext. Sc. Village. MAC

C   **Gift of the fairies.** Very, A. 18 char. Sc. Log cabin. KAM

C   **Gift for the elves.** Woolsey, J. 9 char. Sc. Workshop. WO

  Giglo & gigolette. Maughan, W. S. 18m. 4w. Sc. Int. MAU

  Girls are home. Huber, L. J. 1m. 1w. Sc. Int. HU

C   **Girls in books.** Miller, H. L. 13g. Sc. School stage. MIN PLG

J   **Girls whose fortune sought her.** Clapp, P. 3b. 3g. Sc. Yard. PLH

  Girls will be girls. Molnar, F. 2m. 2w. Sc. Int. MOL

C   **Give the book a chance.** Malone, M. 7b. 4g. Sc. Library. PLB

R   **Give us leaders.** Hastings, F. V. Nar. 5w. Sc. Int. WE

J   **Glamour & grease.** Richmond, S. S. 2m. 2w. Sc. Service station. RIC

  Glamous pattern 479823. Teasdale, V. 2w. Sc. Int. TE

T   **Glass slipper.** Ayer, A. 1m. 1w. Sc. Dance floor. ARM

C   **Glorious whitewasher.** Mark Twain. 68. 1g. Sc. Fence. PLB

  Glory day. Lake, G. 3m. 2w. 2c. Sc. Negro farm. MAYL

J   **Glory & the dream.** Du Bois, G. 4b. 4g. Sc. Farmhouse. PLE

C   **Goblin parade.** Folmsbee, B. 9 char. Sc. Schoolrm. BUF

  God & Texas. Aedrey, R. 8m. ext. Sc. Int. GR

  God of our fathers. Emurian, E. K. 2m. 2w. 10b. ext. Sc. Stage. EM

  Gods of the mountain. Dunsany, Lord. 10 char. ext. Sc. Wall. KN

  Going home. Gainfort, J. 3m. 3w. Sc. Suburbs. MAYJ

  Gold feathers. Lovelace, W. R. 5m. Sc. Barrack's rm. MIL

T   **Goldbergs.** Berg, G. 3m. 4w. Sc. Int. KAV

C   **Golden bell for mother.** Very, A. 14 char. Sc. Mice hole. BUF

  Golden boy. Odets, C. 6m. 1w. Sc. Boxing arena. SEK

  Golden doom. Dunsany, Lord. 8m. 4c. ext. Sc. Outside King's door. GR.

C R   **Golden touch.** Kissen, F. 2b. 1g. Ann. Nar. Ancient Greece. KIC

  Golden wedding anniversary. Drummond, R. 1m. 2w. Sc. Int. com. PLU

  Goldfish. Andrews, I. 5m. 4w. Sc. Club. MARQ

J   **Good egg.** Du Bois, G. 3b. 4g. Sc. Int. PLE

c **Guide for Washington.** Barbee, L. 4b. 3g. Sc. River. BUF
Gypsy. Hord, P. 2m. 2w. Sc. Dressingrm. ROW
J **Gypsy look.** Heath, A. L. 3b. 3g. Sc. Int. PLF

H

J **Hail — the Genie.** Richmond, S. S. 6b. 5g. Sc. Boy's rm. RIC
Half hour, please. Richards, S. 4m. 4w. Sc. Theatre. MAYP
c **Halloween gets a new look.** Pyle, M. T. 10b. Sc. Clubrm. PLD
c **Halloween night.** Carlson, B. W. 5 char. Sc. Int. CAR
J **Halloween scarecrow.** Spamer, C. 2b. 3g. Sc. Field. PLJ
c **Handwriting on the wall.** Wight, L. 4b. 4g. Sc. Colonial int. PLE
Handy man. Teasdale, V. 2m. 1w. Sc. Int. TE
Hangs over thy head. Purkey, R. A. 4m. 2w. Sc. Stage. MAYR
c **Hans who made the Princess laugh.** Rowland, E. 7b. 6g. ext. Sc. Market place. BUF
c **Hansel & Grethel.** Simonds, N. 2b. 3g. Sc. Woodcutter's home. BUF
c **Hansel & Grethel.** Wall, L. V. 2b. 3g. Sc. Woodcutter's home. WA
C R **Hansel & Grethel.** White, M. R. Nar. 2b. 3g. Sc. Stage. WH
T **Hard as flint.** Armer, A. 1m. 1w. Sc. Ranch. ARM
Harlequin bridge. Slauden-Smith, F. 2m. 1w. Sc. Bridge. MARO
c **Have a heart.** Pyle, M. T. 3b. 4g. Sc. Playrm. PLB
Havana moon. Hughes, G. 3m. 2w. Sc. Int. com. ON
Have you seen My Lady? Skelton, G. 2m. 2w. Sc. Int. Farce. ARL
Happy as Harry. MacDonagh. 4m. 2w. ext. Sc. In Ireland. NEWA
T **Happy birthday.** Huber, L. J. 1m. 3w. Sc. Kitchen. HUB
c **Happy Christmas to all.** Nolan, J. C. 3b. 3g. Sc. Int. BU BUF
R N–R **Happy haunts.** Hark, M. 7 char. voices. Sc. Int. HAT PLD
J **Happy hearts.** Hark, M. 3b. 3g. Sc. Int. HAT PLC
c **Happy holiday.** Newman, D. 12b. 5g. Sc. Workshop. PLF
T **Happy housewife.** Rosten, H. 11m. 10w. Sc. Int. MAYL
c **Happy hygiene.** Clark, J. Any number of children. Sc. Int. CLA
Happy journey to Trenton & Camden. Wilder, T. Stage manager. 2m. 3w. Sc. Stage. GR WIN
Happy life. St. Clair, R. 4m. 2w. ext. Sc. Int. BRIN
J **Happy New Year.** Hark, M. 3b. 2g. Sc. Int. PLC
R **Happy Prince.** Wilde, O. Nar. 18 char. Sc. Outdoors. PLH
Happy Valentine's Day. 3m. 2w. Sc. Int. PLG
J **Hat for mother.** Phillips, M. K. 6g. Sc. Int. PLG
J **Hats & rabbits.** Hark, M. 3b. 2g. Int. com. HAS PLC
c **Haunted bookshop.** Nicholson, J. 12b. 1g. Sc. Shop. PLF
J N–R **Haunted clothesline.** Miller, H. L. 4b. 3g. Sc. Back yard. MIO PLC
Haunted suitcase. Thalimer, F. L. 4m. 4w. Sc. Int. com. DEN
c **He who eats cabbage.** Marsh, W. A. 3b. Sc. Int. MARS
He who gets hooked. Carriere, A. 1m. 1w. Sc. River. ON
He who gets slapped. Andreyev, L. 1m. 1w. Sc. Curcus. SEG
J **Health offices for a day.** Deming, D. 3b. 3g. Sc. Doctor's office. PLB
Heart of a mother. Molnar, F. 1m, 1w. com. MOL

Heart of age. Bercovici, E. 3m. 1w. Sc. Bar. NEW
J N–R **Heart throbs.** Miller, H. L. 1b. 15g. Sc. Int. com. MIO PLK
J   **Heart trouble.** Hark, M. 3b. 2g. Sc. Int. PLD
J   **Hearts & flowers for mother.** Hark, M. 4b. 3g. Sc. Int. HAR PLF
J   **Hearts & flowers.** Miller, H. L. 4b. 4g. Sc. Int. PLB
Hearts & groceries. Stone, C. 1m. 1w. Sc. Int. FR
Hearts, Inc. Condre, M. 1m. 3w. Sc. Int. CARV
C   **Hearts of oak.** Hall, M. E. 5b. ext. Sc. Colonial int. BUF
C   **Hearts, tarts & Valentines.** Fisher, A. 6b. 3g. Sc. Castle. PLC
J   **Her big crush.** Weiss, M. J. 3b. 3g. Sc. Int. WEI
Here's a Howdy-do. Stone, W. 8m, 2w. Sc. Int. ON
Helena's husband. Moeller, P. 3m. 2w. Sc. Ancient Greece. CER
Hello out there. Saroyan, W. 3m. 2w. Sc. Prison cell. CER
C   **Hello, Mr. Groundhog.** Miller, H. L. 30 char. Sc. Woods. MIN
Help wanted. Lehmann, A. 2m. Sc. Road. LE
Help wanted. Teasdale, V. 1m. 2w. Sc. Int. com. TE
C   **Help wanted for Easter.** MacLellan, E. 4b. 5g. Sc. Forest. PLF
Herbert's hurt. Huber, L. J. 3w. Sc. Sidewalk. HU
Herman's temptation. Howard, V. L. 5b. Sc. Park. HO
C   **Hermes & the two woodsmen.** Bennett, R. 3b. Sc. Glade. PLA
Herme's egg. Yeats, W. B. 5m. 1w. ext. Sc. Ancient Ireland. YE YEA
C   **Heroine of Wren.** Colbo, E. E. 4b. 3g. Sc. Quaker Village. BUF PLA
J N–R **Hero's homecoming.** Miller, H. L. 3b, 5g. Sc. Hotel. MIO PLJ
High pressure. Huber, L. J. 1m. 2w. Sc. Int. com. PLU
The High School. Perl, A. 8m. 3w. Sc. Int. MAYR
High tea. Miller, H. 3m. 3w. 1b. 1g. Sc. Int. MARQ
High window. Powers, V. 2m. 3w. Sc. Study. ROW
J   **Highway trail.** Richmond, S. S. 7b. Sc. Diner. PLC
J   **Highways of tomorrow.** 5b. Sc. Airport. RIC
His daughter's hand. Huber, L. J. 2m. 2w. Sc. Int. HU
J   **His first patient.** Richmond, S. S. 5b. Sc. Doctor's office. RIC
J   **His hand and pen.** Du Bois, G. 4w. Sc. Int. KA
Hitch-hiker, Fletcher, L. 13 char. Sc. Stage. FLE MAK
J   **Hobby for Dad.** Howard, V. L. 8b. Sc. Classrm. HO
Hold the line, please. Donnergraad, L. 6m. 5w. Sc. Int. com. BAK
C   **Holly hangs high.** Barbee, L. 3b. 4g. Sc. Mountain home. BUF
Holy city. Cunningham, G. F. 4m. 2w. Sc. Study. CUN
C   **Holy Grail.** Collins, J. 14b. ext. Sc. Hill. COL
Holy search. St. Clair, R. 8m. 3w. Sc. Int. BRIO
C   **Home in Nazareth.** Kirchner, V. M. 4b. 1g. Sc. In Palestine. WI
Home nursing revue. Kerr, S. 9w. Sc. Int. FR
Home remedy. Huber, L. J. 1m. 3w. Sc. Int. HU
Home, sweet home. Peterson, L. 6m. 2w. Sc. Int. GOL
J   **Home work.** Miller, H. L. 3b. 3g. Sc. Int. PLE
J   **Home work.** Preston, E. E. 8g. Sc. Int. PR
J   **Homecoming.** Hark, M. 2b. 4g. Sc. Int. PLD
J   **Homiest room.** Hark, M. 3b. 2g. Sc. Int. HAS

Home-longing. Bernhart, G. 4m. 4w. Sc. In Norway. SEL

J **Homemakers have a way.** Richmond, S. S. 7w. Sc. School. KA PLB
RIC

J **Hometown Halloween.** Hark, M. 2b. 4g. Sc. Int. HAT PLF

J **Honest Abe Lincoln.** Fisher, A. 4b. 4g. Sc. Cabin. PLK

Honest Injin! Murray, J. 8m. 2w. Sc. Office. PLK

R **Honeymoon.** Maurois, A. 2m. 1w. Sc. Hotel. MAUR

Honor & the glory. Chipp, E. 2m. 1w. Sc. Cottage. ON

J N–R **Hooky holiday.** Miller, H. L. 5b. 5g. Sc. Int. com. MIO

C **Hop, jump, & skip.** Spamer, C. 9b. Sc. Outdoors. PLC

R **Hope for tomorrow: John Keats.** Stewart, M. Nar. 1m. Sc. Int. WE

Hour-glass. Yeats, W. B. 2m. 2w. ext. Sc. Open space. YE YEA

J **House for rent.** MacLellan, E. 4b. 8g. Sc. Forest. PLK

J **House is haunted.** Hark, M. 5b. 6g. Sc. Int. HAR PLB

House of Connelly. Green, P. 2w. Sc. Southern mansion. SEK

R **House of seven Gables.** Hawthorne, N. 4m. 2w. ext. Sc. Int. OF

R **House that didn't want to be lived in.** Brewer, F. 4m. 1w. Sc. Int.
SK

J **House that Jack built.** Richmond, S. S. 4m. 2w. Sc. Int. RIC

Housemaid & the young gentleman. Schnitzler, A. 1m. 2w. Sc. Kitchen
BE

How pleasant to know you Mrs. Lear. Causley, C. 5w. Sc. Vicarage.
ARL

C **How the giraffe got its neck.** Marsh, W. A. 6 char. no. sc. Puppet,
MARS

C **How the old woman furnished the shoe.** Clark, J. 5b. 7g. Sc. Stage.
CLA

How to be happy though married. Preston, E. E. 6m. 4w. Sc. Int. PLU

How to gain peace amid temptation. Switz, T. MacL. voice. 2 groups.
SW

C **How we got our numbers.** Kane, E. B. 7b. 2g. Sc. Int. BUF

J **Howard's forward pass.** Deming, D. 3b. 2g. Sc. Boy's rm. PLC

C **Hubub on the bookshelf.** Woster, A. 9 char. Sc. Stage. BUF

R **Huckleberry Finn.** Mark Twain. 4b. 1g. Sc. Outdoors. PLG

Hugh of the Glen & his clogs are all one. Stephens, P. J. 4m. 2w. Sc.
Welsh farmhouse. MAYL

Humblest place. Du Bois, G. 7m. 3w. Sc. Inn. PLJ

Humai's secret. McCaslin, N. Nar. 8m. 1w. Sc. Throne rm. MAC

The hunger I got. Riggs, L. 6m. Woods. ON

Husband & the little darling. Schnitzler, A. 1m. 1w. Sc. Int. BE

I

C **I can get along.** Asbrand, K. 4b. 6g. Sc. Norwegian int. Puppet. PLC

I love you truly. Birdsall, E. M. 3m. 4w. Sc. Int. Farce. BAK

J **I resolve.** Howard, V. L. 8b. Sc. Stage. HO

I saw the cross. Mattson, J. M. 17m. 5w. ext. Sc. Stage. BRIN

I shall sail again. Du Bois, G. 8m. 1w. Sc. In Spain. DUB

J **I spy.** Marsh, W. A. 2b. 2g. Sc. Int. Puppet. MARS

C   **I want A——.** Carlsob, B. W. 2g. Sc. Int. Puppet. CAR

R   **Ichabod rides again.** Wilde, C. F. Nar. 5b. 1g. Sc. Stage. PLA

J   **Ides of March.** Hark, M. 3b. 2g. Sc. Int. HAS PLB

    Idol & his girl. Molnar, F. 1m. 1w. Sc. Int. MOL

    Idols. Rees, P. M. 1m. 5w. Sc. Int. BAK

    If men played cards as women do. Kaufman, G. S. 4m. Sc. Int. CER

J   **If we could only cook.** Hark, M. 2b. 3g. Sc. Int. PLE

C   **If wishes were horses.** Bathan, B. 5b. 3g. Sc. Yard. BUF

    Ile. O'Neill, E. 5m. 1w. ext. Sc. Ship. DAV, GAS RE

J N–R   **I'll eat my hat.** Miller, H. L. 6b. 4g. Sc. Cafeteria. MIO PLJ

    I'll help Johnny with his lesson. Teasdale, V. 1m. 1w. Sc. Int. TE

C R   **I'll never be late again.** Krausy, G. Nar. 4 char. No sc. WE

C   **I'll share my fare.** Howard, H. L. 5b. 1g. Sc. Market place. BUF PLA

    I'll teach Junior, myself. Teasdale, V. 2w. 1b. Sc. Int. TE

    Immortal memory. Bridie, J. Speaker, Any number of char. Sc. Stage. BRI

    Impasse. Woodress, F. A. 6m. 1w. Sc. Highway. MAYH

T   **Impersonations.** Bailey, A. H. 4m. 1w. Sc. Warehouse. RO

    Imploring flame. Sheffield, J. 7m. 2w. Sc. In the Bronx. MAYN

    Importance of being Earnest. Sliker, H. G. 5m. 4w. Sc. Int. ROW

R   **Importance of being Earnest.** Wilde, O. 5m. 4w. Sc. Stage. PLH OF SEK

R   **Impossible room.** Murray, J. 4m. 4w. Sc. Int. MU

    Incident at a grave. Lake, G. Sc. Graveyard. MAYN

    Incident at Eureka Bumps. Conkle, E. P. 4m. 2w. Sc. Int. ON

J   **Incog.** Keating. E. H. 7b. Sc. Office. KE

C   **Indians for Thanksgiving.** Heiderstadt, D. 4b. 3g. Sc. Fireplace. PLB

    In Camera. Satre, J. P. 2m. 2w. Sc. Int. HAM

T   **In darkened room.** Armer, A. 2m. 1w. Sc. Int. ARM

    In darkness. Stein, H. 2m. 2w. Sc. In darkness. MAYL

    In giving thanks. Huber, L. J. 1m. 3w. Sc. Front porch. HU

C   **In honor of trees.** Newman, D. 4b. 7g. Sc. Outside, PLD

J   **In honor of Washington.** Hark, M. 3b. 2g. Sc. Book store. HAR PLC

J   **In the Doctor's office.** Preston, E. E. 4b. 1g. Sc. Office. PR

J   **In the name of Miles Standish.** Ramsey, H. 7b. 4g. Sc. Street. PLH

    In the suds. Hewett, B. 1m. 2w. Sc. Int. ROW

J   **In the pet shop.** Preston, E. E. 1m. 1w. Sc. Shop. PR

C   **In the witch's house.** Bennett, R. 1b. 2g. Sc. House. KAM

    In the zone. O'Neill, E. 9m. Sc. Forecastle. CER SP

    In triplicate. Pyle, M. T. 5m. 5w. Sc. Int. BAK

    Inner man. Brighouse, H. 2m. 3w. Sc. Kitchen. MARO

    Innermost I Land. Ferrini, V. 3m. 3w. Sc. in Gloucester. MAYN

J   **Ins & outs.** Stirling, N. 3b. 2g. Sc. School. POT

C   **Inside the music box.** Clark, J. Any number of children. Sc. Stage. CLA

T   **Inside Washington.** Burke, C. 3m. no sc. WIN

    Interior. Maeterlinck, M. 2m. 2w. ext. Sc. Old garden. RE

Interlude. Carroll, P. V. 2m. 2w. Sc. Office. BANN

J **Invasion from the stratosphere.** Fisher, A. 7 char. ext. Sc. Space Ship. FIS

J **Inventor's clinic.** Howard, V. L. 5b. Sc. Clinic. HO

Isaiah, the statesman prophet. Nygaard, N. E. 2m. Sc. Church. NY

The Island. Thom, F. 4m. 1w. Sc. Garden. PAYP

It belongs to me. Kern, D. 3m. 2w. Sc. Book store. PL

C **It happened in Bookland.** Clark, J. 3 char. Sc. Int. Puppet. CLA

C **It happened in Egypt.** Ross, F. R. 8b. 6g. Sc. Open space. PLD

C **It's a gift.** Carlson, B. W. 1b. 5g. Sc. Int. CAR

C **It's a problem.** Miller, H. L. 6b. 8g. Sc. Int. MIN

R **It's Greek to me.** Hark, M. 3b. 2g. Sc. Int. HAS

J **It's so complex.** Hark, M. 3b. 2g. Sc. Int. HAS

It's so peaceful. Ward, M. 6m. 2w. Sc. Haunted house. PLK

Ivory tower — two flights down. McKinney, G. 3m. 2w. Sc. Night Club. CARV

J

R **J. M. Barrie.** Bridie, J. 3m. 2w. Nar. Sc. Radio studio. BRI

C **Jack & Jill.** Freudenberger, H. L. 1b. 3g. ext. Sc. Yard. BUF

C **Jack & the beanstalk.** Bufano, R. 4b. 2g. Sc. Outdoors. BRU

C R **Jack & the beanstalk.** Kissen, F. Ann. 3b. 2g. Sc. Studio. KIS

C **Jack & the beanstalk.** Very, A. 4b. 4g. Sc. Garden. PLB

C R **Jack & the beanstalk.** White, M. R. Nar. 3b. 2g. Sc. Studio. WH

C R **Jack Armstrong.** Strong, P. N. 4b. Sc. Field. WE

T **Jack Gleason show.** Marx, M. Letter to the boss. 2m. 1w. Sc. Apt. SET

C **Jack Straw.** Fisher, A. 2b. 1g. Sc. Barnyard. PLC

C **Jack-o-Lantern.** Spamer, C. 2b. 1g. Sc. Woods. PLC

C **Jack's friends.** Spamer, C. 3b. 1g. Sc. Winter scene. PLE

Jacob comes home. Kozlenko, W. 2m. 3w. Sc. Int. In Germany. ROW

James the thunderer. Switz, T. MacL. Nar. 6m. 1w. Sc. Church. SW

R **Jane Eyre.** Bronte, C. Nar. 4m. 4w. Sc. English home. HAC OF PLS

R **Jemmy's wife.** Hackett, W. Nar. 4m. 2w. Sc. Int. HAC

C **Jenny-by-the-day.** Molloy, L. L. 3b. 4g. Sc. Inn. BUF PLB

J **Jerry to the rescue.** Spamer, C. 5b. 1g. Sc. Study. PLB

Jezebel. Ratcliff, N. 8w. ext. Sc. Palace. NEG

Jim & Jennie. Baldwin, M. T. 3m. 2w. Sc. Village. BAL

J **Jimmy Cinders.** Miller, H. L. 8b. Sc. Bunk house. PLK

C **Jimmy Columbus.** Very, A. 8b. 5g. ext. Sc. In Spain. PLB

Jimmy six. Downing, R. 2m. 3w. Sc. Int. PLG

C **Jimmy's garden of words.** Clark, J. 5b. Sc. Garden. CLA

C **Jingle bells.** Hark, M. 3b. 4g. Sc. Outdoors. PLB

C **Jingle bells.** Pendleton, E. 3b. 4g. Sc. Farmhouse. BU

J **Joan makes a sale.** Richmond, S. S. 5w. Sc. Store. RIC

J **John Crown's legacy.** Suerken, E. H. 26b. Sc. Stage. PLF

John Shanahan, me boy. Casey, F. M. 3m. 3w. Sc. Orphanage. FR

John the beloved. Switz, T. MacL. Nar. 4m. 1w. Sc. Church. SW
T **John Turner Davis.** Foote, H. 7m. 4w. Sc. Int. FO MAYO
J **Johnnie jump up.** Hark, M. 6 char. Sc. Boy's bedroom. HAR
C **Johnny did try.** Phillips, M. K. 6b. 2g. Sc. Int. PLE
C **Jonathan's Thanksgiving.** Very, A. 5b. 7g. Sc. Kitchen. BUF
Journey of promise. Kozlenko, W. 7m. 1w. ext. Sc. Ship. BAK
Joy of the world. St. Clair, R. 2m. 2w. ext. Sc. Int. BRIO
J **Judge Monkey.** Colbert, M. 4 char. Sc. Alley. PLH
J N–R **Judge's diary.** Miller, H. L. 5b. 5g. Sc. School stage. MIO PLE
J **Judy takes over.** MacDonald, D. 3b. 6g. Sc. School. DEN
R **Juggler of our Lady.** France, A. Nar. 5m. 2w. Sc. Church. HA PLC
T **Julian Houseman story.** Housman, J. 8m. 2w. ext. Sc. Window. KAV
J N–R **Jump for George.** 6b. 11g. Sc. School Gym. MIO
J **Junction Santa Claus.** Hark, M. 5b. 5g. Sc. Depot. HAR PLE
J **Junior buys a car.** Phelps, P. 5b. 5g. Sc. Int. DEN
J **Junior Prom.** Wilde, C. F. 4b. 4g. Sc. High School. PLB PLF
C **Junk, valuable junk!** Carlson, B. W. 1b. 2g. Sc. Int. CAR
C **Just in time.** Ziefler, E. E. 9b. 7g. Sc. Clock shop. PLF
C **Just like us.** Deming, D. 4b. 3g. Sc. Courtyard. PLB
T **Just plain efficiency.** Huber, L. J. 1m. 2w. Sc. Int. HUB
J N–R **Just what the Doctor ordered.** Miller, H. L. 14b. 3g. Sc. Int. MIO
PLC PLK

K

C **Kachoo!** Newman, D. 7g. ext. Sc. Classroom. KA PLE
Karma. Kocher, E. 3m. 1w. ext. Sc. Plantation. MAYO
C R **Katherine & Frederick.** Kissen, F. Ann. Nar. 3b. 1g. Sc. Int. KI
C **Keeping Christmas.** Peacock, M. 4b. 5g. Sc. Int. PLD
C **Kettle of brains.** Williams, G. M. 2b. 2g. Sc. Outdoors. BUF
R **Stevenson, R. L.** Kidnapping of David Balfour. Nar. 7m. 2w. Sc. In
Scotland. PLJ
R **Killed by Merry Christmas.** Street, J. M. Nar. 5b. 2g. Sc. Int. PLB
Kindled flame. York, E. B. 2m. 2w. Sc. In Jerusalem. BRIN
C **King Alfred the Great.** Collins, F. 4b. 1g. Sc. Stage. COL
C **King in the kitchen.** Slattery, M. E. 4b. 4g. Sc. Kitchen. PLE
King is here. Du Bois, G. 6m. 4w. Sc. Shepherd's hut. DUB
R **King Neptune's court.** Ann. 2m. 2w. voices. Sc. Studio. WE
King of the great clock tower. Yeats, W. B. 4m. 1w. Sc. Curtains. YE
YEA
R **King of the Golden River.** Ruskin, J. Nar. 5b. voices. No sc. PLE
C **King's birthday.** Burger, I. B. 11 char. ext. Sc. Throne rm. BUR
C **King's creampuffs.** Swintz, M. 9 char. Sc. Throne rm. BUF PLJ
C **King's jester.** Leuser, E. 6b. 1g. ext. Sc. Palace. PLF
King's march. John, E. 5m. 1w. Sc. Temple. FA
King's threshold. Yeats, W. B. 9m. ext. Sc. Palace. YE YEA
C **King's toothache.** Fisher, H. L. 7b. 1g. Sc. Throne rm. FI

J **King's weather.** Oser, J. A. 8b. 5g. Sc. Throne rm. PLK
The Kite. Sherriff, R. C. 7m. 4w. Sc. Prison. WIN
C **Knave of hearts.** Saunders, L. 7m. 2w. 6c. Sc. Curtains. CHA CHAO
Known but to God. Du Bois, G. 11 char. Sc. Tomb. DUB PLK
Know your neighbor. Richards, S. 3m. 5w. St. Int. com. BAN

L

Lace handkerchief. Wilson, B. 1m. 4w. Sc. Boarding house. CARV
J **Lacey's last garland.** Miller, H. L. 3b. 2g. Sc. Int. PLK
Ladies with lamps. Wefer, M. 2m. 5w. Sc. Hospital. ROW
Lady from abroad. Constanduros, M. 2m. 5w. Sc. Int. FA
R **Lady Lookout.** Lyman, B. 2w. voices. Sc. Studio. WE
R **Lady of the Lake.** Scott, W. Nar. 6m. 3w. Sc. Studio. PLK
J **Lady with the lamp.** Wren, J. 6g. Sc. Int. Sc
Lamb in the window. Finch, R. 6m. 3w. Sc. Pulpit. ROW
C **Lamp in the forest.** MacLellan, E. 4b. 2g. Sc. Forest. PLC
C **Language shop.** Hall, M. E. 17 char. Sc. Store. BUF
Land of Heart's desire. Yeats, W. B. 2m. 3w. 1c. Sc. Int. RE YE YEA
C **Land of scratches & scribbles.** Clark, J. 5b. 4g. Sc. Int. CLA
C R **Land where balloons grow.** Harris, V. Ann. 4 char. No sc. WE
Landslide for Shakespeare. Dias, E. J. 8m. 8w. Sc. Stage. PLK
R **Larry Gray & the gremlins.** Reynolds, T. M. Ann. 3b. WE
T **Last chance.** Huber, L. J. 2m. 1w. Sc. Street. HUB
Last curtain. Hosey, N. L. 3m. 3w. Sc. Stage. ROW
R **Last drum.** Hackett, W. 4m. Sc. Int. HAC
Last flight over. Lemmon, A. 3m. 2w. Sc. Cabin. ROW
Last laugh. Du Bois, G. 2m. 3w. 2c. Sc. Int. DUB PLC
Last night's supper. Walters, A. 3m. 3w. Sc. Office. ROW
Last of the Lowries. Green, P. 1m. 3w. Sc. Int. DAV
J **Last snake in Ireland.** Nalone, M. 8b. Sc. Stage. PLK
T **Last straw.** Armer, A. 1m. 1w. Sc. Office. ARM
Last supper. Emurian, E. K. k7m. Organist. Sc. Church. EM
J **Late spring.** Petersen, R. 3b. 4g. Sc. Hut. PLH
J R **Laurence boy.** Alcott, L. M. 4b. 3g. Sc. Int. HA PLB
J **Laughing Princess.** Nicholson, M. A. 5b. 2g. ext. Sc. Palace. PLJ
Lavender lie. Jackson, M. R. 15w. Sc. Old Ladies home. DEN
Lawyer of Springfield. Gow, R. Sc. Outside. BAK
T **The Laytons.** Boothe, B. 3m. 5w. Sc. Int. WF
C **Lazy afternoon.** Schwartz, M. K. 5b. 1g. Sc. Back yard. PLA
C **Lazy little raindrop.** Barr, J. 4g. Sc. Cloud. KA PLC
Lazy ones. McCaslin, N. 4m. 3w. Sc. Open place. MAC
Leader of the people. Steinbeck, J. 3m. 2w. 1b. Sc. Ranch. POT
Least one. Conkle, E. P. 4m. 3w. Sc. Outside. MAYL
J N–R **Left-over reindeer.** Miller, M. L. 9b. 5g. Sc. Int. MIO
R **Left-over reindeer.** Miller, H. L. Ann. 6b. 1g. dencer. Sc. Stage. PLJ
J **Legacy.** Richmond, S. S. 3m. 1w. Sc. Office. RIC

Litchen Fair. Corrie, J. 3m. 2w. Sc. Cottage. MARO
Literature. Molnar, F. 1m. 1w. Sc. Int. MOL
Lithuania. Brooke, R. 5m. 2w. Sc. Hut. CER
c Little bell. Spanmer, C. 5b. 4g. Sc. Outdoors. PLA
c Little bird in the tree. Leuser, E. 6b. 2g. ext. Sc. Palace. KAM PLC
J Little bit of heaven. ———. 2m. 2w. 2g. Sc. Stage. NEVI
c Little Bo-Peep's May flowers. Spamer, C. 7b. 3g. Sc. Meadow. PLB
Little by little. Molnar, F. 1m. 1w. Sc. MOL
c Little cake. McCarty, E. C. 2b. 6g. ext. Sc. Int. BUF
c Little Christmas guest. Asbrand, K. 8g. Sc. Nursery. KA
c Little Christmas tree. Spamer, C. 8b. 6g. Sc. Stage. PLA
c Little circus donkey. Howard, H. L. 9 char. Sc. Woods. BUF
c Little clown who forgot to laugh. Leuser, E. 5b. Sc. Road. PLB
Little darling & the poet. Schnitzler, A. 1m. 1w. Sc. Int. BE
c Little February. Spamer, C. 2b. 1g. ext. Sc. Stage. PLE
Little flaw of Ernesto Lippi. Schaefer, L. 3m. 6w. Sc. Int. MAYO
R Little guy back home. Weaver, L. Nar. 3m. ext. Sc. Outdoors. WE
c Little hero of Holland. Asbrand, K. 7b. 4g. ext. Sc. River bank. BUF
c Little Ida & the flowers. Ormandy, E. 9g. Sc. Bedrm. KA PLE
Little man. Galsworthy, J. 9m. 2w. Sc. R.R. station. CER
Little more than kin. Durham, F. 3m. 4w. Sc. Int. ON
c Little new citizen. Preston, E. E. 5b. 5g. Sc. School rm. SH
c Little patriot. Barbee, L. 2b. 2g. Sc. Int. PLB
c Little Polka dot. Asbrand, K. 6b. 5g. Sc. School yard. PLD
c Little pink egg. Spamer, C. 4b. 5g. Sc. Int. PLA
Little prison. Savage, G. M. 5w. Sc. Elevator. ROW
c Little red hen. Barr, J. 4 char. Sc. Kitchen. PLB
c Little Red Riding Hood. Holmes, R. V. 2b. 3g. Sc. Cottage. KAM
c Little Snow White. King, W. Sc. Int. KAM PLA
Little stranger. Craven, R. F. 3m. Sc. Race track. ON
c Little white cloud. Cooper, E. 2b. 3g. Sc. Cabin. KAM
J Little whittler. Asbrand, K. 4b. 2g. Sc. Street. PLG
c Little witch who tried. Leuser, E. 8g. Sc. Kitchen. KA KAM PLC
J Little women. Alcott, L. M. 7g. 2c. Sc. Int. KA
c Littlest artist. Bennett, R. 3b. 1g. ext. Sc. Playrm. KAM
c Littlest fir. Colbo, E. S. 7 char. Sc. Outdoors. BU
c Littlest month. Fox, D. U. 13 char. Sc. Stage. KAM PLD
R Living declaration. Wishengrad, M. 4m. 1w. voices. Sc. Studio. MAL
J N–R Living up to Lincoln. Hark, M. 4b. 3g. Sc. Int. HAT PLA
Lock, stock & barrel. Murray, J. 6m. 6w. Sc. Int. PLK
Lock your car. Kaser, A. L. Sc. Int. DEN
Londonderry air. Field, R. 2m. 2w. Sc. Kitchen. CROP
c Lonely fir tree. Roberts, H. M. 10 char. Sc. Forest. KAM
R Long & short of it. ———. Nar. 5m. ext. Sc. Studio. SK
Long Christmas dinner. Wilder, T. 4m. 4w. Sc. Int. MIR
Long fall. Howe, C. V. 8m. Sc. Shack. MAYJ
c Long live father. Fisher, A. 2b. 3g. Sc. Int. FI

Long stay cut short. Williams, T. 1m. 2w. Sc. Int. MAG
J R **Lorna Doone.** McGowan, J. 8b. 3g. Sc. Int. PLF
Lost Christmas. Kimes, B. 4m. 3w. Sc. Int. FR
Lost kiss. Douglas, M. 5m. 5w. Sc. Outdoors. ROW
Lost letter. Phelps, P. 4m. 4w. Sc. Int. DEN
Lost star. Heicher, M. 13m. 6w. Sc. Curtains. BRIO
Lost voice. Brome, R. 3m. 4w. Sc. Int. DEN
C **Loud-speaker.** Schwartz, M. K. 3b. 1g. Sc. Street. PLD
C **Louisa Alcott's wish.** Goldsmith, S. L. 3b. 4g. 1 dog. Sc. Int. BUF
J **Love from Bud.** Hark, M. 3b. 2g. Sc. Int. HAS
Love honor and obey. Kaser, A. LeR. 6m, 4w. 4c. HAN
Love in the ape house. Sladen-Smith, F. 4m. Sc. Monkey house. SP
T **Love lesson for Scotty.** Armer, A. 1m. 1w. Sc. Int. ARM
Love of Don Perlimplin & Bellsa. Lorca, F. G. 6 char. Sc. Garden.
BE
Love of Ruth. Casey, B. M. 4m. 4w. Sc. Int. BRIN
T **Love scores a touchdown.** Armer, A. 1m. 1w. Sc. Int. ARM
Love triumphant. Maughfling, M. 2m. 3w. Sc. Village green. MAUG
Lovely miracle. Johnson, P. 2m. 2w. Sc. Cottage. DAV
J **Love's young dream.** Preston, E. E. 1m. 1w. Sc. Int. com. PR
C **Luck takes a holiday.** Fisher, A. 9b. 3g. Sc. Int. FI PLF
J **Lucky seven.** Brown, A. M. 7b. Sc. Street. Sc.
Luigi steps aside. Hackett, W. 4m. 2w. Sc. Office. PLK
C **Lullabye Land.** Asbrand, K. 8b. 9g. Sc. Garden. PLA

M

J **Mad Doctor Zing.** Howard, V. L. 6b. Sc. Lab. HO
C **Mad tea party.** Wall, L. V. 4b. 1g. Sc. Under a tree. WA
C **Mad tea party.** Worcester, N. S. 3b. 1g. Sc. Under a tree. PLF
R **Maelduin of Arran.** McCaslin, N. Nar. 10m. 3w. Sc. In Ireland. MAC
J **Magic carpet sweeper.** Miller, H. L. 3b. 3g. Sc. Int. PLK
C **Magic egg.** Hark, M. 9 char. ext. Sc. Woods. BUF
C **Magic formulas.** Fisher, A. 4b. 3g. Sc. Lab. FI
C **Magic goose.** Newman, D. 8b. 5g. Sc. Fair grounds. PLD
C **Magic grapes.** Leuser, E. 6b. 1g. 2c. Sc. Road. PLF
C **Magic Jack-o' Lantern.** Howard, H. L. 5b. 1g. Sc. Int. BUF KAM
C **Magic mirror.** Very, A. 3g. Sc. Int. PLF
C **Magic owl.** Carpenter, F. 6 char. Sc. Woods. CARP
C **Magic pumpkin.** Kingman, L. 10b. 6g. Sc. Bench. BUF
Magic spell. Cooper, E. 1b. 5g. Sc. Int. BUF
C **Magic well.** Leuser, E. 12b. 7g. Sc. Wishing well. PLF
Maiden's prayer. Finch, R. 2m. 3w. Sc. Int. com. ROW
R **Major conflicts.** Maurois, A. 2m. 1w. Sc. Studio. MAUR
C **Make him smile.** Arnold, E. W. 9 char. Sc. Doll shop. BUF
Mille. Deceit. Dickson, G. 2m. 3w. Sc. Dress shop. CARV
Man & woman act. ———. 1m. 1w. Sc. Street. LA

Man at the door. Stevens, H. C. G. 1m. 3w. Sc. Flat. ARL

Man from the fells. Standring, P. 3m. 2w. Sc. Int. BANN

R **Man of strife.** Pollock, S. 12m. 1w. Sc. Church. POL

R **Man without a country.** Hale, E. E. Nar. 6m. 1w. Sc. Studio. HA PLA SC

Man who married a dumb wife. France, A. 7m. 4w. ext. Sc. Int. CER KN

R **Man who stole the freedom train.** Arthur, E. Large no. of Char. no sc. PH

J **Man-trap for mother.** Miller, H. L. 2b. 2g. Sc. Int. PLA

J **Man's eternal quest for the good life.** Eisenberg, H. 4m. ext. Sc. Stage. EI

R **Mantle of Elijah.** Pollock, S. Nar. 2m. 2w. Sc. Church. POL

C **Many a slip.** Fisher, A. 1b. 2g. ext. Sc. Int. FI PLD

Many happy returns. Hollister, L. S. 3m. 5w. Sc. Int. Farce. FR

Many happy returns. Tims, M. 3m. 4w. Sc. Int. ARL

J **Many thanks.** Hark, M. 10b. 10g. Sc. Office. HAR PLH

R **Million-pound banknote.** Mark Twain. 8m. 1w. Sc. Int. HA

R **Marjory Daw.** Aldrich, T. B. Nar. 9m. 2w. Sc. Int. HAC PLA

J **Marko goes a courtin'.** Gross, E. 6g. ext. Sc. Camp. GRO

R **Marriage & friendship.** Maurois, A. Sc. Int. MAUR

Marriage of Pierot. Zeller, A. E. 2m. 1w. Sc. Stage. DEN

C **Martha Washington's spy.** Dias, E. J. 5b. 2g. Sc. Backdrop. PLF

C **Mary Elizabeth's wonderful dream.** Mason, M. E. 6g. ext. Sc. Curtain. KA PLC

Mary Forbisher. Sladen-Smith, F. 4m. 3w. Sc. Int. BANN

C **Mary's cake.** Spamer, C. 2b. 5g. Sc. Outdoors. PLD

T **Mask of guilt.** Mickel, J. 4m. 1w. Sc. Int. MIC

Materia medica. Ryerson, F. 7w. Sc. Hospital. SP

Matrimony bumps. Casey, A. 1m. 1w. Sc. Street. HAN PLU

Matron of Ephesus. Sion, G. 3m. 2w. Sc. Open space. MAYK

C **Matter of business.** Wilkes, E. 4b. 1g. Sc. Int. PLC

R **Matter of taste.** Maurois, A. 1m. 1w. Sc. Int. MAUR

C **May basket.** Hark, M. 7b. 6g. Sc. Outdoors. PLA

C **May day gift.** Barbee, L. 7g. Sc. Classrm. PLB

May eve. Cleveland, E. 2m. 2w. Sc. Int. FR

J R **Mayflower compact.** 11b. 1g. voices. Nar. Sc. Studio. PLE

J **The Mayor.** Howard, V. L. 7b. Sc. Office. HO

J **Meaning of art.** Sylvester, L. 15b. 5g. Sc. Screens. PLA

Meaning of Christmas day. Heicher, M. 9m. 6w. ext. Sc. Church. BRIO

J **Mechanical man.** Murray, J. 6b. 6g. Sc. Classrm. PLG

Medal for Julien. Kocher, E. 3m. 3w. Sc. Int. MAYP

J **Meet Mr. Witch.** Hark, M. 14 char. Sc. Int. HAR PLA

C **Melissa's muffins.** Barbee, L. 4b. 4g. Sc. Outside. PLD

C **Melodious mixture.** Ridge, A. 5 puppets. Sc. Int. RID

Merlin limited. Trentham, V. 2m. 3w. Sc. Shop. ARL

C   **Memorial day for the blue & the grey.** Newman, D. 3b. 2g. Sc. Lawn. PLE

C   **Mermaid club.** Deming, D. 1b. 6g. Sc. Cellar. PLE

R   **Merry adventures of Robin Hood.** ———. Nar. 4b. Sc. Outdoors. NEV

R   **Merry Christmas.** Alcott, L. M. Nar. 3m. 7w. Sc. Int. HAC PLB

C   **Merry Christmas elf.** Fisher, A. 6b. 5g. Sc. Outdoors. PLD

C   **Merry, Merry, Merry.** Carroll, G. H. 16 char. ext. Sc. Int. BUF

J   **The message.** Howard, V. L. 56b. Sc. Fort. HO

    Message for Robin Hood. Colson, J. G. 11b. ext. Sc. Forest. PLF

    Message from John. Spence, W. 4w. Sc. Cottage. BAK

    Message from Khufu. Cottman, H. S. 4m. Sc. Tomb. ROW

C   **Message of the hearts.** Newman, D. 2b. 3g. Sc. Stage. PLE

R   **Message to Garcia.** Hubbard, E. 4m. Sc. Road. PLB

J   **Midge minds her sister's business.** Paradis, M. B. 2b. 8g. Sc. Int. PLA

J   **Midge rings the bell.** Paradis, M. B. 11g. Sc. Int. PA

C   **Midnight burial.** Hill, K. 3b, 5g. Sc. Woods. BUF KA PLA PLK

    Midsummer Night. Molnar, F. 2m. Sc. Summer resort. MOL

C   **Milkmaid & her pail.** Joy, V. 3g. ext. Sc. Highway. KA PLB

J   **Million-dollar recipe.** Howard, V. L. 5b. Sc. Int. HO

R   **Million-pound banknote.** Mark Twain. 6m. Sc. Int. PLC

R   **Mind in the shadow.** Perl, A. Nar. 8m. 5w. Sc. Int. MAYH

C   **Mind your manners.** Asbrand, K. 5b. 6g. Sc. Int. PLA

J   **Mind your P's & Q's.** Hark, M. 17 char. Sc. Stage. HAR PLF

    Minnie Field. Conkle, E. P. 5m. 1w. Sc. Kitchen. GAS

J   **Minor developments.** Huntsberry, W. E. 10b. 3g. Sc. Int. PLA

R   **Minor friendship.** Maurois, A. 3m. 1w. Sc. Int. MAUR

    Minor miracle. Powers, V. 4m. Sc. Curtains. ROW

    Miracle. Molnar, F. 2m. Sc. Int. com. MOL

C   **Miracle of the fishes.** Marsh, W. A. 4b. Sc. Int. MARS

T   **Miracle of the sack of barley.** Tooley, H. Ann. 6m. Sc. Studio. TO

    Miracle of St. Anthony. 8m. 2w. ext. Sc. Church. CER

J   **Miraculous tea party.** McGowan, J. 7b. 8g. Sc. Lawn. PLK

C   **Mirror children.** Spamer, C. 6g. Sc. Bedrm. KA

C   **Mischievous clock.** Clark, J. 2b. 3g. Sc. Int. CLA

    Mish-mosh bird. Murray, J. 9m. 5w. ext. Sc. Int. PLK

J   **Miss Barton is needed.** Nolan, J. C. 7b. 2g. ext. Sc. Hospital. PLD

    Miss fixit. McCoy, P. S. 3m. 4w. Sc. Summer resort. PLJ

    Miss Haffner. Crown, P. 3m. 3w. 2c. Sc. Bedrm. ARL

    Miss Julie. Strindberg, A. 1m. 2w. Sc. Kitchen. CER

C   **Miss Liberty protests.** Williams, H. V. 1b. 1g. ext. Sc. N. Y. harbor. WI

J   **Miss Lonely heart.** Miller, H. L. 5b. 3g. Sc. Int.

C   **Miss Robin's school.** Spamer, C. 5b. 2g. Sc. Int. PLC

C   **Missing Easter eggs.** Barr, J. 5b. 2g. Sc. Forest. PLB

J   **Mister A. Lincoln.** Paradis, M. B. 8g. Sc. Int. PA

C   **Mr. Bates goes to the polls.** Reay, N. B. 3b. 1g. Sc. Front porch. KAM PLD

   Mr. Bell's creation. Richards, S. 3m. 3w. Sc. Telephone. FR
C   **Mister Catchy Cold.** Deming, D. 15 char. Sc. Stage. PLD
   Mr. Fothergill joins the Angels. Dinner, W. 5m. 4w. Sc. Int. MARO
J   **Mr. Lincoln's beard.** Newman, D. 5b. 4g. Sc. R.R. station. PLK
C   **Mr. Lazy man's family.** Ward, M. 3b. 3g. Sc. Int. PLD
C   **Mr. Longfellow observes Book Week.** 4b. 6g. Sc. Study. BUF
C   **Mister Owl.** Spamer, C. 4b. 2g. Sc. Forest. PLC
C   **Mr. Rabbit's Easter jamboree.** Bufano, R. 3b. Sc. Forest. Puppet. BRU
J   **Mr. Smooch's trap.** Werner, S. 10 char. Sc. Forest. PLH
J   **Mr. Snow White's Thanksgiving.** Miller, H. L. 3b. 4g. Sc. Int. PLJ
C   **Mr. Thanks has his day.** Kingsman, L. 11 char. Sc. Street. BUF
   Mister Vincent. Bec, M. 3m. 4w. Sc. Int. ROW
J   **Mrs. Claus' Christmas present.** Urban, C. 5b. 1g. Sc. Int. PLJ
C   **Mrs. Santa's Christmas gift.** Newman, D. 11b. 1g. Sc. Workshop. BU PLC
C   **Mrs. Sniffit's Christmas.** Brown, A. V. 1b. 3g. Sc. Int. PLD
C   **Mixing stick.** Leuser, E. 6b. 5g. Sc. Kitchen. BUF PLB
R   **Mob scene.** Fylstre, A. Ann. 6 char. Sc. Studio. WE
C   **Mock turtle's story.** Wall, L. V. 3b. 1g. Sc. Seashore. WA
J   **Models for health.** Gordon, C. 3b. 7g. Sc. Classrm. PLE
J N–R **Mom's a grandmother now.** Hark, M. 4b. 3g. Sc. Int. HAT PLC
J   **Money talks.** Weiss, M. J. 5b. 4g. Sc. Outside school. WEI
   Monkey's paw. Jacobs, W. W. 4m. 1w. Sc. Int. CER
R   **Monsieur Beaucaire.** Tarkington, B. 6m. 1w. ext. Sc. Int. OF
   Monsieur Le Marquis. Janes, H. 3m. 1w. Sc. Cell in Paris. MAR MARC
   Moon keeps shining. Hark, M. 3m. 2w. Sc. Int. BAK HAT PLD
J   **Moon maidens.** 6 char. voices. Sc. Int. EI
J   **Moonbeam dares.** Lee, S. Ann. 4b. 5g. Sc. In China. PLK
J R **Moonrise island.** Preston, E. E. 4b. 5g. ext. Sc. Int. Farce. PR
C   **Morning maker.** Campbell, C. 4b. ext. Sc. Road. KAM PLC
   Moses, the law-giver. Nygaard, N. E. 5m. Sc. Mountain. NY
R   **Most indestructible man.** Rush, M. E. 2m. 1w. Sc. Int. Farce. SK
J   **Most memorable voyage.** Blakeless, K. L. 10b. ext. Sc. Deck. PLJ
J   **Mother beats the band.** Miller, H. L. 5b. 10g. Sc. Int. PLH
J N–R **Mother for Mayor.** Miller, H. L. 4b. 4g. Sc. Int. MIO PLF
J   **Mother Goose gives advice.** Woolsey, J. Ann. 9 char. Sc. Stage. WOO
C   **Mother Goose gives a dinner.** Vandevere, J. L. 6b. 5g. Sc. Kitchen. KAM
C   **Mother Goose's children.** Woosley, J. 16 char. Sc. Curtains. WOO
J   **Mother of the town.** Woolsey, J. 1b. 8g. Sc. Int. WOO
   Mother remembers. Huber, L. J. 3w. Sc. Int. HU
J   **Mother saves the day.** Hark, M. 3b. 2g. Sc. Int. HAS
C   **Mother saves the day.** Pendleton, E. 3b. 3g. Sc. Int. PLA
J   **Mother's apron strings.** Miller, H. L. 5b. 3g. Sc. Int. MIM PLD
J N–R **Mother's big day.** Miller, H. L. 1b. 7g. Sc. Int. MIM
J   **Mother's day for Susan.** Barr, J. 8g. Sc. Bedrm. PLG

c **Mother's day off and on.** Fisher, A. 2b. 3g. Sc. Int. PLB

J **Mother's fairy godmother.** Miller, H. L. 2b. 4g. Sc. Int. PLK

c **Mother's gift.** Howard, H. L. 7 char. Sc. Curtains. BUF

J **Mother's hidden talent.** Miller, H. L. 8b. 3g. Sc. Int. PLG

    Moving on tomorrow. Phillips, M. K. 8w. Sc. Int. PLK

    Mozart & the gray Stewart. Wilder, T. 3m. Sc. Int. SP

c **Much ado about ants.** Heath, A. L. 3b. 2g. Sc. Int. BUF

    Muletail prime. Conkle, E. P. 2m. Sc. Bar. MAYK

    Mummy limps at midnight. ———. Large number of char. Sc. Tomb.
      KO

J **Murder in the kitchen.** Fisher, A. 2b. 4g. Sc. Stage. FI PLC

T **Murder of Shakespeare.** Tooley, H. 8m. 3w. Sc. Theatre. TO

    Museum of man. Sinclair, L. Any number of char. Sc. Museum. GOL

J **Music hath charms.** Hark, M. 3b. 2g. Sc. Int. HAS PLF

    Music on the menu. Donovan, A. D. 4m. 6w. Sc. Int. DEN

J **Musical notes.** Preston, E. E. 2w. Sc. Street. com. PR

R **My client Curley.** Corwin, N. 27 char. Ann. Sc. Studio. GR

R **My double & how he undid me.** Hale, E. E. 4m. 3w. Sc. Int. HA PLB

J **My honest friend.** Woolsey, J. 2b. 2g. Sc. Kitchen. WOO

    My mirror tells me. Lehmann, A. 1w. Sc. Boudoir. LE

R **My Uncle Willy.** Sweeney, B. 4m. 3w. Sc. Int. MAK

c **Mysterious stranger.** Nicholson, J. 4b. 3g. Sc. Int. PLE

R **Mystery in the Lab.** 4m. 3w. Sc. Lb. MU PLF

    Mystery of the silver-backed hairbrush. Crane, B. 4m. 2w. ext. Sc.
    Int. BAK

J **Mystery ring.** Gross, N. F. 8g. Sc. Front Lawn. PLK

N

J N–R **"N" for nuisance.** Miller, H. L. 3b. 3g. Sc. Studio. MIO PLF

J **Names to remember.** Ramsey, H. Nar. 10 char. Sc. Stage. PLK

c **Naming the flowers.** York, M. A. 12b. 10g. Sc. Throne rm. PLE

    Nangsa. Duncan, M. Any number of char. Sc. In Tibet. DUN

c **Naomi-of-the-inn.** Waite, H. E. 8b. 5g. Sc. Inn. BU PLB

T **Narration for V J Day.** Any number of char. no. sc. HE

J **Narrow squeak.** Deming, D. 1b. 4g. Sc. Stage. PLC

T **Native dancer.** Shaw, D. 2m. 3w. Sc. Atop building. SET

    Natives are restless tonight. Dias, E. J. 10m. 3w. Sc. Camp. DIA

R **Nature's most precious gift.** Probst, G. 2m. Sc. Int. MAL

c **Naughty Susan.** Slingluff, M. O. 3b. 4g. Sc. Int. KAM PLB

c **Nautical sheep.** Nicholson, J. 1b. 1g. Sc. Meadow. PLD

R **Navy & the pirates.** Kane, E. B. Ann. 5b. 2g. Sc. Studio. PLA

R **The necklace.** Maupassant, G. de. Nar. 4m. 3w. Sc. Int. HA PLC

c **Needle fights for freedom.** MacLellan, E. 3b. 6g. Sc. Int. KAM PLD

    Neighbors. Gale, Z. 1m. 7w. Sc. Kitchen. COO CROP

    Nerve of it! Kirkpatrick, J. 3m. 3w. Sc. Int. Farce. ON

J **Nervous father.** Eisenberg, H. 1m. 1w. Sc. Int. EI

J **Never any excuse.** 10b. 2g. Sc. Colonial int. PLA

Never miss a trick. Gurney, M. 3m. Sc. Graveyard. SEK

J New broom. Hark, M. 3b. 7g. Sc. Deserted house. HAR

New Colossus. Emurian, E. K. 4m. 5w. Sc. Int. EM

J New-fangled Thanksgiving. Hark, M. 4b. 3g. Sc. Int. HAR PLB

C New hearts for old. Fisher, A. 3b. 3g. Sc. Int. PLD

J New home for mice. Werner, S. 7 char. Sc. Barnyard. PLJ

New look. Hackett, W. 3m. 6w. Sc. Gown shop. BAK

New secretary. Huber, L. J. Sc. Office. HU

C New shoes. Miller, H. L. 4b. 1g. ext. Sc. Store. MIN PLG

J New Washington. Newman, D. 4b. 6g. Sc. Classrm. PLH

C New worlds. Gould, J. 9b. 1g. Sc. Kitchen. PLD

J N–R New worlds to find. Hark, M. 4b. 1g. Sc. Museum. HAT

Newly weds. George, C. Ann. 1m. 1w. Sc. Int. PLU

Next of kin. Hackett, W. 3m. 4w. Sc. Int. BAK

Next-to-last-rites. Thomas D. 3m. 2w. 2c. ext. Sc. Farmhouse. MAYP

J Nickel & a dime. Fisher, A. 11 char. Sc. Park bench. FIS

Night at an inn. Dunsany, Lord. 8m. Sc. Inn. CER CRO

R Night in Plainville. Cowgill, R. Nar. 5m. 4w. Sc. Int. COW

Night's high noon. Moretonhampstead Drama Class. 3m. 3w. Sc. Int.
    KEL

J Nine cheers for Christmas. 5b. 5g. Sc. Stage. PLJ

C No braver soldier. Bierling, J. C. 8b. 3g. Sc. Kitchen. BUF

T No fight tonight. Huber, L. J. 2m. 1w. Sc. Int. HUB

J No order in the court. Howard, V. J. 6b. Sc. Court rm. HO

J No room at the inn. Patterson, E. L. 14b. 1g. Sc. Inn. BU BUF PLC

J No sale. Richmond, S. S. 3b. 1g. Sc. Store. RIC

T No shoes. Du Pont, L. 3m. 1w. Sc. Hospital. KAV

J T No time for Dames. Armer, A. 1b. 2g. Sc. Playrm. ARM

Noble lord. Wilde, P. 2m. 1w. Sc. Woods. KN

Nobody sleeps. LePelley, G. 1m. 4w. Sc. Int. ROW

C No-mother land. Speacker, L. 8 char. Sc. Woods. KAM PLB

Non Nobis. Aske, L. 4m. 1w. Sc. Sanitorium. MARP

J None so blind. Du Bois, G. 4b. 4g. Sc. Colonial int. PLC

C North wind & the sun. Bennett, R. 6b. 1g. Sc. Stage. PLA

R The nosebag. MacNeice, L. Ann. 29 char. Sc. Studio. GR

J Not fit for man or beast. Hark, M. 3b. 4g. Sc. Shack. HAR

C Not for girls. Miller, H. L. Ann. 3b. 6g. Sc. Int. MIN PLH

C Not for the menu. Pyle, M. T. 3b. 5g. Sc. Sun porch. BUF

C Not only the strong. Waite, H. E. 4b. 6g. Sc. Blockhouse. BUF

Not without honor. Getzinger, E. W. 10w. Sc. In Nazareth. BRIN

J Not worth a continental. Miller, H. L. 4b. 2g. Sc. Store. PLF

J Not-so-crooked man. Fisher, A. 4b. 4g. Sc. Int. FI

C Nothing ever happens. Fisher, A. 5b. 4g. Sc. Int. FI

J Nothing to be thankful for. Hark, M. 3b. 2g. voice. Sc. Int. HAR
    PLD

C Number play: the poison plot. Marsh, W. A. 2b. no. sc. Puppet. MARS

J R Numbers game. Preston, E. E. 5m. 5w. ext. Sc. Radio station. PR

C R **Nurenberg stove.** Mack, N. Ann. 8b. 7g. Sc. Studio. WE
R **Nurse Henrietta.** Kesser, H. 1w. Sc. Int. Monologue. FIV
C **Nursery rhyme diet.** Hark, M. 8b. 8g. Sc. Int. HAR PLE
  Nursing in the mountains. Deming, D. 1m. 4w. Sc. Cabin. PLB
  Nurse's day out. Teasdale, V. 1m. 3w. 2c. Sc. Int. TE

O

  O distant land. Richards, S. 7m. 3w. ext. Sc. Outdoors. BAN MAYH
  "O let him pass!" August, E. 1m. 4w. Sc. Country house. NAFF
J **O little town of Bethlehem.** Moleley, O. J. 8. 3g. Sc. Village. PLJ
J **Ode to spring.** Hark, M. 5b. 6g. Sc. Drug store. PLH
R **Odyssey of Runyon Jones.** Corwin, N. 16 char. no sc. RE
  Of all the years. Hess, M. B. 6m. 8w. Sc. Int. ROW
J **Of gods & men.** Fisher, A. 3m. 5w. Sc. Office. FIS
  Of social significance. Aklom, M. 1m. 2w. Sc. Boudoir. MARO
C **Off the shelf.** Hark, M. 8 char. Sc. Public Library. BUF HAR
J **Ogre of Rashamon.** Balm, C. M. Storyteller. 4m. Sc. Stage. EI
  Oh, H-e-n-r-y-y! Teasdale, V. 1m. 2w. Sc. Garage. TE
  Oh, Mrs. Morton, you're so patient. Teasdale, V. 2w. Sc. Int. TE
  Oh, that golden wedding anniversary. Drummond, R. Ann. 1m. 1w. ext. Sc. Int. PLU
T **Old beginning.** Foote, H. 7m. 4w. Sc. Int. FO
  Old English play. ————. 2m. 2w. ext. Sc. Medieval London. KO
C **Old fashioned Thanksgiving.** Roberts, H. M. 6g. Sc. Attic. KA
  Old lady shows her medals. Barrie, J. M. 1m. 4w. Sc. Int. BAK HAL IN KN
  Old maid. Akins, Z. 2w. Sc. Int. SEK
C **Old man river.** Deming, D. 2b. 5g. Sc. Int. BUF
C **Old mother Hubbard.** Barr, J. 5b. 3g. Sc. Kitchen. PLC
  Old music. Gunn, N. M. 3m. 3w. Sc. Cottage. BANN
J **Old woman & the tramp.** Carlson, B. W. 1b. 1g. Sc. Int. CAR
C R **Old woman in the shoe.** White, M. R. Nar. Any number of char. Sc. Studio. WH
C **On a bicycle built for one.** Richmond, S. S. 3b. 3g. Sc. Outside. PLB
C **On a roof top.** Goodwin, R. V. 8 char. Sc. Int. WI
  On Baile's strand. Yeats, W. B. 5m. ext. Sc. Ancient Ireland. YE YEA
C **On strike.** Fisher, A. 8 char. Sc. Woods. PLD
C **On such a night.** Fisher, A. 4b. 1g. Sc. Farmhouse. PLF
J **On the air.** Richmond, S. S. 4b. 4g. Sc. Radio station. PLB RIC
C **On the fence.** Beach, M. M. 4b. 3g. Sc. Back yard. PLD
  On the sentimental side. Kirkpatrick, J. 3m. 4w. Sc. Int. FR
J **On trial.** Richmond, S. S. 2b. 1g. Sc. Office. RIC
  Once a thief. Perrini, A. 9m. 2w. Sc. Island. MAYP
  Once to every boy. Richards, S. 7m. 4w. Sc. Int. BAN
J **Once upon a time.** Fisher, A. 11b. 5g. Sc. Int. PLD
  One hour alone. Holland, N. 1m. 4w. Sc. Palace. MARO
T **One in twelve.** Latham, J. 3m. 2w. Sc. Court rm. KAT

One man's word. Huber, L. J. 3m. 1w. Sc. Bench. HU
One of these days. Kozlenko, W. 3m. 2w. Sc. Int. BAN
R One special for Doc. Geiger, M. 3m. 1w. Sc. Int. COO POT
T One year after. Armer, A. 1m. 1w. Sc. Int. ARM
C R One-inch fellow. Kissen, F. Ann. Nar. 3b. 3g. Sc. Temple. KIC
C One-ring circus. Fisher, A. 6b. 3g. Sc. Vacant lot. BUF PLA
Only jealousy of Emer. Yeats, W. B. 3m. 2w. Sc. In Ireland. YE YEA
T "Only once blow the fuse." Van Aernam, J. H. 4m. 3w. Sc. Farm. HE
Open-air drama. Bridie, J. 2m. 2w. ext. Sc. Outdoors. BRI
Opened by mistake. Seller, T. 3m. 4w. Sc. Int. BAK
T Operation Coral. Brown, S. P. 9m. Sc. On the beach. KAV
Ophelia. Morris, T. B. 7w. Sc. Bedrm. MARQ
J Opportunity unlimited. Hackett, W. 4b. 3g. Sc. Int. BAK
The option. Baldwin, M. T. 4m. 1w. Sc. Office. BAL
Orange blossoms. Johnson, P. 2m. 5w. Sc. Int. MARO
Original sin. ————. 1m. 1w. Sc. Garden of Eden. KO
Othello. Eisenberg. H. 2m. 2w. ext. Sc. Stage. EI
Other apostles. Callahan, G. E. 7m. Sc. Church. ROW
Other side. Knapp, J. S. 4m. Sc. Prison. GR
Our dream house. Morrish, P. 3b. 3g. Sc. Int. JON
J Our famous ancestors. Hark, M. 2b. 3g. Sc. Int. HAT PLG
J Our four walls. Hark, M. 3b. 3g. Sc. Int. HAR
Our preparation for the future. Switz, T. MacL. 8 char. Voice. ext.
  Sc. Church. SW
Out at the home plate. Bennick, H. R. 2m. 4w. Sc. Int. DEN
Out of the darkness. McGreevey, J. 4m. 3w. ext. Sc. Garden. BRIN
Out of the shadows. Honiton Drama Class. 6w. Sc. Farm. KEL
Out of this world. Dias, E. J. 2m. 4w. Sc. Int. DIA PLA
J Outgoing tide. Hackett, W. 4b. 3g. Sc. Classrm. PLC
J Over the counter. Richmond, S. S. 3m. 5w. Sc. store. RIC
Overtones. Gerstenberg, A. 4w. Sc. Int. CER
J Owl & the young man. Conkle, E. P. 2m. Sc. Outdoors. com. SP

P

Palmer way. Baker, N. E. 3m. 1w. Sc. Int. FR
J Paloma, Princess of Phito. Howard, V. L. 4b. Sc. Observatory. HO
C Panic in the palace. Swintz, M. 8b. 5g. Sc. Throne rm. PLE
J Papa Pepper's bombshell. Miller, H. L. 3b. 3g. Sc. Int. PLF
C Paper Princess. Draper, C. C. 1b. 2g. Sc. Woods. PLD
Paradise enow. Bridie, J. 2m. 5w. Sc. Booth. Farce. BRI
Paradise inn. Apstein, T. 6m. 2w. Sc. In Mexico. MAYL
Parents are people. Weiss, M. J. 2m. 3w. Sc. Int. WEI
Parting tear. Stahl, LeR. 1m. 1w. Sc. Stage. com. HAN
J N–R Party is born. Gross, E. 5b. 5g. Sc. Int. GRO
J Patched coat. Phelps, P. 4b. 5g. Sc. Int. DEN
C Patchwork Princess. Slattery, M. E. 3b. 4g. Sc. Courtyard. PLE

Paths of glory. Sidney, H. 2m. Sc. War. SEK

Patrick Bronte & the saint. Packer, B. 3m. 1w. ext. Sc. Int. MAYH

c **Patrick Pumpkin.** Spamer, C. 3b. 2g. Sc. Outside. PLA

j **Patriotic minstrels.** Ruggles, R. 12b. 12g. Sc. Stage. SC

c **Patriotic Teddy Bear & the U N.** Miller, H. L. 7b. 3g. Sc. Playrm. MIN

Paul before King Agrippa. Nygaard, N. E. 3m. 1w. Sc. Church. NY

Paul Bunyan: Lumber jack. McCaslin, N. 6m. 1b. 1g. Sc. Stage. MAC

Paul in the Areopagus. Nygaard, N. E. 2m. Sc. Rostrum. NY

c **Paul Revere rides again.** Miller, H. L. 30 char. Sc. Stage. MIN

Paul Thompson forever. Gorelik, M. 2m. 2w. Sc. Int. BAK

t **"The pay-off."** Beebe, T. 2m. 1w. Sc. Int. HE

The peacemaker. Huber, L. J. 3m. 1w. Sc. Park. HU

j **Perambulating pie.** Pyle, M. T. 5b. 5g. Sc. Community house. BU PLC

r **Perfect crime.** Lamont, J. 4m. Sc. Int. WE

Perfect gift. Du Bois, H. G. 10b. 2g. Sc. Inn. BU

Period house. Eaton, W. P. 2m. 1b. 1w. 2g. Sc. Int. MAYJ ON

c **Perfect understanding.** Marsh, W. A. 7g. Sc. Int. KA PLB

j **Persistent Musician.** Marsh, W. A. 8b. 2g. Sc. Int. Puppet. MARS

Peter at Penticost. Nygaard, N. E. 2m. Sc. Church. NY

c **Peter Rabbit.** Simonds, N. 5b. 1g. Sc. Rabbit hole. BUF

c r **Peter Rabbit changes his name.** White, M. R. 3b. 3g. Sc. Outdoors. WH

c r **Peterkins try to become wise.** Kissen, F. 2b. 2g. Sc. Int. KIS

j **Peter's Easter basket company.** Blaine, B. G. 5b. 2g. Sc. Woods. PLK

c **Petrified Prince.** Miller, H. L. 7b. 1g. Sc. Throne rm. MIN

t **Pharmacist's mate.** Schulberg, B. 5m. ext. Sc. Submarine. PO

Philip, the desert evangelist. Nygaard, N. E. 3m. Sc. Rostrum. NY

j **Place to begin.** Hark, M. 3b. 3g. Sc. School auditorium. PLB

j **Play without a name.** Fisher, A. 16b. 5g. Sc. Stage. PLD

Player Queen. Yeats, W. B. 6m. 3w. Sc. Open space. YE YEA

Playwright's dilemma. 4m. 3w. Sc. Int. com. ON

j **Pleasant dreams.** Hark, M. 7 char. Sc. Stage. HAR

j **Plot of Potzentausend.** Keating, E. H. 10b. Sc. Int. com. KE

c **Plot thickens.** Fisher, A. 2b. 3g. Sc. Woods. PLC

r **Pickwick papers.** Dickens, C. Nar. 8m. 2w. Sc. Int. OF PLK

c r **Pied Piper.** Kissen, F. Ann. Nar. 14 char. Sc. Town. KIC

c **Pied Piper.** Kennedy, L. 5b. 2g. Sc. Street in Hamlin. BUF PLF

c **Piffle! It's only Sniffle!** Kaufman, T. 11 char. Sc. Stage. BUF PLA

Pilate, the Roman governor. Nygaard, N. E. 3m. Sc. Court yard. NY

c **Pilgrim parting.** Miller, H. L. 9b. 5g. Sc. Beach. MIN PLH

c **Pilgrims & pebbles.** MacLellan, E. 4b. 2g. Sc. In Holland. PLE

Pilot who weathered the storm. Rose, K. 4m. 3w. Sc. Ballrm. ROS

c **Pinata.** MacLellan, E. 2b. 4g. Sc. Roof. PLC

j **Pinch-hitter.** Paradis, M. B. 2b. 4g. Sc. Int. PLC

Pink dress. Elser, D. 2m. 3w. Sc. Int. ROW

c **Pink parasol.** Miller, H. L. 3b. 5g. Sc. Garden. BUF MIO

J **Pink roses for Christmas.** Campbell, J. E. 2b. 3g. Sc. Int. BU
C **Pinocchio.** Miller, M. 8 char. Sc. Int. MILL
J **Pin-up pals.** Miller, H. L. 5w. ext. Sc. Club rm. KA
C **Pioneer Valentine.** Cooper, E. 1b. 2g. Sc. Int. PLA
   Pirates & the ladies. Maughfling, M. 2m. 2w. Sc. Beach. MAUG
J **Pipistrella of Aquitaine.** MacLellan, J. M. 7b. 2g. Sc. Castle. JON
   Poet & the actress. Schnitzler, A. 1m. 1w. Sc. Inn. BE
C **Poet's nightmare.** 4b. 4g. Sc. Int. PLS
   Poison ivy. Du Bois, G. 1m. 1w. 6c. Sc. Int. DUB
C **Polka dot pup.** Miller, H. L. 9b. 7g. Sc. Classrm. MIN PLH
   Polly in the park. Maughfling, M. 2m. 2w. Sc. Park. MAUG
J **Pollywogs.** Howard, V. L. 4b. Sc. Office of psychiatrist. HO
   Poor Aubrey. Kelly, G. 1m. 3w. Sc. Int. GAS
   Poor Maddalena. Saunders, L. 2m. 1w. Sc. Int. KN
   Poor man, rich man. Brome, R. 2m. 2w. Sc. Int. DEN
J **Poor relations.** Keating, E. H. 7b. Sc. Int. KE
C **Pop-up books.** Spamer, C. 14 char. Sc. Schoolrm. KAM PLE
J **Portrait of an American.** Hark, M. 4b. 4g. Sc. Int. PLF
   Pot of broth. Yeats, W. B. Sc. Country kitchen. YE YEA
C **Pot of gold.** Spamer, C. 9 char. Sc. Outdoors. BUF
C **Pottery lane.** Asbrand, K. 3b. 5g. Sc. Int.
C **Precedent in pastries.** Rowland, E. 12 char. ext. Sc. Courtrm. BUF
R **Prelude for posterity.** Hastings, F. V. Ann. 2m. ext. Sc. Studio. WE
J **Prescription for success.** Richmond, S. S. 4m. Sc. Drug store. RIC
C **Present for Abe.** Newman, D. 5b, 4g. Sc. Schoolrm. PLY
C **Present for mother.** Barr, J. 7 char. Sc. Woods. BUF KAM PLA
   The president. Molnar, F. 23 char. Sc. Bank. MO
C **President Lincoln's children.** Very, A. 4b. 2g. Sc. White house. KAM
J **Press photographer.** Richmond, S. S. 4b. 1g. Sc. Office. PLA RIC
C **Pretty maid, where have you been?** Marsh, W. A. 3b. 4g. no. sc. MARS
   The preview. Chalmers, V. 1m. 1w. Sc. Hospital. PLU
J **Price of eggs.** Nicholson, M. A. 2b. 2g. Sc. Village. PLH
R **Pride & prejudice.** Austen, J. Nar. 5m. 2w. PLD PLK
R **Priming the pump.** ———. Nar. 3m. voices. Sc. Studio. SK
C R **Prince & the pauper.** Mark Twain. Nar. 6b. 2g. Sc. Studio. PLF
C **Prince Charming smiles again.** Urban, C. 3b. 2g. Sc. Garden. PLA
C **Prince with no crown.** Spamer, C. 8b. 1g. Sc. Garden. PLB
C **Princess & the horse.** Hourihane, U. 2b. 3g. Sc. Garden. PLA
C **Princess & the pumpkin.** Streacher, L. 3b. 2g. Sc. Palace. PLB
J **Princess & the rose-colored glasses.** Hark, M. 4b. 3g. ext. Sc. Throne rm. HAR PLG
C **Princess who couldn't dance.** Barbee, L. 6g. Sc. Palace. KAM
   Printer's devil. Dias, E. J. 3m. 3w. Sc. Office. PLK
J **Prize for mother.** Hark, M. 4b. 4g. Sc. Int. HAR
C **Prize shamrock.** Newman, D. 7b. 5g. Sc. Stage. PLF
   Prodigal comes home. Parker, M. M. 5m. 3w. Sc. In ancient Palestine. BRIN
C **Professor Willy's wisher-switcher.** Oser, J. 4b. 4g. Sc. Lab. PLF

8   **Prologue for tomorrow.** Hackett, W. 3m. 1w. Sc. Int. HAC
8   **The promise.** Mickel, J. Ann. 1m. 2w. Sc. Studio. MIC
    Promise of the angels. Getzinger, E. W. Nar. 4m. 3w. Sc. Jerusalem. BRIN
    Promised ones. St. Clair, R. Nar. 4m. 3w. Sc. Ctage. BRIN
8   **Prophet of fire.** Pollock, S. Nar. 7m. 4w. Sc. Church. POL
    The proposal. Chekhov, A. 2m. 1w. Sc. Russian int. MAG RE
R   **The proposal.** Johnson, C. 2m. 3w. Sc. Bedrm. JOH
    Prostitute & the soldier. Schnitzler, A. 1m. 1w. Sc. Bridge. BE
J   **Proud Prince.** Balm, C. M. 3m. 1w. ext. Sc. Int. EI
J   **Publicity expert.** Howard, V. L. 5b. Sc. Office. HO
C   **Pumpkin eater's pumpkin.** Newman, D. 4b. 4g. Sc. Meadow. PLD
R   **Puppet master.** Bonett, E. 6m. 6w. Sc. Studio. FIV
J   **Puppet play for mass education.** Wall. L. V. 18 char. Sc. Int. WA
J   **Puppy love.** Miller, H. L. 3b. 4g. Sc. Int. BU MIM PLC
    Purgatory. Yeats, W. B. 1m. 1b. Sc. Church. YE YEA
J   **Push button tuning.** Eisenberg, H. 1m. 13 voices. Sc. Studio. EI
J   **Puss-in-boots.** Elfenbein, J. A. 4b. 2g. Sc. Castle. PLG
C   **Puss-in-boots.** Miller, M. 4b. 2g. Sc. Forest. MILL
C   **Puss-in-boots.** Very. A. 14 char. Sc. Mill. BUF
C   **Pussy pleases.** Spamer, C. 5b. 2g. Sc. Zoo. PLC
    Putting first things first. Posegate, E. D. 3w. 1c. Sc. Stage. BRIN
    Pyramus & Thisbe. Shakespeare. 9m. 2w. Sc. Wood. KN
C   **Pytheas the Greek explorer.** Collins, F. 5b. 1g. Sc. Stage. COL

Q

    Quality of mercy. O'Brien, K. 5w. Sc. Cottage. NEG
    Quare medicine. Green, P. 3m. 1w. Sc. Farm house. SP
    Question period. Molnar, F. 2m. Sc. Int. com. MOL
R   **Queen is dead.** Arthur, M. 4w. Sc. Int. PH
C   **Queen of hearts.** Barr, J. 4b. 2g. Sc. Kitchen. PLB
C   **Queen of hearts.** Burger, E. B. Sc. Kitchen. BUR
C   **Queen with the broken heart.** Urban, C. 2b. 4g. Sc. Palace. BUF KAM
T   **Queen of Heart's party.** Woolsey, J. 15 char. ext. Sc. Throne rm. WOO
R   **Quentin Durward,** Scott, W. Nar. 5m. 2w. Sc. Studio. OF
J   **Quiet Christmas.** Hark, M. Ann. 4b. 5g. Sc. Int. HAT PLD
J   **Quiet evening at home.** Preston, E. E. 1m. 1w. Sc. Int. com. PR
    Quiet rest. Teasdale, V. 1m. 4w. 1b. Sc. Int. com. TE
J   **Quiz for high I Q's.** Preston, E. E. 3b. Sc. School. PR

R

    R U R. Kapek, K. 1m. 1w. Sc. Lab. SEK
J   **Rabbit foot.** Miller, H. L. 5b. 4g. Sc. Int. MIM PLC
C   **Rabbit's reading lesson.** Clark, J. 2b. 3g. Sc. Woods. CLA
J   **The race.** Eisenberg, H. Ann. 3b. 2g. Sc. Stage. EI

Radiance streaming. Emurian, E. K. 2m. 9w. Choir. Sc. Church. EM

8 **Radio: how to abuse it.** Weaver, L. Ann. 2 char. Sc. Studio. WE

8 **Radio Jerusalem.** Magee, C. Ann. 4 char. ext. Sc. Studio. BRIN

J **Radios versus doughnuts.** Woolsey, J. 15b. Sc. Boy Scout rm. WOO

Railroad accident. Molnar, F. Sc. Railroad. 1m. 1w. com. MOL

C **Railroad rhymes & rhythms.** Miller, H. L. Ann. 8b. ext. Sc. Outdoors. MIN

J **Rain & rebellion.** Du Bois, G. 6b. 2g. Sc. Colonial home. PLD

J **Rainbow colors.** Hark, M. 10 char. Sc. Yard. HAR PLC

C **Rapunzel.** Barr, J. 2b. 3g. Sc. Int. PLC

C **Rapunzel.** Wall, L. V. Story teller. Any number of char. Sc. Outdoors. WA.

Readings from the Imitation of Christ. Switz, T. MacL. Nar. ext. SW

C **Red apple.** Marsh, W. A. 1b. 1g. Sc. Int. Puppet. MARS

R **Red death.** Barth, R. Nar. 4m. 3w. Sc. Lab. SP

C **Red 'n green treasure hunt.** Deming, D. 1b. 2g. ext. Sc. Barn. PLF

C R **Red Riding Hood.** White, M. R. Nar. 2b. 4g. Sc. Int. WH

C **Red Riding Hood & the wolf.** Nutter, C. F. 6b. 3g. ext. Sc. Int. PLE

Red velvet goat. Niggli, J. 4m. 5w. ext. Sc. Patio. SEL

J **Red wagon.** Paradis, M. 3b. 3g. Sc. Playrm. PLA

J **Red, white & blue.** Paradis, M. 5b. 5g. Sc. Int. PLB

J **Regulars are out.** Du Bois, G. 5b. 3g. Int. PLA

J **Reindeer on the roof.** Hark, M. 5b. 5g. Sc. Roof. PLF

R **Relax & enjoy it.** Neher, J. Nar. 1m. 3w. 2m. Sc. Int. NE

C **Reluctant ghost.** Brydon, M. W. 10g. Sc. Stage. KA PLE

Rembrandt — master painter of Holland. Chandler, A. C. 11m. 1w. Sc. Workshop. PLB

Remittance from Spain. Apstein, T. 3m. 3w. Sc. Cocktail lounge. MAYO

Rented tux. Murray, J. 4m. 4w. Sc. Int. PLG

J **Rest for Mr. Winkle.** Howard, V. L. 4b. Sc. Int. com. HO PLH

Resurrection. Emurian, E. K. 15m. 3w. Sc. Garden. EMU

Resurrection. Yeats, W. B. 4m. Musicians. Sc. Curtains. YE YEA

R **Return of a patriot.** Geiger, M. Nar. 4m. 2w. Sc. Int. MAL

Return of Benjamin. Mickel, J. Ann. 2m. 2w. Sc. Int. MIC

Return of Chandra. Wilson, D. C. 5m. 2w. Sc. Village. WAYP

C **Return of the Nina.** MacLellan, E. 7b. 4g. Sc. Harbor. KAM PLD

Reunion. Tayleur, W. St. J. 6m. Sc. Hotel. MARQ

Riders to the sea. Synge, J. M. 1m. 3w. ext. Sc. Island. CER CRO HAL IN JA KN MIR RE SEK

C **Ride a cock-horse.** Marsh, W. A. 11 char. Sc. Int. Puppet. MARS

Ridiculous & sublime. Jacobson, P. 2m. 3w. Sc. Int. BAK

C **Right by adoption.** 5b. 8g. Sc. Int. MIN

Ring in the new. Donovan, A. D. 4m. 3w. Sc. Int. DEN

J R **Rip Van Winkle.** Irving, W. Nar. 4m. 2w. ext. HA PLC

Rise of her bloom. Hughes, E. W. 3w. Sc. River bank. MAYK

Rising of the moon. Gregory, Lady. 4m. Sc. Side of Quay. BRE BER

J **Rival for Dad.** Hark, M. 3b. 2g. Sc. Int. HAS

J **Road to Bethlehem.** 4b. 3g. Sc. Hut. PLE

c **Roaring March lion.** Streacker, L. 3b. 1g. Sc. Garden. PLE
c **Robin that wouldn't fly.** Spamer, C. 5b. 1g. Sc. Robin's nest. PLA
c **Robinson Crusoe.** Miller, M. 5b. Sc. Island. MILL
c **Robots to the rescue.** Fisher, A. 5b. Sc. Factory. FI
  Rock dust. Summer, M. R. 5m. 2w. Sc. Camp. ROW
c r **Rock in the sea.** Kissen, F. Ann. 5b. 2g. Sc. Studio. KIS
  Rockers. Johnson, C. 3m. 3w. Sc. Old people's home. JOH
c **Roddy's candy bar.** Barr, J. 6b. 5g. Sc. Woods. PLE
  Romance a la mode. Stahl, L. LeR. Ann. 2b. 2g. Sc. Garden. HAN
j r **Romeo & Juliet.** Shakespeare. Nar. 9m. 2w. Sc. Outside. PLK SEK
j **Room for a King.** Du Bois, G. 5b. 5g. Sc. Yard. PLF
j **Room for Mary.** Thurston, M. B. 6w. Sc. Int. KA
  Room service. Huber, L. J. 3m. 3w. Sc. Hotel. HUB
t **Rootie Kazoote Club.** Carlin, S. 5b. 1g. Sc. Studio. WF
  Rose for Madame Calva. McClintock, F. 4m. 2w. 3c. Sc. Office. CARV
c **Roses for mother.** Newman, D. 3b. 4g. Sc. Stage. PLD
  Rouge atomique. Nash, N. R. 2w. telephone. Sc. Space. MAYP
c **Round & round & round.** Carlson, B. W. Storyteller. 1b. 2g. Sc. Int. CAR
  Royal button-maker. Rose, K. 4m. 1w. Sc. Palace. ROS
  Royal favour. Housman, L. 7m. 2w. Sc. Castle. RE
c **Royal magic.** Slattery, M. E. 4b. 3g. Sc. Workshop. PLF
  Royal pathway of the holy cross. Switz, T. MacL. voices. ext. Sc. Church. SW
j **Royal touch.** Gowan, E. P. 3b. 3g. ext. Sc. Church. JON
c **Ruler of all — but one.** Carlson, B. W. 6b. ext. Sc. Outside. CAR
c **Rumpelstiltskin.** Bennett, H. C. 8b. 1g. Sc. Courtrm. BUF
c r **Rumpelstiltskin.** Kissen, F. Ann. 6b. 1g. Sc. Studio. KIS
c **Runaway pirate.** Bennett, R. 4b. ext. Sc. Harbor. PLD
j **Running the country.** Oser, J. 6b. 5g. Sc. Street. PLG

S

  Safecracker's pride. Bela, N. 2m. 3w. Sc. Int. MAYL
c **Safety patrol.** Barbee, L. 6b. 5g. Sc. Platform. PLA
c **Saga of little Fritjof.** Asbrand, K. 4b. 7g. Sc. Outdoors. PLA
r **Saga of Simon Curle.** Hatton, C. Large number of char. Sc. Studio. HAU
c **Sailing West to find the East.** Parsons, M. 8b. Sc. Castle. BREW
c **St. Alban.** Collins, 6b. Sc. Curtains. COL
c **St. Augustine of Canterbury.** Collins, F. 5b. ext. Sc. Slave market. COL
c **St. Birinus.** Collins, F. 8b. 2g. ext. Sc. Church. COL
c **St. Boniface.** Collins, F. 5b. ext. Sc. Stage. COL
c **St. Chad & Archbishop Theodore.** 5b. Sc. Stage. COL
c **St. Columbo.** Collins, F. 6b. ext. Sc. Stage. COL
c **St. Columba says his last words.** Collins, F. 4b. 4g. Sc. Village. COL
c **St. Columba visits King Brude.** Collins, F. 4b. 1g. Sc. Castle. COL

c **St. Cuthbert.** Collins, F. 2b. ext. Sc. Stage. COL
c **St. Dunstan.** Collins, F. 4b. 2g. ext. Sc. Stage. COL
c **St. Edmund Kink & Martyr.** Collins, F. 2b. ext. Sc. Stage. COL
c **St. Edward the Confessor.** Collins, F. 4b. ext. Sc. Church. COL
c **St. Hilda & Caedmon.** Collins, F. 2b. 2g. ext. Sc. Int. COL
c **St. Oswald & St. Aidan.** Collins, F. 6b. ext. Sc. Int. COL
c **St. Patrick.** Collins, F. 4b. 2g. Sc. Int. COL
c **St. Patrick & the last snake in Ireland.** Davis, L. R. 13 char. Sc. Wooded spot. KAM
J **St. Patrick saves the day.** Du Bois, G. 6b. 5g. Sc. Int. PLE
c **St. Paulinus & King Edwin.** Collins, F. 2b. ext. Sc. Stage. COL ,
c **Saint Peter & the birds.** Woolsey, J. Nar. 3 char. groups. Sc. Kitchen. WO
c **Salesmanship.** Deming, D. 2b. 3g. Sc. Information desk. PLE
Salome. Wilde, O. 9m. 1w. ext. Sc. Palace. CER
Salt for savor. Wilde, P. 7m. Sc. Office. MAYO
c **Salt in the sea.** Colbert, M. 10b. 2g. ext. Sc. Store. BUF
Sam 'n' Ella. Felton, N. Sc. Kitchen. com. ON
T **Sammy Kaye show.** Raymond, J. 2m. 2w. Sc. Int. WF
Sands of time. Dias, E. J. 3m. 3w. Sc. Int. Melodrama. DIA
c **Santa Claus for president.** Miller, H. L. 6b. 1g. ext. Sc. Workshop. PLE
J **Santa Claus parade.** Hark, M. Any number of char. Sc. Street. HAR
c **Santa forgets Christmas.** Carlson, B. W. 2b. 1g. Sc. Int. CAR
J **Santa goes to town.** Paradis, M. B. 10g. Sc. Boarding school. BU PA
c **Santa Claus parade.** Pendelton, E. 2b. ext. Sc. Street. PLE
c **Santa's robbers.** Blanton. C. 2b. 2g. Sc. Int. PLB
Sausages & General Washington. Du Bois, G. 5m. 2w. Sc. Headquarters. DUB PLB
J **Saving the old homestead.** Fay, M. 7b. 3g. Sc. Int. PLF
J **Say it with flowers.** Miller, H. L. 6b. 3g. Sc. Int. MIM PLE
Scene from the Prologue to glory. Conkle, E. P. 4m. 2w. Sc. Log cabin. SP
School act. ———. 6m. 1w. Sc. School rm. LA
8 **School for marriage.** Neher, J. School for marriage. Nar. 3m. 3w. Sc. Int. NE
8 **Sea saves Leyden.** Cowgill, R. Nar. 2m. 2w. voices. Sc. Int. COW
Sea-shell. Chown, P. 1m. 6w. Sc. Tenement. MARP
Second Sunday in May. Downing, R. 6w. Sc. Int. PLK
The secret. Lehmann, A. 1m. 2w. Sc. Hospital. LE
Secret agent. Madley, H. L. 10w. Sc. Int. com. DEN
R **Seduction.** Maurois, A. 3m. 3w. Sc. Int. MAUR
c **See the parade.** Hark, M. 5b. 2g. Sc. Int. BUF HAT
Self-preservation. Huber, L. J. 5m. Sc. Office. HU
Settled out of court. Kavanaugh, K. 2m. 2w. Sc. Int. DEN
c **Seven little seeds.** Gould, J. 3b. 7g. Sc. Home. PLE KAM
Seventh man. Redgrave, M. 6m. Sc. Log hut. FA
Shadow of the Cathedral. Kocker, E. 2m. 1w. Sc. In France. MAYL

Shadowy waters. Yeats, W. B. 2m. 1w. ext. Sc. Sailing vessel. YE YEA

c **Shady shadows.** Miller, H. L. 6 char. Sc. Bedrm. BUF

J N–R **Shakespeare touch.** Miller, H. L. 10b. 6g. Sc. Classrm. MIO PLH

T **Shall we dance?** Parker, K. T. 4m. 5w. Sc. Dance studio. PARK

Shall we join the ladies? Barrie, J. M. 1m. 7w. Sc. Int. CROS

c **Sharing the circus.** Campbell, C. 4b. 3g. Sc. Circus. PLC

J **She also serves.** Paradis, M. B. 5b. 7g. Sc. Int. PLD

J **She laughs last.** Paradis, M. B. 10g. Sc. Bedrm. PA PLD

J N–R **She loves him Yes.** Gross, E. 5b. 3g. Sc. School. GRO

R **She stoops to conquer.** Goldsmith, O. 5m. 4w. Sc. Int. PLK

c **Sheep Skin Po.** Winsatt, H. G. 9b. 5g. Iut. PLF

c **Shepherd of Bethlehem.** Knox, J. 8b. 8g. Sc. Int. BRIO

R **Shepherd of Tekoa.** Pollock, S. Nar. 14m. 2w. Sc. Church. POL

Shepherds & wise men. Phillips, A. L. 9m. 2w. 1b. ext. Sc. Curtains. BRIO

R **Sheherazade kept on talking.** Bridie, J. Nar. 4m. 2w. Sc. Palace. BRI

Shepherd's trove. West Hill Women's Institute. 3m. 8w. Sc. Cottage. KEL

R **Shipment of mute fate.** Crutchfield, L. 4m. 1w. ext. Sc. Ship. POT

c **Ship's boy to the Indies.** MacLellan, E. 7b. 3g. Sc. Inn. PLE

c R **Shiro & his master.** Kissen, F. Ann. 3b. 1g. Sc. Int. KIS

c **Shoemaker & the elves.** Very, A. 6b. 2g. Sc. Shop. PLB

c **Shy Prince.** Spamer, C. 4b. 4g. Sc. Throne rm. KAM

c **Sick fox.** Carpenter, F. 6 char. Sc. Outdoors. CARP

c **Sidewalk elves.** Clark, J. Any number of char. Sc. Street. CLA

J **Sign on the door.** Preston, E. E. 4b. 1g. ext. Sc. Studio. PR

R **Silas Marner.** Eliot, G. Nar. 3m. 5w. ext. Sc. Int. OF

R **Silent city.** Obey, N. 7m. 6w. 2c. Sc. Nar. FIV

J **Silent night.** Hollingsworth, L. 3b. 4g. Sc. Study. BU

Silver key. Hayes, J. 5w. Sc. Near sea. MARQ

Silver lining. Mackay, C. D'A. 1m. 2w. Sc. Int. NEV

Silver star of Christmas. York, E. B. 3m. 5w. Sc. Ancient Judea. BRIO

Silver threads among the gold. Emurian, E. K. 5m. 1w. Sc. Int. EM

R **Silver wedding.** Maurois, A. 2m. 1w. Sc. Int. MAUR

Silvered rope. Sigmund, T. G. 3m. 2w. Sc. Cottage. BRIN

J **Singing shark.** Howard, V. 8 char. Sc. Palace. PLK

R **Singing wind.** Capps, R. D. Nar. 3m. Sc. Outside. WE

R **Sire de Maletroit's door.** Stevenson, R. L. Nar. 5m. 1w. Sc. Int. HA ME PLB

Sisters under the skin. Hughes, B. 8w. Sc. Int. com. ON

Sitters in revolt. Hartman, Z. 4b. 5g. Sc. Int. DEN

Sitting ducks. Baldwin, M. T. 4m. Sc. Office. BAL

J R **Skills to share.** Fisher, A. 3b. 5g. Sc. Int. FIS

Skin deep. Young, M. B. 7w. Sc. Beauty shop. ROW

Sky-fodder. Reynolds, J. 3m. Sc. Curtains. ROW

Sky's the limit. Brome, R. 4m. 3w. Sc. Int. DEN

c   **Sleeping Beauty.** Bennett, H. C. 6b. 11g. Sc. Palace. BUF

c r   **Sleeping Beauty.** Kissen, F. Ann. 3b. 3g. ext. Sc. Studio. KIS

c   **Sleeping Beauty in the woods.** Very, A. 4b. 15g. Sc. Stage. PLA

t   **Small sale.** Huber, L. J. 2m. w. Sc. Store. HUB

c   **Small shoes & small tulips.** MacLellan, E. 4b. 3g. Sc. Int. PLF

c   **Snow White & red rose.** Miller, M. 6 char. Sc. Forest. MILL

c   **Snowdrop.** Spamer, C. 14g. Sc. Outdoors. KA

    So I heard. Fisher, A. M. 14w. Sc. Int. com. Sc. Int. DEN

    So shines a good deed. Du Bois, G. 2m. 4w. Sc. Int. DUB

c   **So this is China.** Asbrand, K. 6b. 14g. Sc. Int. PLC

j   **Society page.** Allred, J. 2b. 6g. Sc. Newspaper office. PLE

j   **Socrates saves the day.** Paradis, M. B. 8b. 3g. Sc. Terrace. PLK

    Sod. Hunter, S. 2m. 2w. Sc. Farm. DEN

j   **Sofapillio.** Eisenberg, H. 2b. 3g. Sc. Int. Farce. EI

j   **Soft-hearted ghost.** Miller, H. L. 5b. 3g. Sc. Int. PLE

c   **Softy the snow man.** Miller, H. L. 9b. 4g. Sc. Display rm. PLF

    Soldier & the housemaid. Schnitzler, A. 1m. 1w. Sc. Park. BE

c   **Soldier, soldier.** Carlson, B. W. 1b. 1g. ext. Sc. Curtains. CAR

j   **Some are teachers.** De Marco, L. 3b. 4g. Sc. Int. PLA

j   **Some tricks are treats.** Kroll, F. L. 2b. 2g. Sc. Int. PLH

r   **Somebody do something!** Neher, J. Nar. 5m. 4w. no. sc. NE

c   **Somebody's Valentine.** Lawrence, J. 3b. 6g. Sc. Shop. PLF

t   **Something in the wind.** Coes, F. 4m. 3w. Sc. Office. KAV

c   **Something new for Halloween.** Newman, D. 5b. 4g. Sc. Cottage. PLF

j   **Something to read.** Preston. E. E. 4w. Sc. Int. PR

    Something unspoken. Williams, T. 2w. Sc. Int. MAYR

j   **Sometimes it's right to fight.** Brown, A. M. 6b. Sc. Back yard. SC

c   **Somewhat forgetful.** Schwartz, M. K. 4b. Sc. Int. PLC

    Son of America. Du Bois, G. Doctor's office. DUB PLA

c   **Son of Liberty.** Lipnick, E. 5b. 2g. Sc. Colonial home. BUF

    Song for a hero. Schafer, L. 10m. 1w. 3c. Sc. Curtains. MAYP

    Songysan Gampo. Duncan, M. Any number of char. Sc. Tibet. DUN

r   **Sons & husbands.** Neher, J. Nar. 1m. 3w. Sc. Int. NE

    Sons of the prairie. Rehmer, H. A. 9m. 3w. Exr. Ballet. Sc. Auditorium. ROW

    Sophocles—King Oedipus. Yeats, W. B. 5m. 3w. Sc. Palace. YE YEA

    Sophocles—Oedipus Colonus. Yeats, W. B. 5m. 2w. Ext. Sc. Ancient Greece. YE YEA

    Sorry, wrong number. Fletcher, L. 7m. 1w. Sc. Telephone. COW FLE

j   **Soup stone.** Peterson, M. N. 4b. 4g. Sc. Street. PLK

c   **South of the border.** Shenker, R. W. 5b. 5g. Sc. In Mexico. PLB

c   **Space unlimited.** Carlson, B. W. 1b. 1g. Sc. Space. CAR

c   **Speaking of speech.** Miller, H. L. 2b. 3g. Sc. Office. MIN

c   **Special edition.** Fisher, A. 4b. 4g. Sc. Stage. BUF PLA

    Special guest. Elser, D. 3m. 2w. Sc. Int. Tragedy. ROW

r   **Spinney under the rain.** Heath, T. 5m. 2w. Sc. Int. FIV

c   **Spirit of Christmas.** Fisher, A. 2b. 4g. Sc. Curtains. PLC

J R **Spirit of Christmas.** St. Clair, R. Ann. 7g. Sc. Int. BU

  C **Spitball.** Carlson, B. W. 6b. ext. Sc. Field. CAR

  R **Spoiled darlings.** Barclay, E. Ann. 4m. 3w. Sc. Studio. RE

  J **Spook shop.** Howard, V. L. 7b. Sc. Haunted house. HO

J N–R **Spooks in books.** Miller, H. L. 5b. 3g. Sc. Library. MIO PLJ

J N–R **Spooky spectacles.** Miller, H. L. 5b. 6g. Sc. Int. MIO PLH

    The sportsmen. Wilde, P. 6m. 3w. Sc. Outdoors. FR

  C **Spot of onion tea.** Carlson, B. W. 1b. 3g. Sc. Int. CAR

    Spreading the news. Gregory, Lady. 7m. 3w. Sc. Fair. CHAM NEV

  J **Spring daze.** Hark, M. 2b. 2g. Sc. Int. PLD

  J **Spring fever.** Hark, M. 3b. 2g. Voice. Sc. Int. HAS PLC

  J **Spring is here.** Hark, M. 20 char. Sc. Stage. HAR

  C **Spring magic.** Ridge, A. 5b. 1g. Sc. Int. RID

  C **Spring neighbors.** Newman, D. 5b. 11g. Sc. Outdoors. PLD

  C **Spring secrets.** Lee, S. 3b. 7g. Sc. Stage. PLE

  C **Spring to the rescue.** Newman, D. 5b. log. Sc. Stage. PLD

    Spring will come. Du Bois, G. 3m. 3w. Sc. Int. DUB

  R **The spy.** Cooper, J. F. Nar. 6m. 1w. Sc. Int. HA PLC

    Square box. Hall, M. 4b. 3g. Sc. Stage. PLK

    Stage bore. Dias, E. J. 2m. 5w. Sc. Boarding house. DIA

  T **Stage entrance.** Paige, M. 1m. 1w. Sc. Theatre. WF

  T **Stand up to death.** Parker, K. T. 3m. 2w. Sc. Int. PARK

    Stand-in for murder. Peterson, L. 4m. Sc. Alaska. GOL

  C **Standing up for Santa.** Fisher, A. 12g. ext. Sc. Stage. KA

  C **Star cadets.** Miller, H. L. 11b. 2g. Sc. Open field. MIN

    Star gazer. West, M. K. 2m. 5w. Sc. Int. PL

J N–R **Star in the window.** Hark, M. 4b. 3g. Sc. Shop. HAT PL

  J **Star in the window.** Pendleton, E. 4b. 3g. Sc. Shop. PLD

  C **Star light & the sandman.** Smith, G. V. 17 char. Sc. Woods. KAM PLA

  T **Star minded.** Parker, K. T. 1m. 3w. voices. Sc. Int. com. PARK

    Star of wonder. Preston, E. E. 8m. 8w. 1b. Sc. R.R. station. BRIO

    Star spangled banner. Emurian, E. K. 17m. Organ. Sc. Tavern. EM

    The starlings. Bridie, J. 3m. Sc. Rustic seat. BRI

  C **Stars & stripes.** Newman, D. 5b. 9g. Sc. Colonial int. PLF

  J **Star-spangled Midge.** Paradis, M. B. 5b. 5g. Sc. Dormitory. PLB

    Stephen, the first martyr. Nygaard, N. E. 9m. ext. Sc. Temple. NY

    Stepmother. Bennett, A. 2m. 2w. Int. KN

  J **Sterling silver tree.** Fisher, A. 4b. 2g. Sc. Road. PLH

    Sticks & stones. Peterson, L. Any number of char. Sc. Curtains. GOL PLG

  C **Stolen heart.** Newman, D. 9g. Sc. Workshop. KA PLC

    Stolen Prince. Totheron, D. 7m. 1w. 2c. Sc. Curtains. GR

  C **Stolen pumpkin.** Arnold, E. W. 9 char. Sc. Garden. PLF

  C **Stolen tarts.** Molloy, L. L. 6b. 1g. Sc. Royal kitchen. PLA

  J **Storm in a tea cup.** Marsh, W. A. 7 char. Sc. Int. com. MARS

Stormy passage. Newton Ferrers Dramatic Class. 3m. 3w. 1b. Sc. Kitchen. KEL

c **Stone age.** Collins, F. 3b. 2g. Sc. Cave. COL

Stop the presses! Dias, E. J. 6m. 2w. Sc. Newpaper office. DIA

J R **Story of a well.** Fisher, A. 5b. 2g. ext. Sc. In Mexico. FIS

c **Story of light.** Miller, H. L. Nar. 5 char. ext. Sc. Int. MIN

c R **Story of Peter Rabbit.** White, M. R. Nar. 18 char. Sc. Curtains. WH

Straight & the Jew. ———. 3m. Sc. Stage. LA

Strained relations. Helsby, A. 5w. Sc. Int. NEG

Strange road. Houston, J. M. 1m. 3w. Sc. Int. ROW

R **Strange traditions.** Hamre, J. Ann. 3m. 1c. Sc. Int. WE

Strange victory. Neuenburg, E. 3w. ext. Sc. Bell tower. BAK

Strangers. Veness, M. 1m. 1w. Sc. Book shop. MAR MARC

c R **Straw ox.** Kissen, F. Ann. 6b. 1g. Sc. Curtains. KIS

J **Strictly for relatives.** Phillips, M. K. 3b. 4g. Sc. Stage. PLF

c **Strictly Puritan.** Miller, H. L. 3b. 9g. Sc. Recreation rm. PLF

Strolling clerk from Paradise. Wayne, P. 2m. 1w. Sc. Curtains. BUS

Strong & silent. Dias, E. J. 4n. 3w. Sc. Bunk house. DIA

c **Stubborn elf.** Leuser, E. 5b. 2g. Sc. Outdoors. PLB

J **Stuff of heroes.** Hark, M. 4b. 2g. Sc. Int. HAR

Submerged. Cottman, H. S. 6m. Sc. Submarine. ROW

Substitute bride. Drummond, R. 4m. 3w. ext. Sc. Int. HAN

Such stuff as dreams. Ferguson, J. A. 2m. 3w. Sc. Cottage. FA

c **Sugar & spice.** Nicholson, J. 2b. 5g. Sc. Pastry shop. PLE

Sukie has an air. Maughfling, M. 2m. 2w. Sc. Countryside. MAUG

Summer comes to Diamond O. Finch, R. 8m. Sc. Cook-shack. ROW

Sun deck. Richards, S. 3m. 4w. Sc. Coney Island. BAN MAYL

Sun is dead man's weapon. Carroll, R. F. 2m. 2w. Sc. Int. FR

Sunday costs five pesos. Niggli, J. 1m. 4w. Sc. In Mexico, COOK, KN RI

Sunday edition. Preston, E. E. 1m, 2w. Sc. Int. com. PLU

Sunny morning. Quintero, S. 2m. 2w. Sc. Park. CER GR JA SP

Sunset in the dust. Davies, R. E. 3m. 2w. Sc. Int. SI

J **Super-sleuths.** Paradis, M. B. 10b. Sc. Dormitory. PA

Suppressed desires. Glaspell, S. 1m. 2w. Sc. Apartment. CER SEK

T **Sure as fate.** Armer, A. 1m. 1w. Sc. Int. ARM

J N–R **Surprise guests.** Hark, M. 4b. 6g. Sc. Int. HAT PLC

c **Surprise package.** Deming, D. 2b. 3g. Sc. Int. PLA

Surprising story of Alfred. Peach, L. du G. 7m. 1w. Sc. Tower of London. BUS

Survival. Hallman, E. S. 4m. Sc. Arctic flight. GOL

Swan-song. Norris, T. B. 9w. Sc. Theatre. NEF

Sweeney Agonistes. Fra. I. Eliot, T. S. 9 char. Sc. Curtain. BE

Sweeney Agonistes. Eliot, T. S. Fra. II. 6 char. Sc. Curtain. BE

R **Swing shift 1830.** ———. Nar. 7m. 2w. ext. Sc. Int. SK

R **Swiss chalet mystery.** Murray, J. 5m. 4w. Sc. Swiss chalet. MU

Switch to Mitch. Preston, E. E. 3m. 2w. Sc. Int. com. PLU

c   **Synod of Whitby.** Collins, F. 7b. 1g. ext. Sc. Stage. COL
J   **T. for turkey.** Hark, M. 4b. 4g. Sc. Kitchen. HAR PLG
c   **Tale of good faith.** Carpenter, F. 5 char. Sc. Farmyard. CARP

T

J R   **Tale of two cities.** Dickens, C. Nar. 6m. 1w. Sc. Int. HA PLD
J   **Talent scouts.** Deming, D. 4b. 3g. Sc. School. PLA
c   **Talent tree.** Brown, T. L. 8 char. Sc. Woods. BUF
J   **Talisman.** Keating, E. H. 6b. ext. Sc. Garden. KE
c   **Talk on teeth.** Clark, J. 6c. Sc. Stage. CLA
    Tarantula. Jurgensen, K. 5m. 2w. Sc. Rertaurant. SEL
c   **Tavern meeting.** Jones, R. C. 5b. 5g. Sc. Tavern. PLD
c   **Tea for six.** Steele, J. 7g. Sc. Int. KA
    Tea with a legend. Holland, N. Sc. Int. MARQ
c   **Teapot trouble.** Nicholson, J. Sc. Antique shop. PLD
J   **Television-itis.** Hark, M. 3b. 2g. Sc. Int. HAS PLC
    Tell it not in Gath. Corrie, J. 3m. 3w. Recory. MARQ
    Telling of the North Star. Ferrini, V. 5m. 2w. ext. Sc. Sea. MAYO
J   **Tempest in a teapot.** 3b. 2g. voices. Sc. Int. HAS
J   **Ten-minute whiteface minstrel show.** Preston, E. E. Any number of char. Sc. Stage. PR
T   **Tenting tonight.** Huber, L. J. 5m. 1w. Sc. Stage. HUB
c   **Terrible tale of terrible tempers.** Clark, J. 9c. Sc. Curtain. CLA
c   **The test.** Tobey, L. C. 11 char. ext. Sc. Throne rm. BUF
    The test. Vance, L. 2m. 1w. Sc. Int. CARV
J   **Test for a witch.** MacLellan, E. 4b. 7g. Sc. Park. PLJ
    Thank you Louise. Lehmann, A. 1m. 1w. Sc. Int. LE
J   **Thankless Tate.** Draper, C. C. 2b. 2g. Sc. Corn field. PLH
J   **Thanks a million.** Fisher, A. 2m. 3w. ext. Sc. Int. FIS
J   **Thanks to Billy.** Hark, M. 3b. 2g. Sc. Int. HAS PLC
J   **Thanks to butter-fingers.** Miller, H. L. 2b. 3g. Sc. Int. PLG
J N–R   **Thanks to George Washington.** Hark, M. 4b. 3g. Sc. Int. HAT PLK
J   **Thanks to George Washington.** Pendleton, E. 4b. 3g. Sc. Int. PLD
c   **Thanks to Sammy Scarecrow.** Howard, H. L. 3b. 1g. Sc. Corn field. GUF KAM
c   **Thanks to the Indians.** Newman, D. 6b. 5g. Pilgrim home. PLE
J   **Thankful hearts.** Paradis, M. B. 7g. Sc. School office. PA PLA
J N–R   **Thanksgiving a la carte.** Miller, H. L. 9b. 3g. Sc. Lunch rm. MIN PLD
c   **Thanksgiving feast.** Fisher, A. 4b. 3g. Sc. Little town. PLC
c   **Thanksgiving for everybody.** Gould, J. 3b. 4g. Sc. Front of home. KAM PLE
c   **Thanksgiving night.** Very, A. Large number of children. Sc. Stage. KA
J   **Thanksgiving proclamation.** Woolsey, J. 6b. 2g. Sc. Office. WOO
c   **Thanksgiving scarecrow.** Leuser, E. 5b. 4g. Sc. Road. PLB
    Thanksgiving through the ages. Emurian, E. K. 10m. 4w. Ext. Sc. Curtains. EMU

J **Thanksgiving wishbone.** Hark, M. 5b. 6g. Sc. Int. PLK
R **That evening air.** Brewer, F. Ann. 5m. ext. Sc. Studio. SK
   That woman. Lehmann, A. 2m. 1w. Sc. Int. LE
R **That's my old man!** Neher, J. Nar. 4m. 2b. Sc. Int. NE
   That's the spirit. Murray, J. 4m. 6w. Sc. Int. PLJ
R **There ought to be a law.** ———. Nar. 4m. 2w. ext. No sc. SK
J **There's talent tonight.** Howard, V. L. 9b. Sc. Office. HO
C **Theseus & the Minotaur.** Carlson, B. W. Reader, 2b. 1g. Sc. Int. CAR
   They banish our anger. Du Bois, G. 3m. 4w. Sc. Int. DUB
   They that walk in darkness. Smith, W. S. 8m. 2w. Sc. In Jerusalem
   BRIN
R **Things we know.** Mickel, J. Nar. 3m. 1w. Sc. Int. MIC
T **Thinking heart.** Faulkner, G. H. Nar. 3m. Sc. War scene. SET
C **Thirsty flowers.** Barr, J. 2b. 1g. Sc. Garden. PLB
   This music crept by me upon the waters. MacLeish, A. 5m. 5w. Sc.
   Garden. MAYP
J R **This, our America.** Schoenfeld, B. C. Ann. 4b. 2g. ext. Sc. Int. NEVI
T **This is our Kathie.** Tooley, H. 3m. 4w. 1b. Sc. Int. TO
   This strange night. McGreevey, J. 16m. 5w. Sc. Outdoors. DRA
   Thomas the doubter. Switz, T. MacL. Nar. 7m. 1w. Sc. Curtain. SW
   Those in glass houses. Brome, R. 2m. 2w. Sc. Int. DEN
   Those Monday blues. Martens, A. C. 3m. 4w. Sc. Int. com. BAK
J **Three & the dragon.** Fisher, A. 5b. 5g. Sc. Street. PLB
C **Three aunts.** Rowlands, E. 5b. 10g. Sc. Throne rm. BUF
J N **Three cheers for Mother.** Miller, H. L. 6b. 8g. Sc. Int. MIO
   Three dying swans. Pyle, M. T. 3m. 6w. Sc. Int. com. ROW
C R **Three golden oranges.** Kissen, F. Ann. 12 char. Sc. Ranch. KIC
C R **Three little pigs.** White, M. R. Nar. 4b. 1g. Sc. no. WH
C **Three little kittens.** Barr, J. 3b. 1g. Sc. Stage. PLB
C **Three little kittens.** Very, A. 9 children. Sc. Schoolrm. PLB
   Three meals a day. McCaslin, N. Ann. 7m. 3w. Sc. Kitchen. com.
   MAC
R **Three Musketeers.** Dumas, A. 5b. 2g. Nar. Sc. Int. PLF
   Three on a bench. Estrado, D. 2m. 2w. Sc. Bench. com. ROW
   Three parsons. Agoston, G. 3m. Sc. Seminary. MAYK
   Three people. Gurney, A. R. 1m. 1w. Sc. Int. MAYR
C **Three pigs catch the wolf again.** Marsh, W. A. 4 char. no. sc. MARS
   Three royal R's. Pyle, M. T. 14 char. ext. Sc. School. PLK
C R **Three sillies.** Kissen, F. Nar. Ann. 6b. 3g. Sc. Curtains. KI KIS
C **Three sillies.** Very, A. 5b. 3g. Sc. Farm yard. BUF
C **Three wishes.** Burlingame, C. 6b. 3g. Sc. Int. BUF
C **Three wishes.** Carlson, B. W. 1b. 1g. Sc. Kitchen. CAR
J **Three wishes.** Mackay, C. D. 2b. 1g. Sc. Kitchen. NEVI
   Three wishes. Parker, T. M. 2m. 2w. 1cat. Sc. Cottage. BUS
C R **Three wishes.** White, M. R. Nar. 1b. 1g. voice. Sc. Studio. WH
J **Three wishes for mother.** Hark, M. 8 char. Sc. Garden. HAR PLE
C **Three wishing bags.** Swintz, M. 5b. 4g. Sc. Kitchen. PLC

Through a glass, darkly. Richards, S. 4m. 3w. Sc. Int. BAN

c **Twelve days to Christmas.** Wright, D. Large number of char. Sc. Stage. PLE

c **Tick tock.** Asbrand, K. 14b. 12g. Sc. Stage. PLF

t **Tick tock.** Huber, L. J. 3m. 1w. Sc. Int. HUB

c **Tick tock.** Very, A. 9g. Sc. Nursery. KA

j **Tiger who wanted a boy.** Hall, M. G. 3b. 3g. Sc. Forest. PLK

c **Tiger in the wood.** Carpenter, F. 6 char. Sc. Wood. CARP

Tilt of stein. Byers, J. 4m. 1w. Sc. Camp. CARV

Time is a thief. Carroll, R. F. 1m. 1w. Sc. Cafe. ON

c **Time out for Christmas.** Fisher, A. 3b. 1g. Sc. Stage. PLB

t **Time out for dreams.** Armer, A. 1m. 1w. Sc. Office. ARM

t **Timeless second.** Armer, A. 1m. 1w. Sc. Penthouse. ARM

j **Timid little witch.** Urban, C. 1b, 2g. ext. Sc. Woods. PLH

c r **Tinder box.** Kissen, F. Ann. 3b. 4g. Sc. Curtains. KI

r **Tinker of Toledo.** McCaslin, N. Nar. 5m. 4w. Sc. Studio. MAC

Tinsel Duchess. Johnson, P. 3m. 2w. Sc. Country home. MARQ

c **Tit for tat.** Carlson, B. W. 3b. Sc. Int. CAR

c **Tit-for-tat.** Fisher, A. 2b. 3g. Sc. Int. PLC

t **To be alone.** Armer, A. 1m. 1w. Sc. City. Arm.

j **To be or not to be.** Hark, M. 3b. 2g. Sc. Int. HAS

To my Valentine. Hark, M. 4m. 2w. Sc. Int. PLG

r **To secure these rights.** Mindel, J. 4m. 3w. voices. No sc. MAL

To what purpose. Boissonneault, L. 1b. 3w. Sc. Shop. JON

j **To you the torch.** Marcus, I. H. 8b. 2g. Sc. Stage. PLC

t **Tom Corbett space cadet.** Weinstock, J. Nar. 4m. Sc. Curtain. WF

c **Tommy's adventure.** Leuser, E. 10 char. Sc. Farm. BUF PLA

j **Tomorrow is Easter.** Hark, M. 6b. 1g. Sc. Florist shop. PLB

Tomorrow's vengeance. Ready, S. 2m. 2w. Sc. Int. BAK

Too many hands on a watch. Morgan, W. H. 2m. 2w. Sc. Int. com. SP

j **Too many kittens.** Hark, M. 2b. 5g. Sc. Int. HAR

t **Too many types.** Huber, L. J. 2m. 2s. Sc. Park. HUB

c **Too much of a good thing.** Parsons, M. 15 char. Sc. Int. KAM

Tooth or shave. Niggli, J. 2m. Sc. Mexico. SEK

c **Top of the bill.** Colson, J. G. 5b. Sc. Woods. PLF

Totentanz. Switz, T. MacL. 8m. 5w. voice. Sc. Stage. SW

Tour of duty. Kelley, A. 1m. 2w. Sc. Highway. MAYL

Tourist trouble. Hollister, L. D. 5m. 5w. Sc. Motel. DEN

Tovarish. Deval, J. 1m. 1w. Sc. Hotel rm. SEK

c **Town mouse & his country cousin.** Muse, V. 8 char. Sc. Barn. BUF

t **Toys and science.** Fenwick, R. 2m. 1b. Sc. Toy shop. SET

Tragic muse. Rose, K. 2w. Sc. Stage of Drury Lane. ROS

Tragi-comedy of Don Cristobita. Lorca, F. G. 21 char. Sc. In Spain. NEWB

r **Transferred ghost.** Stockton, F. 2m. 1w. Sc. Int. PLC

A trap is a small place. Perry, M. 2m. 2w. Sc. Apartment. MAYN

C **Travel game.** Miller, H. L. 26 char. Sc. Conference table. MIN
J **Treasure chest.** Bond, V. 8b. Sc. Island. PLK
C **Treasure hunt.** Fisher, A. 13b. 11g. Sc. Sidewalk. PLC
C **Treasure in the Smith house.** Barrett, G. T. 2b. 3g. Sc. Int. PLC
R **Treasure island.** York, M. A. 5b. No sc. PLE
The tree. Arlett, V. I. 2m. 2w. Sc. Garden. MARQ
The tree. McMartin, E. L. 4m. 4w. Sc. Int. BRIO
J **Tree of hearts.** McGowan, J. 2b. 1g. Sc. Hut. PLK
C **Trial by jury.** Barbee, L. 2b. 4g. Sc. Study rm. PLB
C **Trial of Billy Scott.** Hall, M. E. 13 char. Sc. Judge's desk. BUF
C **Tricky rhymes for sale.** Clark, J. 9c. Sc. Int. CLA
Trifles. Glaspell, S. 3m. 2w. Sc. Kitchen. GAS SEK
R **Trip to the moon.** Robertson, M. 2m. 2w. Sc. Int. PH
C **Tropical island.** Ridge, A. 4b. 1g. Sc. Island. RID
Trouble in tunnel nine. Simon, S. S. 5m. Sc. Mine. ME
Tudor thorns. Morris, T. B. 8w. Sc. Palace. MARO
J **Tulips & two lips.** Du Bois, G. 2b. 5g. Sc. Int. Sc. Flower show. PLF
Tunnel of love. Richards, S. 7m. 4w. Sc. Coney Island. HAYN
J **Turkey, anyone?** Garver, J. 2b. 6g. Sc. Int. PLJ
J **Turkey for all.** Howard, V. L. 6b. Sc. Outdoors. HO PLG
J N–R **Turkey gobblers.** Hark, M. Ann. 3b. 4g. Sc. Int. HAT PLF
J N–R **Turkey turns the tables.** Miller, H. L. 2b. 2g. Sc. Int. MIO
Turn down the empty jug. Packer, B. 2w. Sc. Shabby rm. MAYK
J **Turning the fables on Aesop.** Preston, E. E. 2b. 2g. ext. Sc. Back yard. com. PR
J **Turning the tables.** Fisher, A. A. 5b. 2g. Sc. Int. FIS PLH
'Twas the night before Christmas. Emurian, E. K. 4m. 1w. 1b. ext. Sc. Bedrm. EMU
J **'Twas the night before Christmas.** Hark, M. 3b. 2g. Sc. Int. HAS
'Twas the night before Christmas. Lee, H. 1m. 1w. Sc. Int. FR
R **Twelve hours in Mr. Smith's life.** ———. Ann. 3m. ext. NEW
Twelve pound look. Barrie, J. M. 1m. 2w. Sc. Int. CER JA
Twenty thousand leagues neath the sea. Verne, J. Any number of char. Sc. Below the sea. KO
C **Twin cousins.** Schwartz, M. K. 4b. 1g. Sc. Street. BUF
C **Twinkle.** Spamer, C. 4b. 3g. Sc. Sky. PLF
Two crooks & a lady. Pillot, E. 4m. 2w. Sc. Library. KN
Two hundred thousand dollars. Baldwin, M. T. 6m. 1w. Sc. Study. BAL
Two slaps in the face. Molnar, F. 2m. Sc. Street. BRE SP
Two-woman act. ———. 2w. Sc. Stage. LA

U

R **Ugliest man in the world.** Obler, A. Ann. Large number of char. Sc. Semi-darkness. SP
C R **Ugly duckling.** Kissen, F. Ann. Nar. 15 char. Sc. Farm. KIC
Ulysses. Phillips, S. 8m. 4w. ext. Sc. Seashore. KN
C **Umbrella magic.** MacLellan, E. 7b. 2g. Sc. Street. PLE

c **Una fools the fighting giant.** Carlson, B. W. 2b. 1g. 1g. puppet. CAR
J **Unaccustomed as I am.** Hark, M. 3b. 2g. Sc. Int. HAS
c **Uncolored Easter eggs.** Spamer, C. 5b. 4g. Sc. Orchard. PLD
R **Under milkwood.** Thomas, D. Any number of char. Any place. TH
   Undercurrent. Zeller, E. A. 3m. 1w. Sc. Int. DEN
c **Unexpected guests.** Fisher, A. 6b. 6g. Sc. Flower shop. PLF
c **Unhappy Santa.** Simonds, N. 2b. 1g. Sc. Int. BU
   Unicorn from the stars. Yeats, W. B. 6m. 2w. Sc. Workshop. YE YEA
J **Uninvited guests.** Miller, H. L. 3b. 3g. ext. MIM
R **University of the U.S.** Geiger, M. 6m. voices. Sc. Int. MAL
   Unjust steward. Cunningham, G. F. 4m. 4w. Sc. Church. CUN
J **Unsuspected fruit.** Dias, E. J. 4b. 2g. Sc. Int. PLD
c **Unusual flower.** Graham, M. S. 4b. 3g. Sc. Cottage. BUF
   Unto us the living. Sliker, H. G. 7 char. ext. Sc. Curtain. ROW
R **Ups & downs.** Murray, J. 4m. 2w. Sc. Hotel. MU
J **Useful plough.** Marsh, W. A. 5b. Sc. Int. MARS
c **Useless little wind.** Barr, J. 5b. 6g. Sc. Yard. PLB

V

J **Valentine box.** Howard, V. L. 5b. Sc. Outdoors. HO PLG
c **Valentine family.** Spamer, C. 5b. 4g. Sc. Shop. PLB
c **Valentine star dust.** Nicholson, J. 4b. 5g. Sc. Shop. PLE
   Valient. Hall, H. 5m. 1w. Sc. Office. CER HE KN
J **Valley Forge was never like this.** Howard, V. L. 5b. Sc. Int. HO PLG
   Valley of the shadow. Trevisan, A. F. 1m. 2w. Sc. Kitchen. MAYK
J N–R **Vanishing Easter egg.** Miller, H. L. 4b. 4g. Sc. Int. com. MIO
   Vast experience. Huber, L. J. wm. 1w. Sc. Int. com. PLU
c **Venerable Bede.** Collins, F. 7b. ext. Sc. Church. COL
   Venus & Adonis. Obey, A. 7 char. Sc. Curtains. BF
J **Veterinarian in the family.** Richmond, S. S. 3m. 2w. Sc. Kitchen. RIC
J **Veterinarian in time.** Richmond, S. S. 3m. 2g. Sc. Kitchen. PLA
J **Vicky gets the vote.** Miller, H. L. 8b. 5g. Sc. Int. PLK
J **Violets for Christmas.** Phillips, M. K. 1b. 4g. Sc. Office. PLE
   Violin maker of Cremona. Coppee, F. 3m. 1w. Sc. Work shop. CHAM
J **Virus V.** Preston, E. E. 12b. 8g. Sc. Int. PR
R **Vision of the silver belle.** Weathers, W. Nar. 4b. 3g. Sc. Int. BU
   Visionary farms. Eberhart, R. 17m. 6w. Sc. Stage. NEW
J **Visit of Johnny Appleseed.** Hark, M. 3b. 3g. Sc. Cabin. HAR PLB
c **Visit of the cotton maids.** Clark, J. Any number of Children. Sc. Platform. CLA
J **Visit of the plants.** Melchoir, H. K. 9b. 7g. ext. Sc. Play ground. PLK
c **Visit to Vitamin village.** Clark, J. 5b. 5g. Sc. Village. CLA
J **Visitor to Gettysburg.** Dias, E. J. 4b. 3g. Sc. Int. PLE
c **Visitor to Mount Vernon.** Miller, H. L. 5b. 1g. ext. Sc. Curtains. MIN PLG

c **Visitors from the air.** Clark, J. 10 children. Sc. Int. CLA
R **Vitamin trail.** Armquist, M. Ann. 5 char. Sc. Int. WE
J **Voice of liberty.** Fisher, A. 6b, 4g. Sc. Int. PLB
T **Voice of the machines.** Parker, K. T. 4m. 2w. Sc. Hospital. PARK
R **Voice of the wizard.** Barnouw, E. 3m. 1w. Sc. Work shop. SK
Voice that failed. Preston, E. E. 6m. 3w. ext. Sc. Church. BRIN
J **Voices of America.** Hark, M. 11b. 3g. Sc. Park. HAT
J N–R **Vote for Uncle Sam.** Hark, M. 19 char. Sc. Office. HAT PLD
J **Vote for your hero.** Pendelton, E. 5b. 3g. Sc. Int. PLF

W

Wagging tongues. Allyn, M. C. 7w. Sc. Int. DEN
Waiting for Lefty. Odets, C. 14m. 3w. Sc. Stage. CER
A wake for me & thee. Costello, W. 9m. Sc. Ship. MAYH
J **Walk into my parlor.** Boyer, J. 2b. 2g. Sc. Int. JON
c **Wandering Christ-child.** Carlson, W. 8 char. Sc. Church. Pageant. CAR
Wandering dragon. Shun, T. W. 9m. 3w. Sc. In China. SEL
J **Wanted — a stenographer.** Richmond, S. S. 3m. 4w. Sc. Office. RIC
"Wanted — Mr. Stuart." Watkyn, A. 5m. Sc. Inn. FA
Wantin' fever. Hughes, E. W. 1m. 3w. Sc. Farm. MAYH
J **Was her face red!** Paradis, M. B. 5g. Sc. Dormitory. PA PLB
Washed in de blood. Bailey, R. 3m. 2w. Sc. Woods. SEL
J **Washington marches on.** Fisher, A. 26b. 7g. Sc. Stage. PLG
J **Washington shilling.** Miller, H. L. 8b. 6g. Sc. Int. PLK
c **Washington's gold button.** Newman, D. 2b. 6g. Sc. Colonial int. PLC
J **Washington's leading lady.** 7b. 13g. Sc. Stage. PLK
J **Washington's sacrifice.** Roberts, H. M. 4b. 2g. Sc. Rm. in Mt. Vernon. KAM
J **Watch out for Aunt Hattie.** Shore, M. 2b. 2g. Sc. Attic. PLE
J **The way.** Runnette, H. V. 9b. 8g. Sc. Fireplace. PLJ
c **Way to Norwich.** Fisher, A. 10 char. Sc. Outdoors. BUF
c **Way to the inn.** Gordon, C. 5b. 5g. Sc. Stage. PLE
Way, way down East. Dias, J. Nar. 5m. 3w. Sc. Farm. DIA
J **Wayfarers.** Stinetorf, L. A. 7b. 1g. Sc. Stage. PLA
J **We but teach.** Richmond, S. S. 3m. 4w. Sc. Classrm. RIC
c **We three.** Mash, W. A. 3 char. puppets. No. sc. MARS
c **Weaver's son.** Fisher, A. 3b. 2g. Sc. In Italy. PLF
Wedding. Kirkpatrick, J. 4m. 3w. Sc. Country house. KN
R **Wedding journey.** Maurois, A. 2m. 1w. Sc. Train. MAUR
c **Wee Willie Winkle.** Marsh, W. A. 3b. 2g. No sc. Puppet. MARS
J **Weeping willow's happy day.** Oser, J. A. 10 char. Sc. Outdoors. PLG
The well. Vandwer, I. 3m. 2w. Sc. Frontier. DEN
What did I say? Huber, L. J. 1m. 2w. Sc. Int. com. PLU
What do I do now, Mr. McLeod? Teasdale, V. 1m. 1w. Sc. Club. TE
R **What every woman wants.** Neher, J. 2m. 3w. Sc. Int. NE
T **What had God wrought.** Blake, R. 9m. ext. Sc. Square. RO

c **Who's necessary?** Porter, E. W. 3b. 4g. Sc. Int. PLC

j **Who's old-fashioned?** Hark, M. 4b. 3g. Sc. Int. PLE PLK

c **Who's who?** Heath, A. L. 3b. 3g. Sc. Int. PLA

Who's your butler? Huber, L. J. 1m. 2w. Sc. Int. HU

c r **Why the sea is salt.** Kissen, F. Ann. 5b. 2g. No sc. KI

c **Why the sleepy dormouse.** Fisher, A. 3b. 3g. Sc. Wood. FI

j **Wig for my lady.** Fowke, H. S. 4b. 1g. Sc. In Scotland. JON

c **Wilbur, the sleepy little ghost.** Frey, H. 1w. 1b. voices. COW

r **Wilbur's birthday gift.** Mickel, J. Ann. 5m. 1w. Sc. Int. MIC

c **Wilderness birthday.** Carlson, B. W. 3b. 2g. Sc. Int. CAR

The will. Barrie, J. M. 6m. 1w. Sc. Lawyer's office. COOK GR MIR RI

Will you marry me? Chalmers, V. 1m. 1w. Sc. Int. com. HAN

j **Willoughby's window.** Preston, E. E. 5m. 10w. ext. Sc. Show window. PR

r **Will-o-wisp.** Murray, J. 3m. 3w. Sc. Inn. MU PLE

c **Wind wand.** Dennis, A. 5 char. Sc. Garden. KAM

Window shopping. Huber, L. J. 2m. 1w. Sc. Street. HU

Winter cruise. Maughan, W. S. 11m. 3w. Sc. Ship. MAU

Winter of our discontent. Du Bois, G. 7m. 2w. Sc. Office. DUB

j **Winter thaw.** Barr, J. 5b. 2g. Sc. Snow outside. PLD

Winter's tale. Rose, K. 2m. 2w. Sc. Theatre. ROS

c **Wise men of Gotham.** Holmes, R. V. 6b. ext. Sc. Market. BUF

c r **Wise men of Gotham.** Kissen, F. Ann. 14 char. Sc. Town. KIC

Wise wife. Nicholson, M. A. 4m. 2w. Sc. Farm house. PLJ

Wisely chosen. McCaslin, N. 1m. 2w. Sc. Cabin. MAC

Wishful Taw. Hughes, E. W. 8m. 7w. ext. Sc. In the Ozarka. MAYO

j **Wispy.** Spamer, C. 6b. 3g. Sc. Outdoors. PLH

c **Witch doctor.** Lehman, J. F. 4b. 1g. Sc. Stage. PLA

c **Witch who wasn't.** Howard, H. L. 2b. 3g. Sc. Stage. PLB

j **Witches' complaint.** Woolsey, J. 11 char. Sc. Int. WOO

j **Witches' delight.** MacLellan, R. 3b. 3g. Sc. Barn. PLH

c **Witch's pattern.** Lehmann, J. F. 2b. 3g. Sc. Office. PLD

c **Witch's pumpkin.** Cooper, E. 3g. Sc. Int. BUF

With eye of youth. Ramsey, H. 3m. 3w. Sc. Int. DEN

With malice towards none. Du Bois, G. 4m. 3w. Sc. Int. PLH

t **Within the family.** Parker, K. T. 3m. 3w. Sc. Dance hall. PARK

c **Wolf & the kid.** Bennett, R. 6b. 1g. Sc. Woodland. PLA

c **Woman who didn't want Christmas.** Phillips, M. K. 9g. Sc. Int. KA

j **Wonder world of books.** Woolsey, J. 24 char. Sc. Library. WOO

c **Wonders of Storybook Land.** D'Arcy, A. 19 char. Sc. Int. BUF

r **Word in your ear.** Goldschmidt, W. 11m. 3w. Sc. Int. MAYO

r **Word in your ear.** Sinclair, L. 2 nar. 11m. 3w. Sc. Int. GOL

Words upon the window pane. Yeats, W. B. 4m. 2w. Sc. Lodging house. YE YEA

Workhouse ward. Gregory, Lady. 2m. 1w. Sc. Workhouse. CRO

j **Worth his salt.** Molloy, L. L. 1b, 3g. Sc. Attic. PLB

R **Wreath for Apollo.** Weaver, L. Nar. Any number of char. Sc. Studio. WE

   The wrecker. Bellow, S. 2m. 2w. Sc. R.R. NEWA

   Wrong time. Howard, V. 12 char. Sc. Office. PLK

R **Wuthering heights.** Bronte, E. 3m. 3w. Sc. Int. OF

Y

   Yankee Doodle. Emurian, E. K. 8m. Sc. Banks of river. EM

C **Ye good old days.** Roberts, H. M. 6g. Sc. Attic. PLA

J **Ye old book shoppe.** Richmond, S. S. 4b. 3g. Sc. Shop. PLB RIC

   Yes, yes, I see. Lehmann, A. 1m. 1w. Sc. Park bench. LE

   York — Resurrection. Switz, T. MacL. 7m. 3w. Sc. Council hall. SW

C **Yorktown lass.** Gordon, C. 3b. 4g. Sc. Int. PLD

   You are not alone. Salverson, G. 2m. 2w. Sc. Bus. GOL

J **You can't please everybody.** Preston, E. E. 2m. Sc. Hotel com. PR

   You don't belong to me. McCoy, P. S. 3m. 4w. Sc. High School. PLH

   You must start dieting. Teasdale, V. 2w. Sc. Int. TE

   You never can tell. Holloway, P. 2m. 2w. Sc. Int. DEN

   Young as you look. Seller, T. 4m. 3w. Sc. Int. BAK

   Young gentleman & the young wife. 1m. 1w. Sc. Int. BE

C **Young Irving.** Phillips, M. K. 6b. 4g. Sc. Int. PLD

T **Young lady of property.** Foote, H. 3m. 6w. Sc. Int. FO

R **Young man with the cream tarts.** Stevenson, R. L. 6m. Sc. Int. HA PLB

   Young man's fancy. Manning, H. 4m. 2w. Sc. Int. com. DAV

C R **Young Paul Bunyan.** Kissen, F. 11 char. Ann. Nar. Sc. Forest. KIC

   Young wife & the husband. Schnitzler, A. 1m. 1w. Sc. Int. BE

   The youngest shall ask. Shaber, D. 2m. 1w. Sc. Int. MAYN

C **Your country & mine.** Carlson, B. W. Reader, ext. Sc. Int. CAR

J **Your manners & mine.** Howard, V. L. 5b. Sc. Int. HO

J **Your money or your life.** Howard, V. L. 4b. Sc. Give away show. HO

R **Your time will come.** Mickel, J. Nar. 6m. 1w. Sc. Int. MIC

J **Youth day at the UN.** Hackett, W. 14b. 4g. Sc. Headquarters. PLC

Z

T **Zone of quiet.** Larsner, R. 2m. 3w. Sc. Hospital. KAV

AUTHORS

A

Abney, L.
American Thanksgiving

Ade, G.
Aunt Fanny from Chautauqua
Afterpiece

Agoston, G.
The beast
For each man kills
Three persons

Akins, Z.
Old maid

Aklom, M.
Flash-back
Of social significance

Albright, H.
Final word

Alcott, L. M.
Laurence boy
Little women
Merry Christmas

Aldrich, T. B.
Marjory Daw

Allan, D. C.
All in good time

Allred, J.
All this and Alan too
Society page

Allyn, M. C.
Wagging tongues

Ames, G.
Green veil passes

Anderson, H. C.
Emperor's new clothes

Andersson, D.
Cross of gold
Mayflower compact

Andrews, I.
The goldfish

Andeyev, L.
He who gets slapped

Little Polka dot
Little whittler
Lullaby land
Mind your manners
Pottery Lane
Saga of little Fritjof
So this is China
Tick tock
What's a penny?

Ashton, L. S.
Christmas story

Ashton, N.
Amazing Arabella
Campus brides

Aske, L.
Non Nobis

August, E.
'O let him pass!'

Austen, J.
Pride and prejudice

Austin, H.
Almost everyman

B

Baden, R.
Christmas Eve visitor

Badger, A.
Before the dawn

Bailey, A. H.
Impersonations

Bailey, R.
Washed in de blood

Baker, N. E.
Palmer way

Baldwin, M. T.
All seats reserved
George Washington
Jim & Jennie
The option
Sitting ducks
Two hundred thousand dollars

Balm, C. M.
Awful fate of a fibber
Generous fisherman
Proud Princess
Ogre of Rashamon

Bannister, W.
A government job

Barbee, L.
>Beggars can't be choosers
>Christmas for Cinderella
>Columbus sails the sea
>Enter Juliet
>First day of April
>Flag of the U.S.
>Friday foursome packs a box
>Guide for George Washington
>Holly hangs high
>Letter to Lincoln
>Little patriot
>May Day gift
>Melissa's muffins
>Princess who couldn't dance
>Safety patrol
>Trial by jury

Barclay, E.
>Spoiled darlings

Barnett, G. T.
>Treasure in the Smith house

Barnouw, E.
>Voice of the wizard

Barr, J.
>Animal's Thanksgiving
>April fool surprise
>Buried treasure
>Cats and the cheese
>Cinderella
>Fisherman & his wife
>Lazy little raindrop
>Lion and the mouse
>Little red hen
>Missing Easter eggs
>Mother's day for Susan
>Old mother Hubbard
>Present for mother
>Queen of hearts
>Rapunzel
>Roddy's candy bar
>Thirsty flowers
>Three little kittens
>Useless little wind
>White Christmas
>Winter thaw

Barrie, J. M.
>Old lady shows her medals
>Shall we join the ladies?
>Twelve-pound look
>The will

Barth, R.
Red death

Beach, L.
The clod

Beach, M. M.
On the fence

Bec, M.
Mister Vincent

Bechet, R. R.
Canticle of the nativity

Beebe, T.
Crime clues
Narration for V.J. Day
"The pay-off"

Bela, N.
Safecracker's pride

Bellah, M.
Blue toadstool

Bellow, S.
The wrecker

Bembridge, J.
Disconsolate apparition

Bennett, A.
Stepmother

Bennett, H. C.
Rumpelstiltsken
Sleeping beauty

Bennett, R.
Ass and the lap dog
First Easter egg
Granny Goodman's Christmas
Hermes & the two woodsmen
In the witch's house
Lion and the mouse
Littlest artist
North wind and the sun
Runaway pirate
Wolf and the kid

Bennick, H. R.
Out at the home plate

Bercovici, E.
Heart of age

Berg, G.
The Goldbergs

Bernhart, G.
Home-longing

Bierling, J. C. E.
No braver soldier

Briggs, S.
King Neptune's court

Brighouse, H.
Inner man
Let's live in England
Broadhembury Drama group
Dr. Paynter

Brome, R.
A close shave
Lost voice
Poor man, rich man
Sky's the limit
Those in glass houses

Bronte, C.
Jane Eyre

Bronte, E.
Wuthering heights

Brooke, R.
Lithuania

Brown, A. M.
Lucky seven
Sometimes it's right to fight

Brown, A. V.
Mrs. Sniffit's Christmas

Brown, S. P.
Operation Coral

Brown, T. L.
Talent tree

Brownell, J. C.
The closet

Brydon, M. W.
Dreadful dragon
Reluctant ghost

Bufano, R.
Cinderella or the glass slipper
Jack & the beanstalk
Mr. Rabbit's Easter jamboree

Bunton, R. J.
Boo-Hoo Princess

Burger, I. B.
King's birthday
Queen of hearts

Burke, C.
Inside Washington

Burlingame, C.
Beyond ultroviolet
Fountain for a Duke
Three wishes

Childs, C.
Candle in the window

Chipp, E.
Honor and the glory

Chown, P.
Sea-shell

Clapp, P.
Girls whose fortune sought her

Clark, J.
Banner boys
Better be clean, Clara
Captain Tall tells all
Citizens of the garden
Happy Hygiene
How the old woman furnished the shoe
Inside the music box
It happened in Bookland
Jimmy's garden of words
Land of scratches & scribbles
Life of a first grader
Mischievous clock
Rabbit's reading lesson
Sidewalk elves
Talk on teeth
Terrible tale of terrible tempers
Tricky rhymes for sale
Visit of the cotton maids
Visit to Vitamin village
Visitors from the air
When the letter A ran away

Clark, M. G.
Great beginning

Cleveland, A.
May eve

Coe, F.
Something in the wind

Cohan, G. M.
Farrell case

Colbert, M.
Judge Monkey
Salt in the sea

Colbo, E. S.
First New England tree
Hero of Wren
Littlest fir

Collins, F.
Before the light came
Caractacus
Court of the Druids
Death of Boadicea

First Roman invasion
Gift of forgiveness
Holy Grail
King Alfred the great
Light is kindled
Pytheas the Greek explorer
St. Alban
St. Augustine of Canterbury
St. Birinus
St. Boniface
St. Chad & Archbishop Theodore
St. Columba
St. Columba says his last words
    to the people of Ireland
St. Columba visits King Brude
St. Cuthbert
St. Dustan
St. Edmund
St. Edward, the Confessor
St. Hilda & Caedmon
St. Oswald & St. Aiadan
St. Patrick
St. Paulinus & King Edwin
Stone age
Synod of Whitby
Venerable Bede

Colson, J. G.
Black Ivo
Bow to the Queen
Ebenezer Neverspend
Message from Robin Hood
Top of the bill

———

Comedy sketch

Condre, M.
Hearts, M.

Conkle, E. P.
Abbie, the bug boy
China-handled knife
Incident at Eureka Bumps
Least one
Minnie Field
Muletail prime
Owl & the young men
Scene from Prologue to Glory

Constanduros, M.
Lady from abroad

Cooper, E.
Little white cloud
Magic spell

Cunningham, M.
    Good old George
Curtis, A.
    When father goes on a diet

D

D'Arcy, A.
    Cinderella
    Wonders of Storybook land
Davies, R. E.
    Sunset in the dust
Davis, L. R.
    David and the second Lafayette
    St. Patrick & the last snake in Ireland
Dawson, N.
    "Can die but once"
De La Torre, L.
    Goodbye, Miss Lizzie Borden
De Marco, L.
    Some are teachers
Denbury/, Drama Class
    Bats in the belfry
Deming, D.
    Big news from Little America
    Crisscross streets
    Defense never rests
    Eyes right!
    Fashion show
    First aid first
    Ghost-layers, Inc.
    Grey ghosts
    Health officers for a day
    Howard's forward pass
    Just like us
    Mermaid club
    Mister Catchy Cold
    Narrow squeak
    Nursing in the mountains
    Old man river
    Red 'n green treasure hunt
    Salesmanship
    Surprise package
    Talent scouts
    Tovarich
    Wind wand
Dias, E. J.
    Abner Crane from Hayseed Lane
    Case of the missing pearls
    A deer of another color
    Express to Valley Forge
    Face is familiar

Feudin' fun
General Gage's chowder
Ghost from Genoa
Landslide for Shakespeare
Martha Washington's spy
Natives are restless tonight
Out of this world
Printer's devil
Sands of time
Stage bore
Stop the presses!
Strong and silent
Unsuspected fruit
Visitor to Gettysburg
Way, way down East
What ho!

Dickens, C.
Christmas carol
David Copperfield
Pickwick papers
Tale of two cities

Dickey, N.
The whistle

Dickson, G.
Mlle. Deceit

Dillon, T. P.
Doctor from Dunmore

Dinner, W.
Mr. Fothergill joins the Angels

Dix, B. M.
Allison's lad

Donnergaard, L.
Hold the line, please

Donovan, A. D.
Music on the menu
Ring in the new

———
Double blackface act

———
Double Dutch act

———
Double Irish act

———
Double wop act

Douglas, M.
Lost kiss

Downing, R.
Jimmy six
Second Sunday in May
Sticks and stones

Dramatic sketch

Draper, C. C.
Emperor's daughters
Paper Princess
Thankless Kate

Draper, W.
Christmas on Main St.

Drummond, R.
Golden wedding anniversary
Substitute bride

Du Bois, G.
An apple from Coles County
Attorney for the defense
Ay, there's the rub
Bind up the nation's wounds
Bunny comes to town
But one life to give
Cause for gratitude
Cause to serve
Child of destiny
Child of her spirit
Corn meal & poetry
Darkest hour
Daughter of the gods
Empty room
End of the road
Every day is Thanksgiving
Fetters & dreams
For the glory of St. Patrick
Glory & the dream
Good egg
Green-eyed monster
His hand & pen
Humblest place
I shall sail again
King is here
Known but to God
Last laugh
Light in the darkness
Lincoln says farewell
Never any excuse
None so blind
Perfect gift
Poison ivy
Rain & rebellion
Regulars are out
Road to Bethelem

Eliot, G.
Silas Marner
Eliot, T. S.
Sweeney Agonistes
Elser, D.
Balcony scene
Concert in the park
Pink dress
Special guest
Emery, C.
Day after forever
Emurian, E. K.
America the beautiful
Battle hymn of the Republic
Christmas traditions
Church in the wildwood
Columbia, the gem of the ocean
Dixie
Famous fathers
God of our fathers
Great women of history
Last supper
New Colossus
Radiance streaming
The resurrection
Silver threads among the gold
Star spangled banner
Thanksgiving through the ages
'Twas the night before Christmas
Yankee Doodle
Erskin, J.
The beacon
Esson, L.
The drovers
Estrado, D.
Three on a bench
Etheridge, K.
Folly of Seithenyn

F

Fagan, J. B.
Doctor O'Toole
Faulkner, G. H.
Thinking heart
Fay, M.
Saving the old homestead
Felton, N.
Sam 'n' Ella

Fenwick, R.
Toys and science

Ferguson, J. A.
Campbell of Kilmhor
Such stuff as dreams

Ferrini, V.
Innermost I Land
Telling of the North Star

Fidel, V.
Wherefore is this night

Field, R.
Londondery air

Finch, R.
A certain man had two sons
Dark rider
Far-distant shore
From paradise to Butte
The lamb in the window
Maiden's prayer
Summer comes to Diamond O

Finian, Brother
Light of the world

Fisher, A.
Abe's winkin' eye
Accident of birth
Alice in Puzzleland
All in U N
All on a day in May
All the world around
Angel in the looking-glass
Best bargain in the world
Black blizzard
Bringing up father
By order of the King
Catch as catch can
Caught at the Narrows
Cavalcade of human rights
Christmas cake
Clean-up club
Courting trouble
Empty bowls
Fresco for Unesco
Getting in line
Get-together dinner
Ghosts on guard
Hearts, tarts & valentines
Honest Abe Lincoln
Invasion from the stratosphere
Jack straw

King's toothache
Let there be bread
Littlest month
Long live father
Luck takes a holiday
Magic formula
Mail goes through
Many a slip
Merry Christmas elf
Mother's day off & on
Murder in the kitchen
New hearts for old
A nickel & a dime
Nine cheers for Christmas
Nothing ever happens
Not-so-crooked man
Of gods & men
On strike
On such a night
Once upon a time
One-ring circus
Play without a name
Plot thickens
Robots to the rescue
Skills to share
So I heard
Special edition
Spirit of Christmas
Standing up for Santa
Sterling silver tree
Story of a well
Thanks a million
Thanksgiving feast
Three & the dragon
Time out for Christmas
Tit-for-tat
Treasure hunt
Turning the tables
Unexpected guests
Voice of liberty
Washington marches on
Way to Norwich
Weaver's son
What happened in Egypt
What happened on Clutter St.
What is a patriot?
What makes Thanksgiving?
Why the sleepy dormouse

Fitzsimmons, E. G.
"Double talk"

Fletcher, L.
Hitch-hiker
Sorry, wrong number

Folk life in ancient Greece
Folmsbee, B.
Goblin parade
Foote, H.
The dancers
Death of the old man
John Turner Davis
Old beginning
Young lady of property
Fossum, M. C.
Letters from home
Foulk, C. W.
Floating stone
Fowke, H. S.
A wig for my lady
Fox, D. U.
Littlest month
Foy, H.
Corfe gate
France, A.
Juggler of Our Lady
Man who married a dumb wife
Francis, J. O.
Birds of a feather

Freedom's forge
Freudenberger, H. L.
Jack & Jill
Frey, H.
Wilbur, the sleepy little ghost
Fylstra, A.
Mob scene

G

Gainfort, J.
Going home
Gale, Z.
Neighbors
Galsworthy, J.
Little man
Garver, J.
Father hits the jackpot
Happy Valentine's Day
Turkey, anyone?

Geiger, M.
Democrat & the Communist
Light & liberty
One special for Doc
Return of a patriot
University of the U. S.

George, C.
Newlyweds
When Shakespeare's ladies meet

George, L. D.
When the little angel sang

Gerstenberg, A.
Overtones

Gertzinger, E. W.
Let your light so shine
Not without honor
Promise of the angels

Glaspell, S.
Suppressed desires
Trifles

Goldschmidt, W.
Word in your ear

Goldsmith, O.
She stoops to conquer

Goldsmith, S. L.
Louisa Alcott's wish

Goodman, K. S.
Game of chess

Goodwin, R. V.
On a roof top

Gordon, C.
Compass for Christopher
Models for health
Way to the inn
Yorktown lass

Gorelik, M.
Paul Thompson forever

Gould, J.
Attic treasure
New worlds
Seven little seeds
Thanksgiving is for everybody

Gow, R.
Lawyer of Springfield

Gowan, E. P.
Royal touch

Graham, M. S.
Call it a day
Unusual flower

Grant, A.
The climber
Don't forget the baking powder

Green, P.
Franklin & the King
House of Connelly
Last of the Lowries
Quare medicine
White dresses

Greene, L. L.
Beyond Thule
Broom market day

Gregory, Lady.
Rising of the moon
Spreading the news
Workhouse ward

Gross, A.
Belle

Gross, E.
Date-time
Dooley & the amateur hour
Marko goes a courtin'
A party is born
She loves him Yes

Gross, N. F.
Mystery ring

Gunn, N. M.
Old music

Gurney, A. R. Jr.
Three people

Gurney, M.
Never miss a trick

H

Hackett, W.
After the fog lifts
Christmas carol
Decision
Freedom train
Jemmy's wife
Last drum
Luigi steps aside
New look
Next of kin
Opportunity unlimited
Outgoing tide
Prologue for tomorrow
Youth Day at U N

Hadlington, R.
Abu Hassan pays his debts

Hagy, J.
Fire in a paper

Hale, E. E.
Man without a country
My double & how he undid me

Hall, H.
The valient

Hall, M. E.
Hearts of oak
Language shop
Trial of Billy Scott

Hall, M. G.
Tiger who wanted a boy

Hall, Mazie
Square box

Hallman, E. S.
Survival

Hamilton, G.
Field of honor

Hammons, R.
Common touch

Hamre, J.
Strange traditions

Harber, B.
Gentleman from Philadelphia

Hare, W. B.
Christmas carol
White Christmas

Hark, M.
A B C for safety
Advice to the lovelorn
Aladdin, inc.
Aladdin steps out
All aboard for Christmas
All is not gold
Alumni dinner
Author of liberty
Bake a cherry pie
Best years
Bobby & the Lincoln speech
A book a day
Book revue
Books to the rescue
Bud for president
Case for books
Change of heart
Clean up, shine up

Many thanks
May basket
Meet Mr. Witch
Mind your P's and Q's
Mom's a grandma now
The moon keeps shining
Mother saves her day
Music hath charms
New broom
New-fangled Thanksgiving
New worlds to find
Not fit for man or beast
Nothing to be thankful for
Nursery rhyme diet
Ode to spring
Off the shelf
Our famous ancestors
Our own four walls
Place to begin
Pleasant dreams
Portrait of an American
Princess & the rose-colored glasses
Prize for mother
Quiet Christmas
Rainbow colors
Reindeer on the roof
Rival for Dad
Santa Claus parade
See the parade
Spring daze
Spring fever
Spring is here
Star in the window
Stuff of heroes
Surprise guests
T for turkey
Television-itis
Tempest in a teapot
Thanks to Billy
Thanks to George Washington
Thanksgiving wishbone
Three wishes for mother
To be or not to be
To my Valentine
Tomorrow is Easter
Too many kittens
Turkey gobblers
'Twas the night before Christmas
Unaccustomed as I am
Visit of Johny Appleseed
Voices of America

Vote for Uncle Sam
What, no venison?
When do we eat?
Who's old-fashioned?

Harris, V.
Land where balloons grow

Hartley, C.
Children of the calendar

Hartman, Z.
Sitters in revolt

Hastings, F. V.
Give us leaders
Prelude for posterity

Hatton, C.
The beard
Saga of Simon Curle

Hawthorne, N.
Great stone face
House of seven gables

Hayes, J.
Silver key

Hazan, L.
Arthritis & rheumatism

Heath, A. L.
Gypsy look
Much ado about ants
Who? who

Heath, T.
Spinney under the rain

Heicher, M.
Lost star
Meaning of Christmas Day

Heiderstadt, D.
Indians for Thanksgiving

Helburn, T.
Enter the hero

Helsby, A.
Strained relations

Herbert, M. D.
For old times sake

Hess, M. B.
Of all the years

Hewitt, B.
In the suds

Hill, K.
Midnight burial

Holland, N.
Day before yesterday
Farewell appearance
Leopard's spots
One hour alone
Tea with a legend

Holler, R. M.
Brave little Indian brave

Hollingsworth, L.
Silent night

Hollister, L. D.
An early start
Tourist troubles

Hollister, L. S.
Many Happy returns

Holloway, P.
You never can tell

Holmes, R. V.
Little Red Riding Hood
Wise men of Gotham

Honiton Drama Class
Out of the shadows

Hoppenstedt, E. M.
Poet's nightmare

Hord, P.
The gypsy

Hosey, N. L.
Last curtain

Houghham, E. B.
America's heritage of song

Houghton, S.
Dear departed

Hourihane, U.
Princess & the horse

Houseman, J.
Julian Houseman story

Houseman, L.
Royal favour

Houston, J. M.
Strange road

Howard, H. L.
Ben Franklin peace-maker
Christmas train
Doctor Know all
I'll share my fare

I

Irving, W.
Legend of Sleepy Hollow
Rip Van Winkle

J

Jackson, M. C.
Perfect understanding

Jackson, M. R.
Lavender lie

Jacob, E.
Crowded house

Jacobs, W. W.
Monkey's paw

Jacobson, P.
Ridiculous and sublime

Janes, H.
Monsieur Le Marquis

Jeafferson, M.
Danger! Women at work

John, E.
King's march

Johnson, C.
Astonishing Mrs. O'Shaugnessy
George Washington's chair
The proposal
The rockers

Johnson, L. E.
A bargain's a bargain

Johnson, P.
Dark brown
Lovely miracle
Orange blossom
Tinsel Duchess

Johnson, R. E.
Dreamlost

Jokai, M.
Which of the nine?

Jones, R. C.
Tavern meeting

Joy, V.
Milkmaid & her pail

Jurgensen, K.
Tarantula

K

Kane, E. B.
Children of Chocolate St.
Elves & the shoemaker
How we got our numbers
The navy & the pirates

Kapek, K.
R U R

Kaser, A Le R.
Come out of it
Fisherman's luck
Forever yours
Lock your car
Love honor and obey

Kauffman, S.
Cow was in the parlor

Kaufman, G. S.
Beggar on horseback
If men played cards as women do

Kaufman, T.
Piffle! It's only sniffle!

Kavanaugh, K.
Settled out of court

Keating, E. H.
Incog
Plot of Potzentausend
Poor relations
Talisman

Kelley, A.
Tour of duty

Kelly, G.
Finders keepers
Flatterinf word
Poor Aubrey

Kennedy, L.
Pied Piper of Hamelin

Kern, D.
It belongs to me

Kerr, S.
Home nursing revue

Kesser, H.
Nurse Henrietta

Kimes, B.
The lost Christmas

King, W.
Easter lily
Little Snow White

Kingman, L.
Magic pumpkin
Mr. Thanks has his day

Kinroy, E.
Good-bye to the clown
Whistle daughter, whistle

Kipling, R.
Captains courageous

Kirchner, V. M.
Home in Nazarath

Kirkpatrick, J.
The nerve of it!
On the sentimental side
A wedding

Kissen, F.
Baba Yaga
Bag of fire
Billy beg & his bull
Birds of Killingworth
Boots & his brothers
Christmas angel
Cinderella
Clever Manka
Crowded house
Feast of lanterns
The flea
Flying ship
Four clever brothers
Fox brings luck
Golden touch
Jack & the beanstalk
Katherine & Frederick
Lenka's little house
One-inch fellow
Peterkins try to become wise
Pied piper
Rock in the sea
Rumpelstilyskin
Shiro & his master
Sleeping beauty
Straw ox
Three golden oranges
Three sillies
Three wishes
Tinder box
Ugly duckling
What the good man does
Why the sea is salt
Wise men of Gotham
Young Paul Bunyan

Knapp, B.
Charge it, please

Knapp, J. S.
Other side

Knight, L.
Flibber turns the tables

Knox, J.
Shepherd of Bethlehem

Kocher, E.
Karma
Medal for Julien
Shadow of the cathedral

Kozlenko, W.
Jacob comes home
Journey of promise
One of these days

Krausy, G.
I'll never be late again

Kring, H. A.
Bird who couldn't sing

Kroll, F. L.
Some tricks are treats

L

Lake, G.
Glory day
Incident at a grave

Lamont, J.
Perfect crime

Langner, L.
Another way out

Lanzl, F.
Fantasia on an old familiar theme

Lardner, R.
Zone of quiet

Latham, J. L.
Gray bread
One of twelve

Lathers, H. Q.
Bonnie Annie

Law, W. T.
Dog in the manger

Lawrence, J.
Somebody's Valentine

Lee, H.
'Twas the night before Christmas

Lee, M.

Dope

Lee, S.

Green piper
Moonbeam dares
Spring secrets
Whirlwind comes

Lee, W. C.

Deadwood

Lehman, J. F.

Biskie the snowman
Good health trolley
Witch doctor
Witch's pattern

Lehmann, A.

Aged but not mellowed
Come home
The confession
Greatest show on earth
Help wanted
My mirror tells me
The secret
Thank you Louise
That woman
Yes, yes, I see

Lemmon, A.

Last flight over

LePelley, G.

Cracked ice
Nobody sleeps

Leuser, E.

Big stone
Broth of Christkindli
Brushes for Benjy
Christmas sampler
Courage piece
Five brothers
George Washington comes to town
King's jester
Little bird in the tree
Little clown who forgot to laugh
Little witch who tried
Magic grapes
Magic well
Mixing stick
Stubborn elf
Thanksgiving scarecrow
Tommy's adventure

Lipnick, E.
Son of liberty

———
Little bit of heaven

Lockridge, I.
Color-conscious conscience

———
Long and short of it

Lorca, F. G.
Love of Don Perlimplin & Bellsa
Tragi-comedy of Don Cristobita

Loudan, J.
The counsellor

Lovelace, W. R.
Gold feathers

Lowe, C. F.
Gooseberry tarts

Lyman, B.
Lady Lookout

Lynch, M.
Ethel & Albert

M

Mabley, E.
Discrimination for everybody

McArthur, J.
Fiesta

McCarty, E. C.
Little cake

McCaslin, N.
Bailiff's wonderful coat
Christmas lamb
Gift of music
Humai's secret
Lazy ones
Maelduin of Arran
Paul Bunyan: lumberjack
Three meals a day
Tinker of Toledo
Rose for Madame Calva

McCoy, P. S.
Lieutenant pays his respects
Miss Fix-it
You don't belong to me

MacDonagh, D.
Happy as Harry

Test for a witch
Umbrella magic
Witches' delight

MacLellan, R.
Carlin moth

Maclennan, J. M.
Pipstrelle of Aquitaine

McMartin, E. L.
The tree

MacNaughton, J. A.
Final edition

MacNeice, L.
The nosebag
Dark town

Madley, H. L.
Secret agent

Maeterlinck, M.
Interior
Miracle of St. Anthony

Maupassant, G. de.
The necklace

Magee, C.
Radio Jerusalem, the story of Jesus

Malone, M.
Give the book a chance
Groundhog's shadow
Last supper
Letter to Charlotte

Maloney, M. J.
Death of the average man

————

Man & woman act

Manley, F.
Best trip ever

Manley, W. F.
Crowsnest

Manning, H.
Young man's fancy

Manning, S.
Background for Nancy

Mantle, M.
Beatrice & Benedict

Marcus, I. H.
To you the torch

Mark Twain
 Adventures of Tom Sawyer
 Connecticut Yankee in King Arthur's Court
 Glorious whitewasher
 Huckleberry Finn
 Million-pound note
 Prince & the pauper

Marsh, W. A.
 Bakers's three daughters
 Bang goes my stocking
 The clock says
 Contrary Mary meets Boy Blue
 Domino family's picnic
 The Dominoes have a fire
 Donkey brays loudly
 He who eats cabbage
 How the giraffe got its neck
 I spy
 Miracle of the fishes
 Number play: the poison plot
 Persistent musician
 Pretty maid, where have you been
 Red apple
 Ride a cock-horse
 Storm in a tea cup
 Three pigs catch the wolf again
 Useful plough
 We three
 Wee Willie Winkle

Martens, A. C.
 Those Monday blues

Marx, M.
 Jack Gleason show

Mason, M. E.
 Mary Elizabeth's wonderful dream

Mattson, J. M.
 I saw the Cross

Mauermann, W. G.
 A cup of kindness

Maugham, W. S.
 Ant & the grasshopper
 Gigolo & gigolette
 Winter cruise

Maughfling, M.
 Auntie & the bull
 Love triumphant
 Pirates & the ladies
 Polly in the park
 Suskie has an air

Maurois, A.
    After ten years
    Catastrophy
    Courtship & conquest
    Good manners
    Honeymoon
    Major conflicts
    Marriage & friendship
    Matter of taste
    Minor friendship
    Seduction
    Silver wedding
    Wedding journey

Melchoir, H. K.
    Visits to the planets

Mella, A.
    Grand slam

Meredith, B.
    Adventures of Mr. Bean

Meredith, G.
    Great inheritance

———

    Merry adventures of Robin Hood

Mickel, J.
    Apartment-hunting
    The curtain
    Freedom's herald
    Let the heaven's decide
    Mask of guilt
    The promise
    Return of Benjamin
    Things we know
    Wilbur's birthday gift
    Your time will come

Millay, E. St. V.
    Aria da Capo

Miller, C. A.
    Moon maiden

Miller, H. L.
    Bar-none trading post
    Be my "Walentine"
    Beany's private eye
    Best policy
    Bewitched & bewildered
    Boomerang
    Boy who didn't belong
    Boys in books
    Bread and butter shop
    Brookstick beauty
    Bunnies & Bonnets
    Case of the balky bike

New shoes
Not for girls
Not worth a continental
Papa Pepper's bombshell
Patriotic Teddy Bear & the U N
Paul Revere rides again
Petrified Prince
Pilgrim parting
Pink parasol
Pinocchio
Pin-up pals
Poka dot pup
Puppy love
Puss in boots
Rabbit foot
Railroad rhymes & rhythms
Right of adoption
Robinson Crusoe
Santa Claus for president
Say it with flowers
Shady shadows
Shakespearean touch
Snow white & rose red
Soft-hearted ghost
Softy the snow man
Speaking of speech
Spooks in books
Spooky spectacles
Star cadets
Story of light
Strictly Puritan
Thanks to butter-fingers
Thanksgiving a la carte
Three cheers for mother
Travel game
Turkey turns the tables
Uninvited guests
Vanishing Easter egg
Vicky gets the vote
Visitors to Mount Vernon
Washington shilling
Washington's leading lady
What makes it tick?
What's cookin'?
Who's who at the zoo

Mills, G. E.
Christmas comes to Hamlin

Mindel, J.
Freeing the land
To secure these rights

Mirabesu, O.
The epidemic

Morrish, P.
Our dream house
———
Mummy limps at midnight
Murdock, M.
The cuckoo
Murray, J.
Be my ghost
Boy next door
Case for Mrs. Hudson
Case for two detectives
Case of the missing poet
Colossal, stupendous!
Contest fever
The door
End of the line
Fabre's little world
Final curtain
Five buttons
Game of chess
Haunted clothesline
Honest Injun!
Impossible room
Lock stock & barrel
Mechanical man
Mish-mosh bird
Mystery in the lab.
Rented tux
Swiss chalet mystery
That's the spirit
Ups and downs
When the hurlyburly's done
Will-o'-wisp
Muse, V.
Town mouse & his country cousin
Myrick, N.
Day is bright

N

Nagel, L.
A debt to pay
Nash, M. R.
Rouge atomique
Nathan, B.
If wishes were horses
Neher, J.
As kids go
Bobby soxer's rebellion
Day dreams go to school
Everybody gets into the act

Relax and enjoy it
School for marriage
Somebody do something!
Sons and husbands
That's my old man!
What every woman wants

Neuenburg, E.
Strange victory

Newman, D.
Bunny of the year
Christmas at the Cratchits
Christmas tree surprise
Election day in the U.S.A.
First Thanksgiving

Newman, D.
Gift for the world
Green leaf's lesson
Happy holiday
In honor of trees
Kachoo!
Magic goose
Memorial day for the blue & the grey
Message of the hearts
Mr. Lincoln's beard
Mrs. Santa's Christmas gift
The new Washington
Present from Abe
Prize Shamrock
Pumpkneters' pumpkin
Roses for mother
Something new for Halloween
Spring neighbors
Spring to the rescue
Stars & stripes
Stolen heart
Thanks to the Indians
Washington's gold button

Newton Ferrers Dramatic Club
Stormy passage

Nicholson, J.
Ghost walks tonight
Haunted bookshop
Mysterious stranger
Nautical sheep
Sugar & spice
Teapot trouble
Valentine stardust

Nicholson, M. A.
Crying clown
Laughing Princess

O

Parsons, M.
 Sailing west to find the east
 Too much of a good thing

Patterson, E. L.
 No room at the inn

Peach, L. duG.
 Surprising story of Alfred, Warder of the Tower

Peacock, M.
 Barefoot boy
 Keeping Christmas

Pendleton, E.
 A B C of safety
 Bobby & the Lincoln speech
 Ghosts in the library
 Hearts & flowers for mother
 In honor of Washington
 Jingle bells
 Mom's perfect day
 Mother saves the day
 Nothing to be thankful for
 Santa Claus parade
 Star in the window
 Thanks to George Washington
 Vote for your hero

Perl, A.
 The High School
 Mind in the shadow

Perrini, A.
 Once a thief

Perry, M.
 A trap is a small place

Petersen, R. I.
 Late spring

Peterson, L.
 Desert soliloquy
 Home, sweet home
 Stand-in for murder
 Sticks & stones

Peterson, M. N.
 Soup stone

Pharis, G.
 Courting of Marie Jenvrin

Phelps, P.
 Junior buys a car
 The lost letter
 Patched coat

Phillips, A. L.
 Shepherds & wise men

Christmas dolls revue
Farmer in the dell
Friendly advice
Home work
How to be happy though married
In the doctor's office
In the pet shop
Little new citizen
Love's young dream
Moonrise island
Musical notes
Number game
Oh! that golden wedding
Quiet evening at home
Quiz for high I.Q.'s
Sign on the door
Something to read
Star of wonder
Sunday edition
Switch to Mich
Ten-minute white-face minstrel
Turning the fables on Aesop
Virus v
Voice that failed
Willoughby's window
You can't please everybody

Priming the pump

Privacty, A. H.
Grey squirrel & white buffalo

Probst, G.
Experiment of a free press
Nature's most precious gift

Purkey, R. A.
Hangs over thy head

Pyle, M. T.
Bright stream
Day the shoemaker came
Halloween gets a new look
Have a heart
In triplicate, please!
Mrs. Gibbs advertises
Not on the menu
Perambulating pie
Three dying swans
Three royal R's

Q

Quintero, S.
Sunny morning

R

Ramsey, H.
Grateful gobbler
In the name of Miles Standish
Names to remember
With eye of youth

Ratcliff, N.
The brothers
Jezebel

Rattigan, T.
The Browning version

Raymond, J.
The Sammy Kaye show

Raynolds, T. M.
Larry Gray & the gremlins

Ready, S.
Tomorrow's vengeance

Reay, N.
Good old summer time
Mr. Bates goes to the polls

Redgrave, M.
Seventh man

Rees, P. M.
Idols

Renner, H. A.
Sons of the prairie

Reynolds, J.
Sky-fodder

Richards, S.
August heat
O distant land
Once to every boy
Half-hour, please
Know your neighbor
Mr. Bell's creation
Sun deck
Through the glass, darkly
Tunnel of love

Richmond, S. S.
A career for Ralph
Albright acres
At the cleaners
Big banker
Born to the soil
Business is business
Buster picks a winner
Career girl
Case of Mr. X
The coach scores

Rogers, J.
Back to Boston
Rogers, J. A.
Charge it to George
Rogers, M.
Book of Job
Rose, K.
Boswell meets Johnson
Death of a hero
First of the Dandies
Pilot who weathered the storm
Royal button-maker
Tragic muse
Winter's tale
Ross, F. R.
It happened in Egypt
Rostand, E.
Cyrano de Bergerac
Rosten, H.
Happy housewife
Rowland, E.
Hans who made the Princess laugh
Precedent in pastries
Three aunts
Ruggles, R.
Patriotic minstrels
Rulon, S.
Elizabeth
Runnette, H. V.
The way
Ruscoll, J.
The creeper
Rush, M. E.
Most indistructible man in the world
Ruskin, J.
King of the golden river
Ryerson, F.
Materia Medica

S

St. Clair, R.
Happy life
Holy search
Joy of the world
Promised ones
Spirit of Christmas
Salverson, G.
You are not alone

Sanderlin, O.
Follow the north star

Sangster, A.
Boney

Saroyan, W.
Hello out there

Satre, J. P.
In camera

Saunders, L.
Knave of hearts
Poor Maddalena

Savage, G. M.
Gratitude
Little person

Sayre, G. M.
Final edition

Schaefer, L.
Little flaw of Ernesto
Song for a hero

Schenkkan, R.
Black Piet

Schnitzler, A.
The actress & the count
Count & the prostitute
Farewell supper
Green cockatoo
Housemaid & the young gentlemen
Husband & the little darling
Little darling & the poet
Poet & the actress
Prostitute & the soldier
Soldier & the housemaid
Young gentleman & the young wife
Young wife & the husband

Schoenfeld, B. C.
This, our America

Schofield, J. A. Jr.
"All hail the power of Jesus name"
"Who is this?"

Schulberg, B.
Pharmacist's mate

Schwartz, M. K.
All in favor
The auction
Lazy afternoon
Loud-speaker
Somewhat forgetful
Twin cousins

Simon, S. S.
Trouble in tunnel nine

Simonds, N.
Hansel & Grethel
Peter Rabbit
Unhappy Santa

Sinclair, L.
All the world's a stage
But I know what I like
Case of the sea-lion flippers
Legend of the Long House
Museum of man
When Greek meets Greek
Word in your ear

Sion, G.
Matron of Ephesus

Skelton, G.
Have you see my lady?

Sladen-Smith, F.
Harlequin bridge
Love in the ape house
Mary Forbusher or realism routed

Slattern, M. E.
King in the kitchen
Patchwork Princess
Royal magic

Sliker, H. G.
Importance of being Earnest
Unto us the living

Slingluff, M. O.
Naughty Susan

Smith, A. C.
Before the dawn
Greater than any man
Whirligig of life

Smith, G. V.
Star light and the sandman

Smith, M.
Best gift of all

Smith, W. S.
Answer
By Christ alone
They that walk in darkness

Snyder, W. H., Jr.
Another summer

Spamer, C.
April showers
Broken doll
Bunnyland

Candy canes
Crocus
First butterfly,
Frolic of the leaves
Halloween scarecrow
Hop, jump & skip
Jack-o-lantern
Jack's friends
Jerry to the rescue
Little bell
Little Bo-Peep's May flowers
Little Christmas tree
Little February
Little pink egg
Mary's cake
Mirror children
Miss Robin's school
Mister Owl
Patrick Pumpkin
Pop-up books
Pot of gold
Prince with no crown
Pussy pleases
Robin that wouldn't fly
Shy Prince
Snowdrop
Twinkle
Uncolored Easter eggs
Valentine family
What Mildred found out
Wispy

Speare, E. G.
The anchor
Forest of Arden

Spence, W.
The bridal bouquet
Message from John

Stahl, Le R.
Parting tear
Romance a la mode

Standring, P.
Man from the fells

Standburg, M.
Easter egg magic

Steele, J.
Tea for six

Stein, G.
Brewsie & Willie
Doctor Faustus lights the lights

Stein, H.
In darkness

Steinbeck, J.
Leader of the people

Stephens, N. B.
Lily

Stephens, P. J.
The changeling
Hugh of the Glen & his clogs are one

Stevens, C.
Fit for vcitory

Stevens, H. C. G.
Man at the door

Stevens, T. W.
Drum head

Stevenson, R. L.
Bottle imp
Kidnapped
Sire de Maletroit's door
Young man with the cream tarts

Stewart, B.
End of the line

Stewart, M.
Hope for tomorrow

Stinetorf, L. A.
Wayfarers

Stirling, N.
Ins and outs

Stockton, F.
Transferred ghost

Stone, C.
Hearts and groceries

Stone, W.
Here's a howy-do

———

Straight & the Jew

Streacher, L.
Bob's Armistice parade
No-mother land
Princess & the pumpkin
Roaring March lion

Street, J. M.
Killed by Merry Christmas

Strindberg, A.
Miss Julie

Strong, A.
Drums of Oude

Strong, P. N.
Jack Armstrong

Stuart, J.
The door

Sturm, R. F.
Playwright's dilemma

Suerken, E. H.
John Crown's legacy

Summer, J. N.
Frightful forest

Summer, M. R.
Red dust

Sweeney, B.
My uncle Willy

————

Swing shift 1830

Swintz, M.
King's creampuffs
Panic in the palace
Three wishing bags

Switz, T. MacL.
Andrew the summoner
Brome — Abraham and Isaac
Digby — Conversion of St. Paul
Everyman
Followers of Christ
How to gain peace amid temptation & adversity
James the thunderer
John the beloved
Our preparation for the future
Readings from the Imitation of Christ
Royal pathway of the holy cross
Thomas the doubter
Totendanz
York — Resurrection

Sylvester, L.
Meaning of art

Synge, J. M.
Riders to the sea

T

Tarkington, B.
Monsieur Beaucaire

Tayleur, W. St. J.
Reunion

Tazewell, C.
Can long endure

Teasdale, V.
Bride's first dinner
Christmas shopping in June
Colonel, you're wonderful!
Drama society meets
Emergency call!
Facts of life
Flobelle goes shopping
Form 1040
Glamour pattern 479823
Good-bye, now!
Handy man
Help wanted
I'll help Johnny with his lesson
I'll teach junior, myself
Nurse's day out
Oh, H-e-n-r-y-y!
Oh, Mrs. Norton, you're so patient
Quiet rest
What do I do now, Mr. McLeod?
You must start dieting

Thalimer, F. L.
Haunted suitcase

There ought to be a law

Thomas, D.
Next-to-last rites

Thomas, Dylan
Under milkwood

Thomas, H.
After the air raid

Thomas, M.
Border folk

Thompson, D. F.
Whose birthday is it?

Thon, F.
The island

Thurston, M. B.
Room for Mary

Tims, M.
Many happy returns

Tobey, L. C.
The test

Tooley, H.
Miracle of the sack of barley
Murder of Shakespeare
This is our Kathie

Totheroh, D.
Stolen Prince

Jimmy Columbus
Jonathan's Thanksgiving
Magic mirror
President Lincoln's children
Puss-in-boots
Shoemaker & the elves
Sleeping beauty in the woods
Thanksgiving night
Three little kittens go to school
Three sillies
Tick-tock
What happened to the cakes

W

Waite, H. E.
Cecily entertains the enemy
Christmas House
Naomi-of-the inn
Not only the strong

Walden, R. S.
Cabin by the lake

Walsh, N.
Let there be farce

Walters, A.
Last night's paper

Ward, M.
Family affair
It's so peaceful
Mr. Lazy man's family

Wall, L. V.
Chinese romance
Drummer boy
Get up and bar the door
Hansel & Grethel
Life in a gold coast village
Mad tea party
Mock turtle's story
Pupet play for mass education
Rapunzel

Watkyn, A.
Wanted — Mr. Stuart"

Wayne, P.
Strolling clerk from Paradise

Wealthers, W.
Vision of the silver bell

Weaver, J. C.
Cloud-burst
For the ladies

Little guy Back home
Radio: how to abuse it
Wreath for Apollo

Webb, C. H.
Legend of the lake

Wefer, M.
April fool
Ladies with lamps

Weinstock, J.
Tom Corbett space cadet

Weiss, M. J.
The actor
Debby's dilemma
Greetings from . . .
Her big crush

Werner, S.
February play
Mr. Smooch's trap
New home for mice

West Hill Women's Institute
Shepherd's trove

West, M. K.
Star gazer

White, M. R.
Aladdin & the wonderful lamp
Cinderella
Hansel & Grethel
Jack & the beanstalk
Old woman in the shoe
Peter Rabitt changes his name
Red Riding Hood
Story of Peter Rabbit
Three little pigs
Three wishes
————
Who do you think you are?

Wight, L.
Handwriting on the wall

Wilde, C. F.
Ichabod rides again
Junior prom

Wilde, O.
Canterbury ghost
Happy Prince
Importance of being Earnest
Salome

Wilde, P.
Among friends
Finger of God
Legend

Noble Lord
Salt and savor
The sportsmen

Wilder, T.
Happy journey to Trenton
Long Christmas dinner
Mozart & the gray Stewart

Wilkes, E.
Matter of business

Williams, G. M.
Kettle of brains

Williams, G. R.
Casanova Jr.

Williams, H. V.
Babe of Bethlem
Miss Liberty protests

Williams, T.
The long stay cut short
Something unspoken

Williamson, C. H.
Family heirloom

Williamson, H. R.
Cardinal's learning

Williamson, S. G.
A bed with others

Wilson, A. J. A.
White train

Wilson, B.
Lace Handerchief

Wilson, D. C.
Return of Chandra

Wilson, M. L.
First flowers

Wimsatt, G.
Sheep skin Po

Wincelberg, S.
The conqueror

Wishengrad, M.
The camel and I
Danger of freedom
Divided we stand
Ground of justice
Living declaration

Woodress, F. A.
Impasse

Woolsey, J.
Charlie's May basket
Each star a state

Sophocles O'edipus at Colonus
Unicorn and the stars
Words upon the window-pane

York, E. B.
Kindled flame
Silver star of Christmas

York, M. A.
Flowers for mother
Lincoln's buckskin breeches
Naming the flowers
Treasure Island

York, M. B.
Skin deep

Z

Zeiger, H.
Five days

Zeller, E. A.
Marriage of Pierot
Undercurrent

Zeigler, E. E.
Cape of feathers
Just in time

Zimmermann, A. L.
A dream

COLLECTIONS

Arlette, Vera I. & Others. Mixed bill. Seven varied one-act plays. Lond. Muller, 1948.

Arlette, V. I. Gentle heart
Crown, Patricia. Miss Haffner
Trentham, W. Merlin limited
Sheklton, Geoffrey. Have you seen my lady?
Stevens, H. C. G. Man at the door
Causley, C. How pleasant to know Mrs. Lear
Tims, Margaret. Many happy returns

T **Armer, A. & Grauman, W. E.** Vest pocket theatre. Twenty television playlets. N. Y. French, 1955.

The last straw
Final curtain
Timeless second
Glass slipper
Closing time
Love scores a touchdown
Dead weight
One year after
Time out for dreams
In darkened rooms
Whatever became of Lola Woods
Love lesson for Scotty
Coral
Sure as fate
To be alone
Beast lies dormant
No time for dames
Black star
Country cousin
Hard as flint

Baldwin, Martin T. George Washington & other one-act plays. N. Y. Exposition, 1952.

George W. Washington
Jim and Jennie
All seats reserved
Sitting ducks
Two thousand dollars
The option

Bannister, Winifred, comp. North light. Ten new one-act plays from the North. Glasgow, Scotland, McLellan, 1947.

Carroll, P. V. Interlude
Corrie, J. Failure
Gunn, N. M. Old music
Loudan, J. Counsellor

Law, W. T. Dog in the manger
Standring, R. Man from the Fells
Bannister, W. Gover'ment job
Sladen-Smith, F. Mary Frobisher
MacLellan, J. Carlin moth
O'Casey S. End of the beginning

Barrows, Marjorie. Quintessense of beauty and romance. Chic., Spences, 1945.

Barrie, J. M. The old woman shows her medals.
And other material.

Bentley, Eric, ed. From the modern repertoire. Sec. I. Bloomington, Indiana, Uni. of Indiana, 1949.

Schnitzler, Arthur. Count and prostitute
Schnitzler, Arthur. Actress and the count
Schnitzler, Arthur. Poet and the actress
Schnitzler, Arthur. Little darling and the poet
Schnitzler, Arthur. Husband and the little darling
Schnitzler, Arthur. Young wife and the husband
Schnitzler, Arthur. Young gentleman and the young wife
Schnitzler, Arthur. Housemaid and the young gentleman
Schnitzler, Arthur. Soldier and the housemaid
Schnitzler, Arthur. Prostitute and the soldier
Eliot, T. S. Sweeney Agonistes
  "   Fragment II
Lorca, F. G. Love of Don Perlimplin and Belisa in the garden
Yeats, W. B. A full moon in March
  Also longer plays.

Bentley, Eric. ed. From the modern repertoire. ser. 2. Bloomington, Indiana, Uni. of Indiana, 1952.

Mirbeau, Octave. Epidemic
Obey, Andre. Venus and Adonis
Macneice, L. Dark tower
Brecht, B. Galileo
  Also longer plays.

Brewton, J. E. & Others. English and Continental literature. Chic., Laidlaw, 1950.

Chekhov, Anton. The beggar
Molnar, Ferenc. Two slaps in the face
Gregory, Lady. Rising of the moon
  Also other material.

Brewton, J. E. ed. Excursions in fact and fancy. Chic., Laidlaw, 1949.

Parsons, Margaret. Sailing West to find the East
Abney, Louise. American Thanksgiving
  Also other material.

Bridie, James. Tedious and brief. Lond. Constable, 1944.

A change for the worse
Ear of Vincent Van Gogh
Immortal memory

Scheherazade kept on talking
Paradise enow
The fat woman
The starlings

Brings, L. M. ed. Golden book of church plays. Minneapolis, Denison, 1955.
Angel in the window
Answer
Before the dawn
By Christ alone
Certain man had two sons
Deadwood
Greater than any man
Happy life
I saw the cross
Kindeled flame.
Let your light so shine
Light of the world
Love of Ruth
Not without honor
Out of the darkness
Prodigal comes home
Promised ones
Putting first things first
Radio Jerusalem, Story of Jesus
Silvered rope
They that walk in darkness
Voice that failed

Brings, L. M. ed. Modern treasury of Christmas plays. Minneapolis, Denison, 1955.
Beggars can't be choosers
Candle in the window
Christmas carol
Christmas dolls revue
Christ Eve visitor
Christmas for Cinderella
Christmas in her eyes
Christmas star
Christmas story
Grandma and mistletoe
Holy search
Joy to the world
Let nothing ye dismay
Lost star
Meaning of Christmas day
Shepherd of Bethlehem
Shepherds and wise men
Silver star of Christmas
Star of wonder
The tree
When the little angel sang
White Christmas

Bufano, Remo. Book of puppetry. N. Y. Macmillan, 1950.

Mr. Rabbit's Easter jamboree
Jack and the beanstalk
Cinderella or the glass slipper
    Also longer plays.

Burack, A. S. ed. Christmas plays for young actors. Bost. Plays, 1950.

Campbell, J. E. Pink roses for Christmas
Patterson, E. No room at the inn
Miller, H. L. Puppy love
Hollingsworth, L. Silent night
Paradis, M. B. Santa goes to town
DuBois, H. G. Perfect gift
Pyle, M. T. Perambulating pie
Hark, M. Christmas snowman
Waite, H. E. Naomi-of-the-inn
Fisher, A. Angel in the looking-glass
Leuser, E. Broth of Christkindli
Nolan, J. C. Happy Christmas to all
Pendleton, E. Jingle bells
Barbee, L. Friday foursome packs a box
Smith, M. Best gift of all
Very, A. Everywhere Christmas
Colbo, E. S. Littlest fir
Newman, D. Mrs Santa's Christmas gift
Simonds, N. Unhappy Santa
Howard, H. L. Christmas train
Spamer, C. Candy canes
St. Clair, R. Spirit of Christmas
Weathers, W. Vision of the Silver bell
Kane, E. B. Elves and shoemaker
Hackett, W. Christmas carol

Burack, A. S. ed. One hundred plays for children. An anthology of non-royalty one-act plays. Bost. Plays, 1949.

Arnold, E. W. Make him smile
Asbrand, K. China comes to you
Asbrand, K. What's a penny?
Blanton, C. The dulce man
Brown, T. L. Talent tree
Chandler, A. C. Chinese Rip Van Winkle
Deming, D. Grey ghosts
Deming, D. Old man river
Fisher, A. One-ring circus
Fisher, A. Special edition
Fisher, A. Way to Norwich
Goldsmith, S. L. Louis Alcott's wish
Graham, M. S. Unusual flower
Hall, M. Language shop
Hall, M. Trial of Billy Scott
Hartley, C. Children of the calendar
Heath, A. L. Much ado about ants
Hill, K. Midnight burial

Howard H. L. Little circus donkey
Kane, E. B. How we got our numbers
Kaufman, T. Piffle! It's only a Sniffle!
Leuser, E. Tommy' adventure
MacLellan, E. Clock's secret
Miller, H. L. Shady shadows
Nathan, B. If wishes were horses
Pyle, M. T. Not on the menu
Rittenhouse, C. Children of the sun
Schwartz, M. K. All in favor
Swintz, M. King's creampuffs
Myrick, N. Day is bright
Barbee, L. Letter to Lincoln
Sealock, T. W. The Lincoln coat
Urban, C. Queen with the broken heart
Very, A. What happened to the cakes
Barbee, L. Guide for Washington
Davis, L. R. David and the second Lafayette
Hark, M. The magic egg
Barr, J. A present for mother
Howard, H. L. Mother's gift
Very, A. Golden bell for mother
Hark, M. See the parade
Miller, H. L. Pink parasol
Barbee, L. Columbus sails the sea
Cooper, E. Magic spell
Cooper, E. Witch's pumpkin
Folmsbee, B. Goblin parade
Howard, H. L. Magic Jack-o-lantern
D'Arcy, A. Wonders of storybook land
Hark, M. Off the shelf
Moore, E. G. Mr. Longfellow observes Book Week
Wooster, A. Hubub on the bookshelf
Streacker, L. Bob's Armistice parade
Howard, H. L. I'll share my fate
Howard, H. L. Thanks to Sammy Scarecrow
Kingman, L. Mr. Thanks has his day
Very, A. Jonathan's Thanksgiving
Barbee, L. Holly hangs high
Carroll, G. H. Merry, Merry, Merry
Colbo, E. S. First New England Christmas tree
McCarty, E. C. The little cake
Mills, G. E. Christmas comes to Hamelin
Nolan, J. C. Happy Christmas to all
Patterson, E. L. No room at the inn
Waite, H. E. Christmas house
Asbrand, K. Crystal flask
Asbrand, K. Little hero of Holland
Bennett, H. C. Rumpelstiltsken
Bennett, H. C. Sleeping beauty
Bennett, R. The lion and the mouse

Burlinghame, C. Three wishes
Colbert, M. Salt in the sea
D'Arcy, A. Cinderella
Flouk, C. W. Floating stone
Freudenberger, H. L. Jack and Jill
Molloy, L. L. Broom market day
Molloy, L. L. Jenny-by-the-day
Holmes, R. V. Wise men of Gotham
Kennedy, L. Pied Piper of Hamelin
Leuser, E. Mixing stick
Miller, H. L. Magic cookie jar
Muse, V. Town house and his country cousin
Rowland, E. Hans, who made the Princess laugh
Rowland, E. A precedent in pastries
Rowland, E. The three aunts
Simonds, N. Hansel & Grethel
Simonds, N. Peter Rabbit
Spamer, C. N. Pot of gold
Tobey, L. C. The test
Very, A. Puss-in-boots
Very, A. Three sillies
Williams, G. M. Kettle of brains
Barbee, L. Flag of the U.S.
Bierling, J. C. No braver soldier
Colbo, E. S. Heroine of Wren
Hall, M. E. Hearts of oak
Lipnick, E. Son of Liberty
Miller, H. L. Dolly saves the day
Waite, H. E. Not only the strong

Burger, Isabel, B. Creative play acting. Learning through drama. N. Y., Barnes, 1950.
Queen of hearts
King's birthday
    Also other material.

Bussell, Jan. ed. Plays for puppets. Lond. Faber, 1951.
Peach, L. du G. Surprising story of Alfred, Warder of the Tower
Wayne, P. Strolling clerk from Paradise
Bussell, J. Brigands of the Black Forest
Parker, T. M. Three wishes
Bussell, D. Cat and the kingdom
Bussell, J. Fly by night

Carlson, Bernice W. Act it out. Nashville, Abingdon, 1956.
Excursions pantomime
Soldier, soldier Pantomime
Androcles and the lion
Theseus and the Minotaur
Santa forgets Christmas
Halloween night
Round and round and round
It's a gift
Spit Ball

A spot of onion tea
Junk, valuable junk'
Ruler of all—but one
Tit for tat
The old woman and the tramp
Dog gone
Wilderness birthday
Legend of the Christmas rose
Wandering Christ Child
Your country and mine

Carpenter, Frank. Six animal plays. Lond. Methuen, 1954.
Tale of good faith
Sick fox
Magic owl
Tiger in the wood
Day of good deeds
Doctor fox

Carver, Charles, ed. New one-act plays. Waco Texas, Baylor Uni. 1948.
Byers, Joe. Tilt of stein
Condre, M. Hearts, Inc.
Dickey, N. The whistle
Dickson, G. Mlle. Deceit
Hammons, R. Common touch
Lockridge, I. Color conscious
McClintock, F. Rose of Madame Calva
McKinney, G. Ivory tower — two flights down
Rogers, J. Back to Boston
Vance, L. The test
Wilson, B. Lace Handkerchief

Cerf, B. A. & Cartmell, Van H., comp. Thirty famous one-act plays.
N. Y. Modern Library, 1949.
France, A. Man who married a dumb wife
Strindberg, A. Miss Julia
Wilde, O. Salome
Gregory, Lady. Rising of the moon
Chekhov, A. The boor
Barrie, J. M. Twelve pound look
Schnitzler, A. Green cockatoo
Maeterlinck, M. Miracle of St. Anthony
Jacobs, W. M. Monkey's paw
Galsworthy, J. Little man
Synge, J. M. Riders to the sea
Quintero, S. Sunny morning
Dunsany, Lord. Night at an inn
Houghton, S. Dear departed
Strong, A. Drums of Oude
Moeller, P. Helena's husband
Glaspell, S. Suppressed desires
Goodman, J. S. Game of chess
Brooke, R. Lithuania
Hall, H. & Middlemass, R. The valient

O'Neil, E. In the zone
Kaufman, G. S. If men played cards as women do
Langner, L. Another way out
Beach, L. The clod
Millay, Edna St. V. Aria da Capo
Gerstenberg, A. Overtones
Coward, N. Fumed oak
Odets, C. Waiting for Lefty
Saroyan, W. Hello out there
Shaw, I. Bury the dead

Chamberlain, R. W., comp. Beacon lights of literature. Bk. 7. Syracuse, Iroquois, 1949.
Saunders, Louise. The knave of hearts
    Also other material.

Chamberlain, R. W., comp. Tales and trails. Bk. 8. Syracuse, Iroquois, 1949.
Gregory, Lady. Spreading the news
Coppee. Violin maker of Cremona
    Also other material.

Chamberlain, R. W., comp. True and otherwise. Bk. 7. Syracuse, Iroquois, 1949.
Saunders, Louise. Knave of hearts

Clark, Jean. Jolly junior assembly plays. Chic., Denison, 1947.
Banner boys
Captain Tall tells all
How the old woman furnished the shoe
Land of scratches and scribbles
Life of a first grader
Mischieveous clock
Rabbit's reading lesson
Sidewalk elves
Terrible tale of terrible tempers
Talk on teeth
Visitors from the air
Visit to vitamin village
When the letter A ran away
Better be clean, Clara
Citizens of the garden
Inside the music box
It happened in Bookland
Happy hygiene
Jimmy's garden of words
Tricky rhymes for sale
Visits of the cotton maids

Collins, Freda. Put on the armour of light. Lond. Nat'l. Soc. SPCK. 1955.
St. Columba visits King Brude
Gift of forgiveness
St. Columba says his last words to the people of Ireland
Before the light came
The stone age

Pytheas the Greek explorer
Court of the Druids
First Roman invasion
Caractacus
Death of Boadicea
Holy Grail
Light is kindled
St. Alban
St. Patrick
St. Columba
St. Augustine of Canterbury
St. Paulinus and King Edwin,
St. Oswald and St. Aidan
St. Birinus
St. Hilda and Caedmon
St. Cuthbert
Synod of Whitby
St. Chad and Archbishop Theodore
Venerable Bede
St. Boniface
St. Edmund King and Martyr
King Alfred the Great
St. Dunstan
St. Edward the Confessor

Cook, Luella B. & Others. Adventures in appreciation. N. Y., Harcourt, 1947. 3rd ed.

Geiger, M. One special for Doc
Gale, Zona. Neighbors
    Also other material.

Cook, Luella B. & Others. Adventures in appreciation. N. Y., Harcourt, 1952. Mercury ed.

Niggli, Josephina. Sunday costs five pesos
Barrie, J. M. The will
    Also other material.

R **Cowgill, Rome.** Fundamental writing for radio. N. Y., Rinehart, 1949.

Sorry, wrong drama
Ethel and Albert
Dr. Heidegger's experiment (adapt)
Wilbur Kenesaw Smith
Night in Plainville
Sea saves Leyden
    Also other material.

Cross, E. A., comp. Literature — Heritage of British literature. rev. ed. N. Y. Macmillan, 1954.

Dunsany, Lord. Night at an inn
Gregory, Lady. Workhouse ward
Synge, J.M. Riders to the sea
    Also other material.

Cross, T. P., comp. American writers. rev. ed. Bost. Ginn, 1946.
Gale, Zona. Neighbors
Field, Rachel. Londonderry air
Also other material.

Cross, T. P., comp. English writers. rev. ed. N. Y., Ginn, 1951.
Barrie, J. M. Shall we join the ladies?
Also other material.

Cunningham, G. F. Unjust steward and other plays. Edinburgh, Oliver & Boyd, 1951.
The unjust steward
Holy city
Behind the house of Obed-Edom

Davis, E. C., ed. Eight popular plays for amateurs in prompt book style. N.Y., Greenberg, 1948.
Manning, H. Young man's fancy
Houghton, S. Dear departed
George C. When Shakespeare's ladies meet
Kelly, G. Flattering word
O'Neill, E. Ile
Manley, W. F. Crowsnest
Johnson, P. Lovely miracle
Green, P. Last of the Lowries

Dias, E. J. Melodramas and farces for young actors. Bost. Plays, 1956.
Way, way down East
Feudin' fun
Sands of time
Stops the presses!
Case of the missing pearls
Strong and swift
Out of this world
Stage bore
Natives are restless tonight
Abner Crane from Hayseed Lane
Face is familiar
What Ho!!

DuBois, Graham. Plays for great occasions. Collection of royalty-free one-act holiday plays. Bost. Plays, 1951.
Lincoln says farewell
Child of her spirit
Spring will come
Winter of our discontent
Corn meal and poetry
Sausages and General Washington
For the glory of St. Patrick
The last laugh
But one life to give
Poison ivy
They banish our anger
So shines a good deed
Child of destiny

I shall sail again
Known but to God
Son of America
Darkest hour
Green-eyed monster
Cause of gratitude
Cause to serve
King is here
Bunny comes to town
Empty room

Duncan, Marion, ed. & trans. Harvest festival, dramas of Tibet. Hong Kong, Orient Pub. 1955.

Drowazzamgmo
Songtsan Gampo
Nangsa

Emurian, E. K. Plays and pageants for many occasions. Bost. Wilde, 1953.

'Twas the night before Christmas
The resurrection
Thanksgiving through the ages
Dixie
America the beautiful
Battle hymn of the Republic
Christmas traditions
Great women of history
Columbia, the gem of the ocean
    Also a longer play.

Emurian, E. K. More plays and pageants for many occasions. Bost. Wilde, 1954.

God of our fathers
The new Colossus
Star-spangled banner
Yankee, Doodle
Silver threads among the gold
The church in the wildwood
Radiance streaming
Last supper
Also a longer play.

Eisenberg, H. & Eisenberg, L. Skits and stunts. comp. N. Y. Association, 1953.

Corn but not forgotten
Sofapillio
Nervious father
Push button tunning
Othello
Farmer's daughter
The race
What would you do?
Folk festival script
Man's eternal quest for the good life

Balm, C. M. Awful fate of a fibber
Balm, C. M. Generous fisherman
Balm, C. M. Ogre of Rashamon
Balm, C. M. Proud Princess
Miller, C. A. Moon maiden

Fagan, J. B. & Others. Modern one-act plays. N. Y. Penguin, 1942.
Fagan, J. B. Doctor O'Toole
John, E. King's march
Watkyn, A. "Wanted — Mr. Stuart"
Constanduros, M. Lady from abroad
Sangster, A. Boney
Ferguson, J. A. Such stuff as dreams
Redgrave, M. Seventh man

Fisher, Aileen. Health and safety plays and programs. Bost. Plays, 1953.
Magic formula
Robots to the rescue
The Not-so-crooked man
Catch as catch can
Long live father
Murder in the kitchen
Why the sleepy dormouse
King's toothache
By order of the king
What happened on Clutter St.
Many a slip
Nothing ever happens
Luck takes a holiday
Courting trouble

Fisher, Aileen & Rabe, O. United nations plays & programs. Bost. Plays, 1954.

Thanks a million
All the world around
Cavalcade of human rights
Alice in puzzleland
Best bargain in the world
Invasion of the stratosphere
Let there be bread
Accident of birth
A nickel and a dime
What happened in Egypt
Of Gods and men
The get-together dinner
Skills to share
Story of a well
A fresco for Unesco
All in U.N.
Getting in line
Empty bowls

R   **Fisher, Aileen & Rabe, O.** Five radio plays. Lond. V.X. Mundi, 1948.
   Obey, N. Silent city
   Bonett, E. Puppet master
   Mella, A. Grand slam
   Kesser, H. Nurse Henrietta
   Heath, T. Spinney under the rain

   Fletcher, Lucille. Sorry, wrong number. N. Y. Dramatists Play Ser. 1952.
   Sorry, wrong number
   Hitch-hiler

T   **Foote, Horton.** Philco television playhouse. Dramatists Play Serv. N. Y.
   (date?)
   Young lady of property
   The dancers
   The old beginning
   John Turner Davis
   Death of the old man

   Gassner, John, ed. Twenty-five best plays of the modern American thea-
   tre. Early ser. N. Y. Crown, 1949.
   Glaspell, S. Trifles
   O'Neil, E. Ile
   Millay, Edna St. V. Aria da Capo
   Green, P. White dresses
   Conkle, E. P. Minnie Field
      Also 19 longer plays.

   Goldschmidt, Walter. comp. Ways of mankind. Bost. Beacon, 1954.
   Peterson, L. Stand-in for murder
   Sinclair, L. Word in your ear
   Hallman, E. S. Survival
   Peterson, L. Desert soliloquy
   Sinclair, L. When Greek meets Greek
   Salverson, G. You are not alone
   Peterson, L. Home, sweet home
   Sinclair, L. Case of the sea-lion flippers
   Sinclaid, L. But I know what I want
   Sinclair, L. All the world's a stage
   Peterson, L. Sticks and stones
   Sinclair, L. Museum of man

   Griffith & Mersand, J. ed. Modern one-act plays. N. Y. Harcourt, 1950.
   Barrie, J. M. The will
   Dillon, T. P. Doctor from Funmore
   Meredith, B. Adventures of Mr. Bean
   Quintero, S. A sunny morning
   Wilder, T. Happy journey to Trenton and Camden
   Ardery, R. God and Texas
   Green, P. Franklin and the King
   Totheroh, D. Stolen Prince
   Dunsany, L. Golden doom

   Knapp, J. S. Other side
   Finch, R. Far-distant shore
   Kelly, G. Finders keepers

Powers, T. Emergency, stand by!
Stevenson, R. L. Bottle imp
Corwin, N. My client Curley
MacNeice, L. The nosebag

Gross, Edwin & Gross, Nathalie. Teen theatre. N. Y. McGraw-Hill, 1953.
Belle
Date-time
Dooley & the amateur hour
She loves him Yes
Marko goes a courtin'
Party is born

R **Hackett, Walter, comp.** Radio plays for young people. Fifteen great stories adapted for royalty-free performances. Bost. Plays, 1950.
Hale, E. E. Man without a country
Mark Twain. Million pound bank note
Wilde, O. Canterville ghost
Maupassant, G. de. The necklace
Dickens, C. Tale of two cities
Irving, W. Rip Van Winkle
Stevenson, R. L. Young man with the cream tarts
Cooper, J. F. The spy
Hawthorne, N. Great stone face
Alcott, L. M. Laurence boy
France, A. The juggler of our Lady
Irving, W. Legend of Sleepy Hollow
Hale, E. E. My double and how he undid me
Stevenson, R. L. Sire de Maletroit's door
Dickens, C. Christmas carol

R **Hackett, Walter.** Radio plays from history and literature. Bost. Baker, 1952.
Bronte, C. Jane Eyre
Alcott, L. M. Merry Christmas
Hackett, W. Last drum
Poe, E. A. Fall of the House of Usher
Hackett, W. Prologue for tomorrow
Aldrich, T.B. Marjory Daw
Hackett, W. Jemmy's wife

Halpin, L. F. & Others. Adventures in English literature. N. Y. Harcourt, 1954.
Synge, J. M. Riders to the sea
Barrie, J. M. The old lady shows her medals
Also other material.

Hamilton, Hamish. Pub. Anthology of 21 years of publishing. Lond. Hamilton, 1952.
Rattigan, T. Browning version
Sartre, J. P. In camera
Also other material.

Haney, Germaine. Showers for all occasions. Minneapolis, Denison, 1954.
Casey, A. Matrimony bumps
Stahl, Le R. Parting tear

Kaser, A. Love honor and obey
Stahl, LeR. Romance a la mode
Chalmers, V. Will you marry me?
Drummond, R. Substitute bride
    Also other material.

Hark, Mildred & McQueen, N. Junior plays for all occasions. Bost. Plays, 1955. Collection of royalty-free, one-act plays for Children.

New broom
House is haunted
Meet Mr. Witch
Off the shelf
Book revue
New-fangled Thanksgiving
Nothing to be thankful for
Many thanks
T for turkey
Junction Santa Claus
Santa Claus parade
Christmas Eve news
Christmas in the woods
Bobby and the Lincoln speech
Lincoln reminders
Cupies and hearts
Cupids post office
In honor of Washington
Day for trees
Enter George Washington
Father's Easter hat
Prize for mother
Hearts and flowers for mother
Three wishes for mother
Father keeps house
Too many kittens
Our own four walls
When do we eat?
Not fit for man or beast
Doctor manners
Mind your P's and Q's
Stuff of heroes
Princess and the rose-colored glasses
Visit of Johnny Appleseed
Nursery rhyme diet
Pleasant dreams
Rainbow colors
ABC for safety
Spring is here
The dolls
Good neighbors
Johnnie jump up

Hark, Mildred & McQueen, N. Modern comedies for young players. Non-royalty. Bost. Plays, 1951.

Unaccustomed as I am
Love from Bud
A game of hearts
A rival for Dad
The Ides of March
Let's go formal
The homiest room
Spring fever
Double exposure
Hats and rabbits
Advice to the lovelorn
To be or not to be
Mother saves the day
Tempest in a teapot
Bud for President
It's Greek to me
Aladdin, incorporated
Thanks to Billy
Music hath charms
'Twas the night before Christmas
It's so complex
All is not gold

Hark, Mildred & McQueen, N. Twenty-five plays for holidays. Collection of non-royalty, one-act plays. Bost. Plays, 1952.

New worlds to find
Happy haunts
Hometown Halloween
Great gift
Ghosts in the library
A book a day
Voices of America
Vote for Uncle Sam
Our famous ancestors
Surprise guests
Turkey gobblers
A quiet Christmas
Star in the window
Christmas shopping early
Living up to Lincoln
Lincoln umbrella
Happy hearts
A change of hearts
Date with Washington
Thanks to George Washington
Easter hope
Life with mother
Mom's a grandmother now
See the parade
Moon keeps shining

R **Hatton, Charles.** Radio plays and how to write them. Eng. Southend-on Sea, Essex, 1948.
The beard
Saga of Simon Curle
Also other material.

T **Heath, Eric.** Writing for television. Los Angeles, Research, 1950.
Van Aernam, J. H. "Only once blow the fuse"
Fitzsimmons, E. G. Double talk
Beebe, T. Narration for V J Day
Beebe, T. Crime clues
Beebe, T. The pay-off
Also other material.

Howard, Vernon L. Short plays for all-boy casts. 30 royalty-free comedies and skits. Bost. Plays, 1954.
The blue serge suit
Your money or your life
Million dollar recipe
Spook shop
The message
When it's moonlight on Pike's Peak
A rest for Mr. Winkle
Turkey for all
Paloma, Princess of Pluto
The blackbird
These's talent tonight
The inventor's clinic
Five boys, and a Santa
Drexel
Publicity expert
The Mayor Doctor
The mad Doctor Zing
I resolve
Pollywogs
Valentine box
No other in the court
Valley Forge was never like this
Athletes all
Herman's temptation
Grizzlegump
Danger — Pixies at work
The best of the old West
A hobby for Dad
The big melodrama

Huber, Louis J. Easy Arena plays. Minneapolis, Northwestern, 1951.
One man's word
First and ten
Mother remembers
Home remedy
Herbert's hurt
Self-preservation
Peacemaker

In giving thanks
Girls are home
Lend me five
Who's your butler?
New secretary
Window shopping
Let's haunt
His daughter's hand
Goodbye, mother
Adventure after midnight

T **Huber, Louis J.** Easy television plays. Minneapolis, Northwestern, 1952.
The black sheep
No fight tonight
Happy birthday
Too many types
Just plain efficiency
Tenting tonight
Small sale
Tick tock
Blank check
Bright world
Date with Kate
Fan mail
Last chance
Room service

Inglis, R. B., comp. Adventures in English literature. N. Y. Harcourt,
1949.
Synge, J. M. Riders to the sea
Barrie, J. M. The old lady shows her medals
Also other material.

James, Thelma G., comp. World neighbors. N. Y. Harper, 1950.
Barrie, J. M. Twelve pound look
Synge, J. M. Riders to the sea
Quintero, S. Sunny morning
Also other material.

R **Johnson, Crane.** Past fifty. San Francisco, International Theatre, 1953.
George Washington's chair
Astonishing Mrs. O'Shaugnessy
The proposal
The rockers

Johnson, E. M., ed. Canadian school plays. ser. I. Toronto, Ryerson,
1948.
Gowan, E. P. Royal touch
Ringwood, G. P. Courting of Marie Jenvrin
MacLennan, J. M. Pipistrelle of Aquitaine
MacNaughton, J. A. Final edition
Boissonneault, L. To what purpose
Shad, B. Blue willow plate
Morrish, P. Our dream house
Fowke, H. S. A wig for my lady
Boyar, J. Walk into our parlor

Kamerman, Slyvia E., comp. Blue-ribbon plays for girls. A Collection of royalty-free . . . all girl cast. Bost. Plays, 1955.
Allred, J. All this and Alan, too
McCoy, P. S. Lieutenant pays his respects
Miller, H. L. Pin-up pays
Alcott, L. M. Little women
Phillips, M. P. Flair for fashion
Thurston, M. B. Room for Mary
Malone, M. A letter for Charlotte
Richmond, S. S. Homemakers have a way
Murdock, M. The cuckoo
Du Bois, G. His hand and pen
Hill, K. Midnight burial
Brydon, M. W. Reluctant ghost
Porter, E. W. Callie goes to camp
Roberts, H. M. Old fashioned Thanksgiving
Hagy, L. Fire in a paper
Barbee, L. The Friday foresome packs a box
Mason, M. E. Mary Elizabeth's wonderful dream
Phillips, M. K. The woman who didn't want Christmas
Barbee, L. A letter to Abraham
Jackson, M. C. Perfect understanding
MacLellan, E. Flowers for Mother's Day
Leuser, E. Little witch who tried
Spamer, C. The mirror children
Asbrand, K. Little Christmas guest
Newman, D. Stolen heart
Ormandy, E. Little Ida and the flowers
Steele, J. Tea for six
Very, A. Thanksgiving night
Joy, V. Milkmaid and her pail
Duggar, F. December gifts
Spamer, C. The snowdrop
Very, A. Tick-tock
Barr, J. Lazy little raindrop
Ficher, A. Standing up for Santa
Newman, D. Kachoo!

Kamerman, Sylvia E., comp. Little plays for little players. 50 non-royalty plays for children. Bost. Plays, 1952.
MacLellan, E. Birthday gift
Very, A. Gift of the fairies
Very, A. President Lincoln's children
Bennett, R. Littlest artist
Urban, C. Queen with the broken heart
MacLellan, E. A needle fights for freedom
Roberts, H. M. Washington's sacrifice
Very, A. Boy who couldn't tell a lie
Davis, LeR. St. Patrick and the last snake in Ireland
Knight, L. Flibber turns the tables
Spamer, C. Bunny brigade
Barr, J. A present for mother
Streacker, L. Return of Nina

MacLellan, H. L. Magic Jack-o-lantern
Leuser, E. Little witch who tried
Cooper, E. Little white cloud
Gould, J. Thanksgiving for everybody
Howard, H. L. Thanks to Sammy Scarecrow
Spamer, C. The pop-up books
Hark, M. Christmas party
Kane, E. B. Children of Chocolate St.
Roberts, H. M. Lonely fir tree
Asbrand A. Friendly as can be
Bellah, M. Blue toadstool
Deming, D. First aid first
Fox, D. U. Littlest month
Gould, J. Seven little seeds
Lehman, J. F. Biskie the snowman
Lehman, J. F. Good health trolley
Hark, M. Doctor manners
Newman, D. Green leaf's lesson
Parsons, M. Too much of a good thing
Reay, N. B. Mr. Bates goes to the polls
Sanderlin, O. Follow the north star
Slingluff, M. O. Naughty Susan
Wilson, M. L. First flowers
Woster, A. All houses are haunted
Barr, J. Cinderella
Barr, J. The lion and the mouse
Barbee, L. Princess who couldn't dance
Bennett, R. In the witch's house
Campbell, C. Morning maker
Dennis, A. Wind wand
Holmes, R. V. Little red riding hood
King, W. Little snow white
Leuser, E. Little bird in the tree
Smith, G. V. Star light and the sandman
Spamer, C. Shy Prince
Vandevere, J. L. Mother Goose goes to dinner

T **Kaufman, W. I., ed.** Best television plays. vol. III. N. Y. Kaufman, 1954.
　Latham, J. One in twelve
　　Also other material.

T **Kaufman, W. I., ed.** Best television plays of the year. N. Y. Merlin, 1950.
　DuPont, L. No shoes
　Lardner, R. Zone of quiet
　Stuart, J. The door
　Brown, S. P. Operation Coral
　Berg, G. The Goldbergs
　Coe, F. Something in the wind
　Houseman, J. Julian Houseman story
　Valency, M. Battleship Bismark

Keating, E. H. Dramas for boys. Lond. French, n.d.
　Plot of Potzentausend
　Incog

    Poor relation
    Talisman

Kelly, Mary, ed. Group play-making. Lond. Harrap, 1948.
    Honiton Drama Class. Out of the shadows
    Broadhembury Drama Group. Dr. Paynter
    Moretonhembury Drama Class. Night's high noon
    West Hill Women's Institute. Shepherd's trove
    Newton Ferrers Dramatic Class. Stormy passage
    Seaton Drama Group. Dungeon of thyself
    Morebath Drama Group. Accounts settled
    Denbury Drama Class. Bats in the belfry
      Also material on teaching group drama.

R   **Kissen, Fan.** Bag of fire & other tales. Bost. Houghton, 1949.
    Fox brings luck
    Bag of fire
    Three sillies
    Katherine and Frederick
    Why the sea is salt
    Cinderella
    Tinder box
    Flying ship
    The flea
    Birds of Killingworth
    Four clever brothers
    Billy Beg and his bull

R   **Kissen, Fan.** Crowded house & other tales. Bost. Houghton, 1950.
    Clever Manka
    One-inch fellow
    Ugly duckling
    Three golden oranges
    Feast of lanterns
    Crowded house
    Golden touch
    Young Paul Bunyan
    Christmas angel
    Baba Yaga
    Wise men of Gothan
    Pied Piper

R   **Kissen, Fan.** Straw ox & other tales. Bost. Houghton, 1948.
    Rumpelstiltskin
    Boots & his brothers
    Three wishes
    Lenka's little house
    Straw ox
    What the good man does is right
    Shiro & his master
    Sleeping beauty
    Rock in the sea
    Peterkins try to become wise

Knickerbocker, Edwin Van B., ed. Short plays. rev. N. Y. Holt, 1949.

Pillot, E. Two crooks and a lady
Goodman, K. S. Game of chess
France, A. Man who married a dumb wife
Synge, J. M. Riders to the sea
Smith, A. G. Whirligig of life
Barrie, J. M. The old lady shows her medals
Saunders, L. Poor Maddalena
Kirkpatrick, J. A wedding
Hall, H. & Middlemass. The valient
Dunsany, Lord. Gods of the mountains
Shakespeare. Pyramus and Thisbe
Dix, B. M. Allison's lad
Wilde, P. Noble Lord
Bennett, A. The stepmother
Phillips, S. Ulysses
Niggli, J. Sunday costs three pesos

Koppe, Richard, comp. Treasury of college humor. N. Y. Penn., 1950.

Folk life in ancient Greece
Mummy limps at midnight
Old English play
Twenty thousand leagues neath the sea
Original sin
    Also other material.

Laurie, Joe Jr., comp. Vaudeville from honky-tonks to the Palace. N. Y. Holt, 1953.

Man & woman act
School act
Dramatic sketch
Double Dutch act
Double Wop act
Double Irish act
Straight & the Jew
Two-woman act
Double blackface act
Comedy sketch
After piece
    Also other material.

Lehmann, Adolph. Vignettes. N. Y. Pageant, 1952.

The secret
That woman
Help wanted
Thank you Louise
My mirror tells me
Aged but not mellowed
Greatest show on earth
Come home
The confession

McCaslin, Nellie. More legends in action. Ten plays of ten lands. Evanston, Ill. Row, Peterson, 1950.

Paul Bunyan, lumberjack
Bailiff's wonderful coat
The tinker of Toledo
Humai's secret
Maelduin of Arran
The lazy ones
Christmas lamb
Three meals a day
Wisely chosen
Gift of music

R **Mackey, D. R.** Drama on the air. N. Y. Prentice-Hall, 1951.

Fletcher, L. Hitch hiker
Sweeney, B. My uncle Willy
Maloney, M. J. Death of the average man
   And other material.

McGaw, Charles. Acting is believing. N. Y. Rinehart, 1955.
Checkhov, A. The proposal
Williams, T. The long stay cut short
   Also other material.

R **Malone, Dumas, ed.** Jeffersonian heritage. Bost. Beacon, 1953.

Wishengrad, M. Living Declaration
Geiger, M. Democrat & Commissar
Wishengrad, M. Divided we stand
Mindel, J. Freeing the land
Mindel, J. To secure these rights
Geiger, M. Light & Liberty
Geiger, M. Return of a patriot
Wishengrad, M. Danger of freedom
Wishengrad, M. Ground of justice
Probst, G. Experiment of a free press
Geiger, M. University of the United States
Geiger, M. Nature's most precious gift

March, Olave. Actor's theatre plays. vol. I. Lond. Favil, 1945.

Erskine, J. The beacon
Janes, H. Monsieur le Marquis
Grant, A. The climber
Bembridge, J. Disconsolate apparition
Veness, M. Strangers
Grant, A. Don't forget the baking powder

Marriott, J. W., comp. Best one-act plays of 1942-3. Lond. Harrap, 1944.

Ustinov, P. Beyond
Morris, T. B. Tudor thorns
Brighouse, H. Inner man
Dinner, W. Mr. Fothergill joins the Angels
Holland, N. One hour alone
Johnson, P. Orange blossom
Corrie, J. Litchen Fair

Sladen-Smith, F. Harlequin bridge
Aklom, M. Of social significance
Foy, H. Corfe Gate

Marriott, J. W., comp. Best one-act plays of 1944-5. Lond. Harrap, 1946.
Johnson, P. Dark brown
Brighouse, H. Let's live in England
Corrie, J. The failure
Holland, N. Leopard's spots
Etheridge, K. Follow of Seithenyn
Ames, G. Green veil passes
Chown, P. Sea-shell
Aklom, M. Flash-back
Aske, L. Non Nobis
Dawson, N. ". . . Can die but once?"

Marriott, J. W., comp. Best one-act plays of 1948-9. Lond. Harrap, 1950.
Morris, T. B. Ophelia
Tayleur, W. St. J. Reunion
Johnson, P. Tinsel Duchess
Corrie, J. Tell it not in Gath
Andrews, I. Goldfish
Williamson, H. R. Cardinal's learning
Holland, N. Tea with a legend
Arlett, V. I. The tree
Hayes, J. Silver key
Miller, H. High tea

Marsh, W. A. Plays & patterns for glove puppets. Lond. Harrap, 1955.
Pretty maid, where have you been?
Ride a cock-horse
Clock says
We three
Three pigs catch the wolf again
We Willie Winkle
Contrary Mary meets Boy Blue
A number play: poison plot
Dominoes have a fire
Domino family's picnic
Red apple
Donkey brays loudly
How the giraffe got its neck
Miracle of the fishes
He who eats cabbage
Useful plough
Bang goes my stocking
Persistent musician
Storm in a tea cup
I spy
Baker's three daughters
   Also other material.

Maugham, W. S. Encore. Original stories & screenplays. N. Y. Double-day, 1952.

Ant and the grasshopper
Winter cruise
Gigolo and gigolette

Maughfling, Mabel. Five mime plays. Original ballad mimes. Lond. French, 1948.

Polly in the park
The pirates & the ladies
Sukie has an air
Auntie & the bull
Love triumphant

R **Maurois, Andre.** The art of being happily married. N. Y. Harper, 1953.

Courtship and conquest
Wedding journey
Honeymoon, or, Treacle moon
Marriage and friendship
Minor conflicts
Matter of taste
Good manners
After ten years
Major conflicts
Seduction
Catastrophy
Silver wedding

Mayorga, Margaret, comp. Best one-act plays, 1948-9. N. Y. Dodd, 1949.

Agoston, G. For each man kills
Apstein, T. Fortunata writes a letter
Williamson, S. G. A bed with the others
Kinoy, E. Whistle, daughter, whistle
Costello, W. A wake for me and thee
Packer, B. Patrick Bronte and the Saint
Perl, A. Mind in the shadow
Richards, S. O distant land
Hughes, E. W. Wantin' fever
Woodress, F. A. Impass

Mayorga, Margaret, comp. Best one-act plays, 1949-50. N. Y. Dodd, 1950.

Stein, G. Dr. Faustus lights the lights
Wishengrad, M. The camel and I
Richards, S. August heat
Gainfort, J. Going home
Agoston, G. The beast
Holland, N. Day before yesterday
Robinson, M. W. Exodus
Eaton, W. P. Period house
Lanzl, F. Fantasia on an old familiar theme
Howe, C. V. The long fall

Mayorga, Margaret, comp. Best one-act plays, 1950-51. N. Y. Dodd, 1951.

Agoston, G. Three parsons
Hughes, E. W. Rise of her bloom
Conkle, E. P. Muletail prime
Trevisan, A. F. Valley of the shadow
Holland, N. Farewell appearance
Kinoy, E. Goodbye to the clown
Lowe, C. F. Gooseberry tarts
Castro, E. Brothers
Sion, G. Matron of Ephesus

Mayorga, Margaret, comp. Best one-act plays of 1951-52. N. Y. Dodd, 1952.

Conkle, E. P. The least one
Apstein, T. Paradise Inn
Stephens, P. T. Hugh of the Glen & his clogs are all one
Kocher, E. Shadow of the Cathedral
Kelley, A. Tour of duty
Lake, G. Glory day
Bela, N. Safecracker's pride
Rosten, H. Happy house wife
Richards, S. Sun deck
Stein, M. In darkness

Mayorga, Margaret, comp. Best plays of 1952-53. N. Y. Dodd, 1953.

Ferrini, V. Innermost I Land
Apstein, T. Beams of our house
Lee, M. Dope
Richards, S. Tunnel of love
Perry, M. A trap in a small place
Conkle, E. P. Abbie, the bug boy
Shaber, D. The youngest shall ask
Lake, G. Incident at a grave
Stephens, P. J. The changeling
Sheffield, J. Imploring flame

Mayorga, Margaret, comp. Best plays of 1953-54. N. Y. Dodd, 1954.

Schaefer, L. Little flaws of Ernesto Lippi
Ferrini, V. Telling of the North Star
Foote, H. John Turner Davis
Apstein, T. A remittance from Spain
Wilde, P. Salt for savor
Sheffield, J. Forgotten land
Goldschmidt, W. Word in your ear
Snyder, W. H. Jr. Another summer
Kocher, E. Karma
Hughes, E. W. Wishful Taw

Mayorga, Margaret, comp. Best short plays of 1954-55. N. Y. Dodd, 1955.

Wincelberg, S. The conqueror
Schaeferm, L. Song of a hero
Stein, G. Brewsie & Willie

Nash, N. R. Rouge Atomique
Richards, S. Half-hour, please
Wilson, D. C. Return of Chandra
Thomas, D. Next-to-last rites
Thon, F. The island
Kocher, E. Medal for Julien
Waldau, R. S. Cabin by the lake

Mayorga, Margaret, comp. Best short plays, 1955-56. Bost. Beacon, 1956.
Perrini, A. Once a thief
MacLeish, A. This music crept by me upon the waters
Williams, T. Something unspoken   ·
Zeiger, H. Five days
Perl, A. The High School
Purkey, R. A. Hangs over thy head
Walsh, N. Let there be farce
Gurney, A. R. Jr. Three people
Seiger, M. L. Blue concerto
    Also longer plays.

Mercedes, Sister Ann & Others. Adventures in reading. N. Y. Harcourt, 1954.
Simon, S. S. Trouble in Tunnel mine
Pharis, G. Courting of Marie Jenvrin
Hall, H. & Middlemass. The valient
Stevenson, R. L. Sire de Maletroit's door
    Also other material.

RT   **Mickel, Joseph.** Radio & television dramas. N. Y. Exposition, 1953.
Let the heavens decide
Wilbur's birthday gift
Return of Benjamin
The promise
Things we know
Freedom's herald
Your time will come
The curtain
Apartment hunting
Return of Benjamin (television version)
Mask of guilt

Miles, D. H. & Keck, C. M. Literature & life. Bk. I. Chic. Scott, 1947.
Lovelace, W. R. Gold feathers
    Also other material.

Miller, Helen Louise. Holiday plays for teen-agers. Collection of one-act, royalty-free plays. Bost. Plays, 1952.
Ghost in the house
Bewitched & bewildered
Father talks turkey
Football hero
Thanksgiving a la carte
Christmas promise
Case of the silent caroler
Puppy love

Boy who didn't belong
The Lincoln heart
Good enough for Lincoln
Beanny's private eye
Hooky holiday
"N" for nuisance
Haunted clothesline
Spooky spectacles
Hero's homecoming
Spooks in books
Just what the Doctor ordered
Turkey turns the tables
Christmas oboe
Left-over reindeer
I'll eat my hat
Lincoln cupboard
Heart throbs
Be my "walentine"
Jump for George
February frenzy
Vanishing easter egg
Mother for mayor
Three cheers for mother
Judge's diary
Pink parasol
What makes it tick?
Shakesperean touch
Say it with flowers
Boomerang
Letter from George Washington
Best policy
Case of the Easter bonnet
Rabbit foot
Mother's big day
Mother's apron strings
Uninvited guests
Day to remember

Miller, H. Louise. Plays for living and learning. Bost. Plays, 1955.
Curious quest
Bar-none trading post
Petrified Prince
Travel game
Polka dot pup
Girls in books
Boys in books
Not for girls
Pilgrim parting
Bread and butter shop
Paul Revere again
Star cadets
Case of the balky bike
Right of adoption

It's a problem
February failure
Lincoln Museum
Visit to Mount Vernon
Patriotic Teddy Bear & the U.N.
Hello, Mr. Groundhog
Speaking of speech
Who's who at the zoo
Railroad rhymes & rhythms
Story of light
New shoes

Miller, Madge. Miniature plays. vol. I. Anchorage, Ky. Children's Theatre Press, 1954.
Pinocchio
Snow White and rose red
Robinson Crusoe
Puss in boots

Millett, F. B., ed. Reading drama. N. Y. Harper, 1950.
Schnitzler, A. Farewell supper
Barrie, J. M. The will
Synge, J. M. Riders to the sea
Yeats, W. B. Cathleen ni Houlihan
Wilder, T. Long Christmas dinner
    Also other material,

Molnar, Ferenc. Romantic comedies. N. Y. Crown, 1952.
Actor from Vienna
Anniversary dinner
    Also longer plays.

Molnar, Ferenc. Stories for two. N. Y. Holizon, 1950.
Little by little
Boys will be boys
Girls will be girls
Dowry
Grey fedora
Alfred, dear
Adventures in Paris
Daring innovation
Heart of a mother
Literature
Easter bonnet
The Admiral
Letter to Ibsen
The idol and his girl
Railway accident
Midsummer night
Question period
Miracle

Murray, John. Mystery plays for young people. Bost. Plays, 1956.
Will-o Wisp
Swiss Chalet mystery
When the hurly burly's done

Mystery in the Lab
Case of the missing poet
Case for Mrs. Hudson
Be my ghost
Boy next door
Game of chess
End of the line
The door
Final curtain
Five buttons
Ups and downs
Case for two detectives

R **Nehr, Jack & Pratt, Dallas.** Hi, neighbor. Ten radio plays for mental
health. Phil. Nat'l. Mental Health Ass'n. 1950.
Bobby soxer's rebellion
School for marriage
What every woman wants
Relax and enjoy it
Day dreams go to school
Somebody do something!
As kids go
Everybody gets into the act
That's my old man
Sons and husbands

Nelson's theatrecraft plays. Bk. 3. Plays for women. Lond. Nelson, 1940.
Box, M. Husbands are a problem
Morris, T. B. Swan-song
Ratcliff, N. The brothers
August, E. "O let him pass!"
Biscombe, M. Favour is deceitful
Jeafferson, M. Danger! women at work

Nelson's theatrecraft series 4. Plays for women. Lond. Nelson, 1941.
OBrien, K. Quality of mercy
Morris, T. Gossip's glory
Helsby, A. Strained relations
Hadlington, R. Abu Hassan pays his debts
Biscombe, M. Eve's delight
Ratcliff, N. Jezebel

Neville, M. A. & Payne, L. W. Jr., comp. Broadening horizons. Chic.
Rand, 1949.
Twelve hours in Mr. Smith's life
Gregory, Lady. Spreading the news
Mackay, C. D'A. Silver lining
Merry adventures of Robin Hood
Adventures of Tom Sawyer
Also other material.

Neville, M. A. & Payne, L. W. Jr., comp. Exploring new fields. Chic.
Rand, 1949.
Mackay, C. D'A. Daniel Boone: Patriot
Mackay, C. D'A. Three wishes

Monkhouse, A. Grand Cham's diamond
Schoenfeld, B. C. This, our America
A little bit of heaven
   Also other material.

New World Writing. 4th Mentor selection. N. Y. New Amer. Lib., 1953
Bercovici, E. Heart of age
Eberhart, R. Visionary farms
   Also other material.

New World Writing. 6th Mentor selection. N. Y. New Amer. Lib., 1954.
MacDonagh. Happy as Harry
Bellow, S. The wrecker
   Also other material.

New World Writing. 8th Mentor Selection. N. Y. New Amer. Lib., 1955.
Lorca, F. G. Tragi-comedy of Don Cristobita and Dona Rosta
   Also other material.

Nygaard, N. E. Bible comes alive. Biblical sermons in costume. Bost.
   Baker, 1947.
Paul before King Agrippa
Fishers of men
Pilate, the Roman governor
Elijah, the firebrand of the Almighty
Philip, the desert evangelist
Paul in the Areopagus at Athens
Christmas story
Stephen, the first martyr
Isaiah, the statesman prophet
Peter at Pentecost
Moses, the law giver

R   **Olafson, Lewy, Adapt.** Radio plays of famous stories. Bost. Plays, 1956.
Bronte. Wuthering heights
Eliot. Silas Marner
Bronte. Jane Eyre
Hawthorne. House of seven gables
Wilde. Importance of being Earnest
Mark Twain. Adventures of Tom Sayer
Mark Twain. Connecticut Yankee in King Arthur's court
Rostand. Cyrano de Bergerac
Scott. Quentin Durward
Tarkington. Monsieur Beaucaire
Dickens. Pickwick Papers
Dickens. David Copperfield
Dickens. Uriah Heep.
Hugo. Bishop's candlesticks
Kipling. Captains Courageous
Jokai. Which of the nine

One-act plays for stage and study. 10th. ser. N. Y. French, 1949.
Rogers, M. Book of Job
Ade, G. Aunt Fanny from Chautauqua
Eaton, W. P. Period house
Stone, W. Here's a howdy-do

Johnson, R. E. Dreamlost
Riggs, L. The hunger I got
Conkle, E. P. Incident at Eureka Bumps
Tazewell, C. Can long endure
Sturm, R. F. Playright's dilemma
Cohan, F. Farrell case
Craven, F. Little stranger
Hughes, B. Sisters under the skin
Zimmermann, A. L. A dream
Felton, N. Sam 'n' Ella
Kirkpatrick, J. The nerve of it!
Hughes, G. Havana moon
Chipp, E. Honor and glory
Albright, H. Final word
Carriere, A. He who gets hooked
Durham, F. A little more than kin
Stevens, T. W. Drum head
Carroll, R. F. Time is a thief

Paradise, Marjorie B. One-act plays for all-girl casts. Collection of royalty-free plays. Bost. Plays, 1952.
Midge rings the bell
Growing pains
Thankful hearts
Was her face red
Alpha Kappa
Santa goes to town
She laughs last
Firebug
Mister A. Lincoln
Admiral's daughter
Super-sleuths

T **Parker, K. T.** Parker's television plays. Minneapolis, Northwestern, 1954.
Cup of tea
Shall we dance
Voice of the machines
Star minded
Within the family
Cry on my shoulder
Stand up to death
Double indemnity

TR **Phillips, D. C. & Others.** Introduction to radio & television. N. Y. Ronald, 1954.
Robertson, M. Trip to the moon
Arthur, E. Man who stole the Freedom Train
Arthur, M. Queen is dead
Stewart, B. End of the line
Also other material.

Plumb, Beatrice & Others. Wedding anniversary. Minneapolis, Denison, 1951.
Huber, L. J. All aboard
Chalmers, V. The preview

Preston, E. B. Berate your mate
Huber, L. J. What did I say?
Huber, L. J. High pressure
Preston, E. E. How to be happy though married
Huber, L. J. Vast experience
Preston, E. E. Sunday edition
Kaser, A. L. R. Second honeymoon
Huber, L. J. Letter to Lola
Casey, A. Matrimony bumps
Drummond, R. Golden wedding anniversary
George, C. Newlyweds
Kaser, A. L. R. Forever yours
Preston, E. E. Oh, that golden wedding
Preston, E. E. Switch to Mitch

R **Pollock, Seton & Granthan, W.** Men of God: Hebrew prophets. Lond. Gollancz, 1947.
Prophet of fire (Elijah)
Shepherd of Tekoa (Amos)
Citizen (Isaiah)
Bands of love (Hosea)
Man of strife (Jeremiah)
Mantle of Elijah (John the Baptist)

Potell, Herbert & Others. Adventures for today. N. Y. Harcourt, 1955.
Starling, N. Ins and outs
Crutchfield, L. Shipment of mute fate
Schulberg, B. Pharmacists mate
Steinbeck, J. Leader of the people
Geiger, M. One special for Doc
   Also other material.

Preston, Effa E. Fun with stunts. Minneapolis, Denison, 1956.
Afternoon of October twentieth
After the day's work
Body, Body, who's got the body?
Census taker
Charity begins at home
Farmer in the dell
Friendly advice
Home work
In the Doctor's office
In the pet shop
Love's young dream
Moonrise island
Musical notes
Number game
Quiet evening at home
Quiz for high I Q's
Sign on the door
Something to read
Ten-minute white face minstrel show
Turning the Fables on Aesop
Virus V

Wiloughby's window
You can't please everybody
   Also other material.

Rees, Leslie C. Modern short plays. Sydney, Australia, Angus, 1951.

Yeats, W. B. Land of Heart's Desire
Synge, J. M. Riders to the sea
Chekhov, A. The proposal
Maeterlinck, M. Interior
Francis, J. O. Birds of a feather
Esson, L. The drovers
Phillpotts, E. Carrier pigeon
Housman, L. Royal favour
Ferguson, J. A. Campbell of Kilmhor
O'Neill, E. Ile
Corwin, N. Odyssey of Runyon Jones
Barclay, E. Spoiled darlings
Meredith, G. Great inheritance

Richard, Brother Basilian & Others. Adventures in appreciation. N. Y. Harcourt, 1954.

Niggli, J. Sunday costs five pesos
Barrie, J. M. The will
   Also other material.

Richmond, S. S. Career plays for young people. Non-royalty vocational guidance plays. Bost. Plays, 1949.

Business is business
A career for Ralph
Hail — The Genie
Wanted — a stenographer
Prescription for success
Highways of tomorrow
Flying high
The legacy
His first patient
Born to the soil
No sale
Joan makes a sale
Over the counter
The crisis
Cub reporter
Press photographer
We but teach
Flag the Limited
On trial
Corner store
House that Jack built
On the air
Glamour and grease
At the cleaners
Veterinarian in the family
Ye olde book shoppe

Homemakers have a way
The coach scores
The experiment
Career girl

Ridge, Antonia. Puppet plays for children. Lond. Faber, 1953.
Spring magic
Melodious mixture
Tropical island
Blue beans
Cure for lions
All aboard the "Bookworm Belle"

T   **Roberts, E. B.** Television writing and selling. Bost. Writer, 1954.
Manley, F. Best trip ever
Blake, R. What had God wrought
Bailey, A. H. Impersonation
    Also other material.

Rose, Kenneth. Georgiana. Seven portraits. Lond. Muller, 1947.
Royal button-maker
Boswell meets Johnson
Winter's tale
Death of a hero
First of the dandies
Tragic muse
Pilot who weathered the storm

Russia — Today. Soc. The theatre is our weapon. Lond. Russia Today
    Soc. n.d.
Bishop, J. Erna Kremer of Ebenstadt
Parsons, G. According to plan

Scarborough, Rehn. V for victory. Bost. Baker, 1952.
Allam, D. C. All in good time
Shyne, E. Man without a country
Hougham, E. B. America's heritage in song
Wren, J. Lady with the lamp
Ruggles, R. Patriotic minstrels
Morley, W. You're in the army now
Brown, A. M. Lucky seven
Brown, A. M. Sometimes it's right to fight
Thomas, H. After the air raid
    Also other material.

Schofield, J. A. & Joudry, R. C. Easter playlets for children and young
    people. Bost. Wilde, 1955.
"Who's is this?"
"Many infallible proofs"
    Also longer play.

T   **Sebby, S. R.** Easter fantasia. Bost. Christopher, 1953.
Easter fantasia
    Also other material.

Selden, Samuel, comp. First steps in acting. N. Y. Appleton, 1947.

Sidney, H. Paths of glory
Gurney, M. Never miss a trick
Niggli, J. Tooth or shave
Shakespeare. Romeo and Juliet
Glaspell, S. Trifles
Green, P. House of Connelly
Akins, Z. Old maid
Wilde, O. Importance of being Earnest
Synge, J. M. Riders to the sea
Andreyev, L. He who gets slapped
Glaspell, S. Surpressed desires
Bland, M. Lighted candles
Kapek, R. R U R
Deval, J. Tovarich
Shakespeare. As you like it
Odets, C. Golden boy
Kaufman, G. S. Beggar on horseback

Selden, Samuel, comp. International folk plays. Chapel Hill, Uni. of No. Carolina, 1949.

Bernhart, G. Home-longing
Jurgensen, K. Tarantula
Schenkkan, R. Black Piet
Seelye, M. Fleas and figs
Shun, T. W. Wandering dragon
Pharis, G. Courting of Marie Jenvrin
Niggli, J. Red velvet goat
Fidel, V. Wherefore is this night
Bailey, R. Washed in de blood

T **Settel, Irving, comp.** Top T V shows of the year. 1954-5 N. Y. Hastings

Fenwick, R. Toys and science
Marx, M. Letter to the boss
Hazam, L. Arthritis and rheumatism
Shaw, D. Native dancer
Faulkner, G. H. Thinking heart
Poole, L. Conquest of pain
Also other material.

Shattuck, Marquis E. Gateway to adventure. Bk. 4. Syracuse, N. Y. Iroquois, 1948.

Preston, E. E. Little new citizen
Also other material.

Six one-act plays by South African authors. Pretorias, Van Schaak, 1949.

Miller, J. Cradle in the dust
Gordimer, N. First circle
Wilson, A. J. A. The white train
Davies, R. E. Sunset in the dust
Thomas, M. Border folk
Sherwin, G. The light is against us

Skornia, H. J. & Others. Creative broadcasting. N. U. Prentice, 1950.
Freedom's forge
There ought to be a law
Who do you think you are?
Swing shift 1830
Long & short of it
Priming the pump
Brewer, F. Cloud that wouldn't rain
Brewer, F. That evening air
Rush, M. E. Most indestructible man in the world
Brewer, F. The house that didn't want to be lived in
Barnouw, E. Voice of the wizard
    Also other material.

Sper, Felix, ed. Modern short plays. N. Y. Globe, 1952.
Molnar, F. Two slaps in the face
Conkle, S. P. Scene from Prologue to Glory
Morgan, W. H. Too many hands on a watch
Wilde, P. Finger of God
Conkle, E. P. The owl and two young men
Sladen-Smith, F. Love in the ape house
O'Neill, E. In the zone
Ryerson, F. Materia Medica
Ober, A. Ugliest man in the world
Green, P. Quare medicine
Barth, R. Red death
Helburn, T. Enter the hero
Quintero. A sunny morning
Wilder, T. Mozart and the Gray Stewart

Switz, T. MacL. Great Christian plays. Greenwich, Conn. Seabury, 1956.
    With music scores.
Brome — Abraham and Isaac
York — Resurrection
Digby — Conversion of St. Paul
Totentanz — Morality play
Everyman — Morality play
Choral readings for acting or radio
Thomas the doubter
John the beloved
Andrew the summoner
James the thunderer
Royal pathway of the holy cross
How to gain peace amid temptation and adversity
Followers of Christ
Our preparations for the future
Good thoughts in solitude
    Also a group of religious services.

Teasdale, Verree. Aren't people funny? N. Y. French, 1947.
Form 1040
Bride's first dinner
Flobelle goes shopping
I'll help Johnny with his lesson

What do I do now, Mr. McLeod?
Facts of life
Oh, H-e-n-r-y-y!
Drama society meets
Glamour pattern 479823
Handy man
Nurse's day out
An emergency call!
I'll teach Junior, myself
Christmas shoppin' — in June
You must start dieting
Help wanted
Oh, Mrs. Morton, You're so patient
Quiet rest
Colonel, You're wonderful!
Flobelle goes to the movies
Goodbye, now!

R **Thomas, Dylan.** Under milkwood. N. Y. New Directions, 1954.

Under milkwood

T **Tooley, Howard.** Television. Minneapolis, Northwestern, 1953.

Miracle of Sack of Barley
Murder of Shakespeare
This is our Kathie
 Also other material

Wall, L. V., comp. Complete puppet book. N. Y. Crowell, 1951.

A mad tea-party
Mock turtle's story
Puppet play for mass education
Life in a gold coast village
Rapunzel
Drummer boy
Hansel & Grethel
Chinese romance
Get up and bar the door
 Also other material.

R **Weaver, Luther.** Technique of radio writing. N. Y. Prentice, 1948.

Briggs, S. King Neptune's court
Lyman, B. Lady Lookout
Raynolds, T. M. Larry Gray & the gremlins
Fossum, M. C. Letters from home
Hamre, J. Strange traditions
Lamout, J. Perfect crime
Fylstra, J. Mob scene
Armquist, M. Vitamin trail
Weaver, L. Radio: how to abuse it
Stewart, M. Hope for tomorrow: John Keats
Weaver, L. For the ladies
Hastings, F. V. Give us leaders
MacGregor, J. J. Bubble bath
Bushnell, M. H. Who listens to what?

Krausy, G. I'll never be late again
Harris, V. Land where balloons grow
Powell, T. T. A day camper's siesta
Strong, P. N. Jack Armstrong
Mack, N. Nuremberg stove
Hastings, F. V. Prelude for posterity
Calls, R. D. Singing wind
Weaver, L. Wreath for Apollo
Weaver, L. Little guy back home
   Also other material.

Weiss, M. J. Guidance through drama. N. Y. Whiteside, 1954.

Parents are people
The actor
Greetings from . . .
Debby's dilemma
Money talks
Her big crush

T   **Weiss, Margaret R.** The T V Writer's guide. N. Y. Pellegrim, 1952.

Ruscoll, J. The creeper
Boothe, B. The Laytons
Paige, M. Stage entrance
Raymond, J. The Sammy Kay show
Carlin, S. Rootie Kazoote Club
Weinstein, J. Tim Corbett space cadet
   Also other material.

R   **White, M. R., comp.** Children's program for radio broadcast. Minneapolis, Northwestern, 1948.

Aladdin and the wonderful lamp
Three wishes
Peter Rabbit
Three little pigs
Old woman who lived in the shoe
Hansel & Grethel
Story of Peter Rabbit
Jack & the beanstalk
Red riding hood
Cinderella

Williams, H. V. Puppets go to school. Chic. Winston, 1955.

Goodwin, R. V. On the roof top
Williams, H. V. Miss Liberty protests
Williams, H. V. Babe of Bethlehem
Kischner, V. M. Home in Nazareth
   Also other material.

Winn, Georgia, G. & Others. Action !! Beaconlights of literature. Syracuse, N. Y. Iroquois, 1952.

Kelly, G. Finders-keepers
Wilder, T. Happy journey to Trenton and Camden
Sherriff, R. C. The kite

Monroe, C. S. Coals to Newcastle
Nat'l. Broadcasting. Inside Washington
Also other material.

Woolsey, Janette & Sechrist, E. H. It's time to give a play. Phil. Macrae, 1955.
Gifts for the elves
Legend of Babouska
St. Peter and the birds
Mother Goose's children
Johnny's birthday surprise
Also many longer plays

Woolsey, Janette & Sechrist, E. H. New plays for Red Letter Days. Phil. Macrae, 1953.
Queen of Heart's party
Great tree council
Charlie's May basket
Mother of the town
Each star a state
Witches' complaint
Thanksgiving proclamation
Mother Goose gives advice
Wonder world of books
Radio versus doughnuts
First aid to first troop
My honest friend
Also many longer plays.

Yeats, W. B. Collected plays. Lond. Macmillan, 1952.
Countess Cathleen
Land of Heart's desire
Cathleen Ni Houlahan
Pot of broth
King's threshold
Shadowy waters
Deirdre
At the Hawk's well
Green helmet
On Baile's strand
Only jealousy of Emer
Hour-glass
Player queen
Dreaming of bones
Cavalry
Cat and the moon
Sophocles' King Oedipus
Sophocles' Oedipus at Colonus
The resurrection
Words upon the window-pane
Full moon in March
Herne's egg
Purgatory

Death of Cuchulain
Unicorn from the stars
King of the Great clock tower

Yeats, W. B. Collected plays. New ed. N. Y. Macmillan, 1953.

Countess Cathleen
Land of Heart's desire
Cathleen Ni Houlihan
Pot of broth
King's threshold
Shadowy waters
Deirdre
At the Hawk's well
Green helmet
On Baile's strand
Only jealousy of Emer
Hour-glass
Unicorn from the stars
Player queen
Dreaming of bones
Cavalry
Cat and the moon
Sophocles — King Oedipus
Sophocles — Oedipus at Colonus
The resurrection
Words upon the window-pane
Full moon in March
King of the Great clock tower
Herne's egg
Purgatory
Death of Cuchulain

SUBJECT LIST

ACTING

Flattering word
Timeless second

ACTOR

The actor
Farewell appearance
High tea

ACTRESS

Tinsel Duchess
Winter's tale

ADAPTATIONS

Abu Hassan pays his debts
Adventures of Tom Sawer
As you like it
Beatrice & Benedict
Beggar on Horseback
Bishop's candlesticks
Bottle imp
Canterville ghost
Captains Courageous
Christmas at the Cratchits
Christmas carol
Cock & the fox
Connecticut Yankee in King Arthur Court
Cyrano de Bergerac
David Copperfield
The door
Fall of the House of Usher
Forest of Arden
Glorious Whitewasher
Golden boy
Great stone face
Happy Prince
The High School
House of Connelly
House of seven gables
Huckleberry Finn
Icabod rides again
Importance of being Earnest
Jane Eyre
Kidnapping of David Balfour
King of the golden river
Lady of the lake

175

THE ADOLESCENT

Admiral's daughter
Bobby soxers' rebellion
Boys will be boys
Candy for your birthday
Debby's Dilemma
Enter Juliet
Enter the hero
Girls will be girls
Growing pains
Her big crush
Hold the line, please
Ides of March
I'll help Johnny with his lesson
Jerry to the rescue
Loud-speaker
Love lessons for Scotty
Midge minds her sister's business
Minor developments
Miss Lonely heart
Money talks
The Moon keeps on shining
Pink dress
Rented Tux
Ridiculous & sublime
Star-spangled Midge
Tenting tonight
When do we eat?
Wilbur's birthday gift

ADVERTISING

Career girl
For the ladies
Mrs. Gibbs advertises

ALASKA

Cracked ice
Seventh man
Stand-in for murder
Survival

ALUMNI

Alumni dinner

AMATEUR HOUR

Dooley & the amateur hour

AMERICANIZATION

Little new citizen
Son of America

ARMY LIFE

End of the line
Time is a thief

ART

But I know what I like
Day is bright
Finger in art
Meaning of art
Mr. Vincent
"N" for nuisance
Rose for Madam Calva
Watch out for Aunt Hattie

ASTRONOMY

Children of the sun
Star cadets

ATHLETICS

Athletes all

AUCTION

The auction

AUTOMOBILE

Bab buys a car
Glamour & grease
Junior buys a car
Lock your car

AVIATION

Emergency, stand by!
Flight completed
Highways of tomorrow
Flying high

BABY SITTER

All is not gold
Baby sitter
Sitters in revolt

BALLADS

Auntie & the bull
Love triumphant
Pirates & the ladies
Polly in the park
Sulie has an air

BALLET

Swan-song
Three dying swans

BEARD

The beard

BEAUTY SHOP

Goo-bye, now!

BAKING

King's creampuffs

BASEBALL

Jack Armstrong
Out at home plate
Spitball

BELLS

Little bell
Voice of Liberty

BETTER ENGLISH

Advice doctor
Almost everyone

BIBLE

Something to read

BIBLE — NEW TESTAMENT

Canticle of the nativity
Digby — Conversion of St. Paul
Followers of Christ
Fishers of men
Home in Nazareth
Last supper
Mantel of Elijah
Other apostles
Our preparation for the future
Out of the darkness
Paul before King Agrippa
Paul in Areopagus
Peter at Penticost
Philip, desert evangelist
Pilate, the Roman governor
The Resurrection
Stephen, the first martyr
York — Resurrection

BIBLE — OLD TESTAMENT

Bands of love
Behind the house of Obed-Edom
Book of Job
Brome — Abraham & Isaac
Citizen

Elijah, the firebrand of the Almighty
Famous fathers
Isaiah, the statesman prophet
It happened in Egypt
Jezebel
Man of Strife
Moses, the law-giver
Prophet of fire
Shepherd of Tekoa

BIOGRAPHICAL

Louisa M. Alcott
Louisa Alcott's wish
Prologue for tomorrow

JOHNNY APPLESEED

Visit of Johnny Appleseed
Wilderness birthday

SIR FRANCIS BACON

The tree

BALBOA

Drum head

DANIEL BOONE

Daniel Boone: patriot

CHARLOTTE BRONTE

Letter for Charlotte
Patrick Bronte and the saint

BEAU BRUMMEL

First of the Dandies

ADMIRAL BYRD

Big news from Little America

WILLIAM JENNINGS BRYAN

Cross of gold

EDMUND BURKE

Who do you think you are?

FANNY BURNEY

Silver lining

ROBERT BURNS

Immortal memory

JOHN CALVIN

Holy city

GEORGE WASHINGTON CARVER

George Washington Carver

COLUMBUS

Weaver's son

DANTE

Gentle heart

EDISON

Voice of the wizard

FABRE

Fabre's little world

FRANKLIN

Ben Franklin, peacemaker
Franklin & the King
Gentleman from Philadelphia

ELIZABETH FRY

Dungeon of thyself

GALILEO

Fountain for a Duke
Galileo

DR. GOLDBERGER

Red death

WASHINGTON IRVING

Young Irving

THOMAS JEFFERSON

Author of Liberty
Democrat & commissar
Danger of freedom
Divided we stand
Freeing the land
Ground of justice
Light & liberty
Living declaration
Men who stole freedom
Nature's most precious gift
Return of a patriot
Tavern meeting

To secure these rights
University of the U S
Whose birthday is it?

JOHNSON

Boswell meets Johnson

JOHN KEATS

Hope for tomorrow: John Keats

FRANCIS SCOTT KEY

Star spangled banner

PAUL KRUGER

Sunset in the dust

EMMA LAZARUS

New Colossus

LINCOLN

Light in darkness

DOLLY MADISON

Jemmy's wife

MORSE

What had God wrought

MOZART

Mozart & the gray stewart

NELSON

Death of a hero

WILLIAM PITT

Pilot who weathered the storm

POCAHONTAS

Bright stream

REMBRANDT

Rembrandt — master painter

PAUL REVERE

Regulars are out
Son of Liberty

RICHELIEU

Three musketeers

SHAKESPEARE

A deer of another color

MRS. SIDDONS

Tragic muse

STRADIVARI

Little whittler

QUEEN VICTORIA

One hour alone
Royal favour

WASHINGTON

In honor of Washington

BENJAMIN WEST

Brushes for Benjy

WHITTIER

Barefoot boy

CARDINAL WOLSEY

Cardinal's learning

BIRDS

Bird who couldn't fly
Bird court
Birds of Killingworth
Little bird in the tree
Mish-mosh bird
Miss Robin's school
Robin that wouldn't fly
The starlings
Yes, yes, I see

BIRTHDAY

Aladdin, incorporated
Happy birthday
Many happy returns
Mirror children
Party is born

BLIZZARD

Black blizzard

BLUES

Those Monday blues

BICYCLE

On a bicycle built for one

CAFETERIA

I'll eat my hat

CALENDAR

Children of the Calendar

CAMP

Beware the bear!
Callie goes to camp
Grey ghosts
Marko goes a courtin'
Midnight burial

CANADA

Courting of Marie Janvrin

CARDS

Grand slam
If men played cards as women do

CAREER

Career for Ralph
The experiment
Hail — the Genie
Highway trail
Talent tree

CARPET SWEEPER

Magic carpet sweeper

CATS

Cats & the cheese
Cat & the kingdom
Puss-n-boots
Pussy pleases
Socrates saves the day
Three little kittens
Too many kittens

CATTLE

The drovers

CENSUS

Census taker

CHARACTER BUILDING

Big stone
Gold feathers

Gray bread
If wishes were horses
I'll never be late again
Impersonations
Johnnie jump up
Man who married a dumb wife
Message to Garcia
Mischievous clock
Prince with no crown
Stubborn elf
Tommy's adventure
Twelve-pound look
Royal touch
Shady shadows
Surprise package
Unusual flower
Who started the fire

CHARACTER STUDY

The failure
Lily
Miss Julie
My Uncle Willy
Nurse Henrietta
Skin deep
Strange road
That evening star
Tilt of stein
Turn down an empty jug

CHARGE ACCOUNT

Charge it, please
Charge it to George

CHAUTAUQUA

Aunt Fanny from Chautauqua

CHESS

Game of chess

CHILD PSYCHOLOGY

Nurse's day out

CHILD WELFARE

When altars burn

CHILDREN'S PROGRAM

Rootie Kazoote Club

CHINA

Bag of fire
Blue willow plate

Chinese Rip van Winkle
China comes to you
Dreadful dragon
Fire in a paper
Home, sweet home
Moonbeam dares
Sheep Skin Po
So this is China
Stolen Prince

CHORAL READING

Andrew the summoner
James the thunderer
John the beloved
Thomas the doubter
Unto us the living

CHRISTMAS

All aboard for Christmas
Angel in the looking glass
Bats in the belfrey
Beggars can't be choosers
Boy who didn't belong
Broth of Christlindli
Bunny comes to town
Cause to serve
Children of Chocolate St.
Christmas comes to Hamelin
Christmas every day
Christmas for Cinderella
Christmas in her eyes
Christmas in the woods
Christmas on Main St.
Christmas recaptured
December gifts
Ebenezer Neverspend
Empty room
Everywhere Christmas
Friday foursome packs a box
Granny Goodman's Christmas
Happy Christmas to all
Holy search
How pleasant to know Mrs. Lear
Humblest place
It's a gift
Joy of the world
Keeping Christmas
Killed by Merry Christmas
King is here
King's march
Let nothing ye dismay
Let's be sensible

Lost Christmas
Merry, merry, merry
Mixing stick
Mrs. Sniffit's Christmas
Naomi-of-the-inn
Nine cheers for Christmas
No room at the inn
O little town of Bethlehem
Of all the years
On such a night
Perambulating pie
Perfect gift
Pinch-hitter
Pink roses for Christmas
Quiet Christmas
Red Wagon
Road to Bethlehem
Room for a king
Room for Mary
Shepherd of Bethlehem
Silent night
Softy the snowman
Tick tock
Twinkle
Violets for Christmas
Wayfarers
When the little angel sang
Which is mine?
White Christmas
Woman who didn't want Christmas

CHRISTMAS BELL

Jingle bells
Vision of the silver bell

CHRISTMAS CAKE

Christmas cake
Little cake

CHRISTMAS CANDLE

Candle in the window

CHRISTMAS CANDY

Candy canes

CHRISTMAS COWBOY

Christmas cowboy

CHRISTMAS DINNER

Long Christmas dinner
'Twas the night before Christmas
Little Christmas guest

CHRISTMAS GUESTS

Christmas eve visitor

CHRISTMAS HOLLY

Christmas house
Holly hangs high

CHRISTMAS LETTER

Christmas eve letter
Christmas eve news

CHRISTMAS, MEANING

Meaning of Christmas

CHRISTMAS MISTLETOE

Gramma & mistletoe

CHRISTMAS NATIVITY

Shepherds & wise men
This strange night
White Christmas

CHRISTMAS PAGEANT

Wandering Christ-child

CHRISTMAS REINDEER

Left-over reindeer
Reindeer on the roof

CHRISTMAS ROSE

Legend of the Christmas rose

CHRISTMAS — SANTA

Five boys & a Santa
Junction Santa Claus
Mrs. Claus' Christmas present
Mrs. Santa's Christmas gift
On the roof
Santa Claus for president
Santa Claus parade
Santa forgets Christmas
Santa goes to town
Santa's robbers
Standing up for Santa
Unhappy Santa

CHRISTMAS SHOPPING

Christmas shopping early
Christmas shopping — in June

CLOUD

Lazy little raindrops

COLLEGE

Cupid's partner
Face is familiar

COLOR

Color-conscious conscience
Rainbow colors

COLUMBUS DAY

Beyond Thule
Child of destiny
Compass of Christopher
Columbus sails the sea
Fetters & dreams
Ghost from Genoa
Great beginning
I shall sail again
Jimmy Columbus
Lazy ones
Most memorable voyage
New worlds
Return of the Nina
Sailing West to find the East
Ship's boy to the Indies

COMMENCEMENT

Moon keeps shining
Place to begin
To you the torch
Who's old-fashioned

COMMUTERS

Period house

CONEY ISLAND

Sun deck
Tunnel of love

COOKING

Bride's first dinner
Million dollar recipe
Mixing stick
Test for a witch

CONTESTS

Contest fever

COOKIE JAR

Magic cooky jar

COURT ROOM

Afternoon of Oct. twentieth
No order in the court
One in twelve

COWBOY

Jimmy Cinders

CRIME

August heat
Black sheep
The creeper
Crime clues
Don't forget the baking powder
Grand Cham's diamond
Julian Houseman story
Mask of guilt
Once a thief
The "Pay-Off"
Perfect crime
Return of Benjamin
Shall we join the ladies?

CROOKS

Decision
Safecrackers' pride
Two crooks & a lady

COURTESY

"Courtesy"
Doctor manners
Mind your manners
Tea for six

CUSTOMS

Man from the Fells

DANCE

Dancers
Dancing Princess
Day the shoemaker came
Exodus
Karma
Native dancer
Princess who couldn't dance
Shall we dance?
Sign on the door

DATING

All this and Alan too
Casanova Jr.

Date with Kate
Ins & outs
Lieutenant pays his respects
Nervous father
She also serves

DEATH

Death of the average man
Stand up to death

DEMOCRACY

All in favor
American family
What is a patriot?

DENMARK

What the good man does

DEPARTMENT STORE

Willoughby's window

DETECTIVE

Beany's private eye
Body, body, who's got the body?
Case for two detectives
Case of the missing pearls
Case of the missing poet
Don't forget the baking powder
Mystery of the silver-backed hairbrush
Tomorrow's vengeance

DIALECT

Dog in the manger
The failure
Forgotten land
Glory day
Incident at Eureka bumps
Least one
Most indestructible man
Muletail prime
The nerve of it!
Owl & two young men
Sam 'N' Ella
Sportsman
White dresses

DIET

Herman's temptation
Rest for Mr. Winkle
When father goes on a diet
You must start dieting

Missing Easter eggs
Uncolored Easter egg
Vanishing Easter egg

EASTER FLOWERS

Easter lily
Hearts & flowers
Tomorrow is Easter

EASTER HOP

Easter hop
Bunny of the year

EASTER RABBIT

Bunny who was always late
Bunnyland brigade
Hats & rabbits
Mr. Rabbit's Easter jamboree
Rabbit foot

EDUCATION

Fortunes of Merry legs
Hour glass
I'll teach junior, myself
Miss Haffner
Shakespeare touch
Some are teachers
Three royal R's
What makes it tick?

ELECTION DAY

Bud for President
Election day in the U.S.A.
Running the country
Vote for Uncle Sam

ELECTRICITY

"Only once blow the fuse!"

ELEVATOR

Little prison

ENGINEERING

Engineering a bid

EPIDEMIC

The epidemic

ESSAY CONTEST

Unsuspected fruit

ETHICAL

Finger of God

EX-CONVICT

Sure as fate

FABLE

Ant & the grasshopper
Androcles & the lion
Hermes & the two woodsmen
Lion & the mouse
Little hero of Holland
Tale of good faith
Theseus & the Minotaur
Town mouse & his country cousin
Turning the Fables of Aesop
Way to Norwich

FAIR

Litchen fair
Magic goose
Milkmaid & her pail are one
Spreading the news

FAIRY

Adalmina's pearl
Aladdin & his wonderful lamp
Carling moth
Children of Chocolate St.
Cinderella
Crystal flask
Elves & the carpenter
Fairy in the dell
Gift for the world
Hans who made the Princess laugh
Hansel & Grethel
In the witch's house
Jack & the beanstalk
Little bird in the tree
Little snow white
Magic cookie jar
Magic well
Magic mirror
Nurenberg stove
Patchwork Princess
Peter Rabbit changes his name
Pinocchio
Pot of gold
Prince Charming smiles again
Proud Princess
Queen of Hearts
Red Riding Hood & the wolf

Young lady of property
Young man's fancy

FANTASY

The dolls
In triplicate, Please!
Interior
Jenny-by-the-day
Knave of hearts
Let the heavens decide
Londonderry air
Lovely miracle
Merlin limited
Old woman & the tramp
Paper Princess
Spinney under the rain

FARCE

Let there be farce

FARM

Abner Cran from Hayseed Lane
Born to the soil
Cow was in the parlor
Farmer in the dell
Sod
Out of the shadows
Visionary farms
You never can tell

FASHION SHOW

Fashion show
Flair for fashions

FATHERS DAY

Bringing up father

FAUST STORY

Dr. Faustus lights the lights

FEMINISM

Letter to Ibsen

FEUD

Fog in the valley

FIRE PREVENTION

Fire bug
Green ghosts
Polka dot pup

FIRST AID

First aid first
Narrow squeak

FISHING

An early start
Fisherman's luck
He who gets hooked
Singing shark

FLAG DAY

Each star a state
Flag of the U S

FLOOD

Caught at the Narrows

FLOWERS

Crimson glory rose
Crocus
First butterfly
Flowers for mother
Girls whose fortune sought her
Green piper
Grey squirrel & white butterfly
Little Ida & the flowers
Naming the flowers
Say it with flowers
Snowdrop
Thirsty flowers
Tulips & two lips

FOLK TALES

Baba Yaga
Billy Beg & his bull
Black Piet
Boys & his brothers
Christmas angel
Clever Manka
Crowded house
Doctor from Dunmore
Feast of lanterns
The flea
Fleas & figs
Flying ship
Folk festival script
Folk life in ancient Greece
Four clever brothers
Fox brings luck
Golden touch

Home-longing
Katherine & Frederick
Lenka's little house
Morning maker
Nosebag
One-inch fellow
Persistent musician
Peterkins try to be wise
Pied piper
Quare medicine
Red velvet goat
Shiro & his master
Straw ox
Sunday costs five pesos
Tarantula
Three golden oranges
Three wishes
Tinder box
Ugly duckling
Wandering dragon
Wantin' fever
Washed in de blood
Wherefore is this night
Why the sea is salt
Wise men of Gotham
Wishful Taw
Young Paul Bunyan

FOOD

A spot of onion tea

FOOTBALL

First & ten
Football hero
Howard's forward pass
Just what the doctor ordered
One man's word
Thanksgiving a la carte
Vote for your hero

FORMAL (DRESS)

Let's go formal

FREE LOVE

Daring innovation

FREEDOM

A dream
Freedom train

FRIENDSHIP

Blue toadstool

FRENCH MODESTE

Mlle. Deceit

FRESH AIR

Home remedy

FUNERAL

Next-to-last-rites

FUR COAT

Window shopping

GANGSTERS

One special for Doc.

GAY NINETIES

Farmer's daughter
Way, way down East

GENIUS

Day before yesterday

GEOGRAPHY

Visit of the Cotton Maids

GHOST

Be my ghost
Back to Boston
Ghost walks tonight
Ghost-layers, Inc.
Ghosts on guard
Granny's ghost
It's so peaceful
Let's haunt
Reluctant ghost
Surprising story of Alfred

GIRL SCOUTS

Give us leaders
Day camper's siesta
First aid to first troop
Perfect understanding

GIVE AWAY SHOW

Your money or your life

GLASSES

Princess & the rose-colored glasses

GOLF

What do I do now, Mr. McLeod?

Halloween scarecrow
Happy haunts
Haunted clothesline
Haunted suitcase
Hometown Halloween
House is haunted
Impossible room
Jack-o-lantern
Little witch who tried
Magic pumpkin
Magic spell
Night's high noon
Soft-hearted ghost
Some tricks are treats
Something new for Halloween
Spook shop
Spooky spectacles
Stolen pumpkin
Timid little witch
Who scared whom?
Wispy
Witch doctor
Witch who wasn't
Witches' complaint
Witches' pattern
Witches' pumpkin

HARLEQUINADE

Aria da Capo
Harlequin bridge

HEALTH

Catch as catch can
Fit for victory
Good health trolley
Health officer for a day
It's a problem
Kachoo!
King's toothache
Long live father
Magic formula
Models for health
Murder in the kitchen
Not-so-crooked man
Nursery rhyme diet
Piffle! It is only Sniffle!
Pleasant dreams
Robots to the rescue
Too much of a good thing
Visitors from the air
Why the sleepy dormouse

ROME, ANCIENT

Cornerstone of freedom

SOUTH AFRICA

Border folk

STONE AGE

Stone age

TIBET

Songtsan Gampo

UNITED STATES

Attorney for the defense
Ah, there's the rub
The beacon
But one life to give
Cecily entertains the enemy
The clod
Coals to Newcastle
The conqueror
Dolly saves the day
Drums in the dusk
Freedom's forge
General Gage's chowder
God & Texas
Hearts of oak
Heroine of Wren
In the name of Miles Standish
Judge's diary
Lacey's last garland
Last drum
Mayflower compact
Melissa's muffins
Narration for V.J. Day
Navy & the pirates
Needle fights for freedom
Never any excuse
No braver soldier
Not worth a continental
Pilgrim parting
Play without a name
Priming the pump
Rain & rebellion
The spy
Swing shift 1830
The well
With malice towards none
Worth his salt
Yankee Doodle
Yorktown lass

WORLD WAR I

Battleship Bismark
Little guy back home

WORLD WAR II

According to plan
Bed with the others
Call me Mac
Can die but once
Erna Kermer of Ebenstadt
Far-distant shore
For each man kills
Leopard spots
Pharmacist's mate
Shadow of the Cathedral
Stormy passage
While we sleep

HITCH-HIKER

Hitch-hiker

HOBBY

Hobby for Dad
Somewhat forgetful

HOLIDAYS

Flibber turns the tables
Happy holidays
Hooky holiday

HOME

Charity begins at home
Homemakers have a way
House for rent
House that didn't want to be lived in
Letters from home
Our dream house
Quiet evening at home
Spring daze
When do we eat?

HOME WORK

Home work
It's Greek to me

HORSE

Princess & the horse
The race

INSURANCE

The legacy

INTERDEPENDENCE

I'll share my fare

INTERIOR DECORATOR

The homiest room

INVENTORS

Inventors clinic
Jim & Jennie

IRISH

At the hawk's well
Countess Cathleen
Death of Cuchlain
Deirdre
Dreaming of bones
End & the beginning
Happy as Harry
Herne's egg
Green helmet
King's threshold
On Baile's strand
Only jealousy of Emer
Player queen
Pot of broth
Rising of the moon
Spreading of the news

ITALIAN-AMERICAN

Little flaw of Ernesto

ITALY

Generous fisherman

JAPAN

Awful fate of a fibber

JEALOUSY

Green-eyed monster
Literature

JESTER

King's jester

JOURNALISM

Cub reporter
Freedom's herald
On the sentimental side

JUNGLE

Natives are restless tonight

JUNIOR PROM

Junior prom

JUNIOR RED CROSS

One-ring circus
Lady with the lamp

JUNK

Junk, valuable junk

JUVENILE DELINQUENCY

As kids go
Night in Plainville

KITTENS

Three little kittens

LABORATORY

Mad Dr. Zing
Mystery in the Lab

LANGUAGE

Petrified Prince
Trial of Billy Scott
Word in your ear

LAW

The counsellor
On trial
That woman
There ought to be a law
The will

LEGENDS

Bailiff's wonderful coat
The brothers
Courage piece
Emperor's new clothes
Floating stone
Humai's secret
Legend of the lake
Lion & the mouse
Legend of Sleepy Hollow
Maelduin of Arran
Magic grapes
Ogre of Rashamon
Paul Bunyan: lumberjack
Pied Piper of Hamelin

Princess & the rose-colored glasses
St. Peter & the birds
Shehrazade kept on talking
Telling of the North Star
Three meals a day
Tinker of Toledo
Wise men of Gotham
Wisely chosen

LEAVES

Frolic of the leaves

LINCOLN

Abe Lincoln — champ
Abe Lincoln goes to school
Abe's winkin' eye
Apple from Coles county
Bind up the nation's wounds
Birthday gift
Bobby & the Lincoln speech
Child of her spirit
China-handled knife
February failure
G for Gettysburg
Gift of the Fairies
Glory & the dream
Good enough for Lincoln
His hand & pen
Honest Abe Lincoln
Last curtain
Lawyer of Springfield
Lincoln coat
Lincoln cupboard
Lincoln heart
Lincoln museum
Lincoln reminders
Lincoln says farewell
Lincoln umbrella
Lincoln's buckskin breeches
Living up to Lincoln
Long & short of it
Mister A. Lincoln
Mr. Lincoln's beard
Present for Abe
President Lincoln's children
Scene from Prologue to Glory
Thinking heart
Visitor to Gettysburg
When Lincoln kept store

LIGHT

Story of light

LONDON — MEDIEVAL

Old English play

LOVELORN

Advice to the lovelorn

LUCK

Luck takes a holiday

MACHINES

Voice of the machines

MAGICIAN

Laughing Princess

MAIL

Mail goes through

MANKIND

Museum of man

MANNERS

Doctor's office
Your manners are showing

MARKET DAY

Broom market day

MARRIAGE

After ten years
All is not gold
Blue concerto
Catastrophy
Grey fedora
Good manners
High pressure
Honeymoon
How to be happy though married
Letter to Lola
Major conflicts
Marriage & friendship
Matrimony bumps
Matter of taste
Minor friendship
Newly weds
Minnie Field
Parting tear
Poor Aubrey
School for marriage

Seduction
Silver wedding
Strained relations
Sunday edition
Vast experience
Wedding journey
What did I say?
Whistle daughter, whistle
Will you marry me?
Wise wife

MATHEMATICS

The Cuckoo
How we got our numbers

MEDICINE

Arthritis & rheumatism
Defense never rests
His first patient

MEDIEVAL LIFE

Folly of Seithenyn

MELODRAMA

Big melodrama

MELTING POT

Imploring flame

MEMORIAL DAY

Can long endure
Day to remember
Judge's diary
Memorial day for the blue & the grey
Pink parasol
Portrait of an American
See the parade
So shines a good deed
They banish our anger
Uninvited guests

MENTAL HEALTH

Day dreams go to school
Mind in the shadow
Somebody do something!
Sons & husbands
What every woman wants

MERCHANT MARINES

Wake for me & thee

MISTAKEN IDENTITY

Adventures of Mr. Bean

MOB

Mob scene

MOCK WEDDING

Substitute bride

MONEY

Bar-none trading post
Two hundred thousand dollars

MONTHS

All on a day in May
April fool
April fool surprise
April showers
Charlie's May basket
December gifts
February frenzy
February play
First day of April
Full moon in March
Little Bo-peep's May flowers
Little February
Littlest month
May basket
May day gift
May eve
Roaring March lion
Second Sunday in May

MOON

Moon maiden

MORAL

Crowded house
Help wanted
He who eats cabbage
Little man

MORALITY PLAY

Everyman
Totentanz

MOTEL

Tourist trouble

MOTHER GOOSE

Jack & Jill
Let it snow

Concert in the park
Gift of music
Music hath charms
Music on the menu
Musical notes
When it's moonlight on Pike's Peak

MYSTERY

Boy next door
Case for Mrs. Hudson
Case for two detectives
Case of the silent caroler
Clock's secret
Dark brown
The door
End of the line
Farrell case
Final curtain
Five buttons
Gratitude
Green veil passes
High window
Midnight burial
Mysterious stranger
Night at an inn
Nobody sleeps
Plot thickens
Queen is dead
Swiss chalet mystery
Ups & downs
The whistle
Will-o'-wisp

MYSTIC

Saga of Simon Curle
Strange victory

MYTH

Venus & Adonis

NARCOTICS

Dope

NATURE

Five senses
Green thumb
Mr. Smooch's trap

NAZI GERMANY

Jacob comes home

Favour is deceitful
The proposal
Strangers
Sunny morning

OLD PEOPLE'S HOME

Lavender lie
Rockers

OPERA

The gypsy
Rise of her bloom

ORPHANAGE

John Shanahan, me

OUTLAWS

Last of the Lowries

OLD AND YOUNG

Disconsolate apparition
Young as you look

PAINTING

Ear of Vincent van Gogh

PANTOMIME

Excursions
Oh! that golden wedding
Soldier, soldier

PARADISE

Paradise anow

PASSOVER

Camel and I
Youngest shall ask

PASTRY

Sugar & spice

PATRIOTIC

After the air raid
All in good time
Lucky seven
Man without a country
Sometimes it's right to fight
This is our America
Visitor to Mt. Vernon
Your country & mine

PSYCHOLOGICAL

Balcony scene
Farewell supper
In camera
It's so complex
Overtones
Sky-fodder
Suppressed desires
Tea with a legend
The wrecker
Things we know
Trifles

PUBLICITY

Publicity expert

PUMPKINS

Patrick Pumpkin

PUPPET

Anyone could but ——
Babe of Bethlehem
Baker's three daughters
Bang goes my stocking
Brigands of the Black Forest
Cinderella or the glass slipper
Domino family's picnic
Dominoes have a fire
Chinese romance
Fly by night
Drummer boy
Contrary Mary meets Boy Blue
Get up & bar the door
Grasshoppers & ants
How the giraffe got its neck
I can get along
I want A ——
I spy
Jack & the beanstalk
Pretty maid, where have you been?
Puppet play for mass education
Red apple
Ride a cock-horse
Storm in a teacup
Three pigs catch the wolf again
Three wishes
Una fools the fighting giant
Useful plough
We three
Wee Willie Winkle
What's your name?

PURITANS

Darkest hour

QUEST

Dark tower

QUESTIONS & ANSWERS

Twelve hours in Mr. Smith's life

QUIZ

Quiz for high IQ's

RABBIT

Peter Rabbit
Rabbit foot

RACE TRACK

Little stranger

RADIO

J. M. Barrie
Numbers game
On the air
Pin-up-pals
Push button tuning
Radio: how to abuse it
Radio Jerusalem, story of Jesus

RAILROAD

Billy's train ride
Flag the Limited
Railroad accident
Railroad rhymes & rhythms

RAIN

Lazy draindrop

RANCH

Cloud burst
Dark rider
Hard as flint
Summer comes to Diamond O

READING

Rabbit's reading lesson

REAL ESTATE

Albright acres
The option

RED CROSS

Home nursing revue
Old man river

REDUCING

Sky's the limit

RELIGIOUS

Angel in the window
The answer
Before the dawn
Before the light came
Calvary
A certain man who had two sons
The confession
Empty room
Gift of forgiveness
Happy life
Holy Grail
Juggler of Our Lady
King Alfred the Great
The lamb in the window
Legend of Babouska
Let your light so shine
Light is kindled
Light of the world
Minor miracle
Not without honor
Paul Thompson forever
Prodigal comes home
Promised ones
Purgatory
Putting first things first
Pytheas the Greek explorer
Royal pathway of the holy cross
Salome
Silvered rope
Synod of Whitby
Three parsons
To what purpose
Unicorn from the stars
Venerable Bede

RELIGIOUS — ANTHROPOLOGY

Sticks & stones

RELIGIOUS — CHURCH

Before the dawn
Greater than any man
Unjust stewart
Voice that failed

RELIGIOUS — WORLD

Man's eternal quest for the good life

REUNION

The reunion

ROBOTS

R U R

ROMANCE

Bridal bouquet
Country cousin
Bubble bath
Glass slipper
Have you seen my lady?
Hearts, Inc.
His daughter's hand
Love scores a touchdown
Marjory Daw
The proposal
Puppy love
Romance a la mode
Spoiled darlings
Three on a bench
Time out for dreams
Walk into my parlor

RUSSIA

The beggar
The boor

REFUGEES

Journey of promise
Tovarich

SAFETY

A B C for safety
All houses are haunted
By order of the king
Case of the Balky Bike
Courting trouble
Crisscross streets
Luck takes a holiday
Many a slip
Nothing ever happens
Red 'n green treasure hunt
Safety patrol
Sidewalk elves
What happened on Clutter street

ST. PATRICK DAY

Boston O'Tooles
For the glory of St. Patrick
Last laugh
Last snake in Ireland
Prize Shamrock

SAINTS

St. Alban
St. Augustine of Canterbury
St. Birinus
St. Boniface
St. Chad & Archbishop Theodore
St. Columba
St. Columba says his last words
St. Columba visits King Brude
St. Cuthbert
St. Dunstan
St. Edmund King & Martyr
St. Edward the Confessor
St. Hilda & Caedmon
St. Oswald & St. Aidan
St. Patrick
St. Patrick & the last snake in Ireland
St. Patrick saves the day
St. Paulinus & King Edwin

SAYINGS

Poor relations
Talisman

SCHOOL

All this, and Alan too
Backward-jumping frog
Boomerang
Browning version
Daughter of the gods
Eyes right!
Crosspatch & Cupid
Goodbye to the clown
Home work
Judy takes over
Luigi steps aside
Mechanical man
"N" for nuisance
Patched coat
Printer's devil
Sands of time
Sticks & stones
Those in glass houses
Trial by jury
What's cookin'?

SCIENCE

Beyond ultraviolet
Conquest of pain
Mystery in the lab
Professor Willy's wisher-switcher
Tom Gilbert, space cadet

SCREEN PLAY

Gigolo & Gigolette

SEA

After the fog lifts
Crowsnest
Ile
In the zone
Riders to the sea
Shadowy waters
Twenty thousand leagues neath the sea

SEASONS OF THE YEAR

Autumn
Green leaf's lesson

SPRING

First flowers
Late spring
Ode to spring
Spring fever
Spring is here
Spring magic
Spring neighbors
Spring secrets
Spring to the rescue
Spring will come

SUMMER

Good old summer time

WINTER

Briskie the snowman
Cloud that wouldn't rain
Jack's friends
Winter thaw

SEEDS

Seven little seeds

SENSES

Five senses
Panic in the palace

SEX

Facts of life

SHOES

Flobelle goes shopping

SHORT WEIGHT

Precedent in pastries

SIN

Original sin

SINGING

The lost voice

SLEEPING

Cross Princess
Lullaby land

SOCIAL BACKGROUND

Background for Nancy
Campus brides
One of these days

SOCIAL SIGNIFICANCE

Discrimination for everybody
Through the glass, darkly

SOCIAL WORK

For the welfare of all

SOCIOLOGY

All the world's a stage
Of social significance
Question period

SOIL CONSERVATION

Great inheritance

SONGS

America the beautiful
America's heritage of song
Battle hymn of the Republic
Bonnie Annie
Church in the wildwood
Columbia the gem of the ocean
Dixie
Radiance streaming
Silver threads among the gold

SORORITY

Alpha Kappa

THE SOUTH

The long stay cut short
Something unspoken

SOUTH AFRICA

Black star
Cradle in the dust
Life in a Gold Coast village
The light is against us
White train

SPACE TRAVEL

Space unlimited

SPAIN

Tragi-comedy of Don Cristobita

SPEECH

Speaking of speech
Unaccustomed as I am

SPELLING

Tricky rhymes for sale
When the letter A ran away

SPIRITUALISM

Words upon the window pane

SPY

A government job

STARS

Follow the North Star
Golden doom
Non Nobis
Paloma, Princess of Phito
Star light & the sand man
Star minded

STAMP COLLECTING

Johnny did try

STENOGRAPHER

Wanted — a stenographer

STORY TELLING

Wilbur, the sleepy little ghost

Father talks turkey
First Thanksgiving
Grateful gobbler
If we only could cook
I'll share my fare
Indians for Thanksgiving
Jonathan's Thanksgiving
Just what the doctor ordered
Little white cloud
Many thanks
Mr. Thanks has his day
Mr. Snow White's Thanksgiving
New-fangled Thanksgiving
Nothing to be thankful for
Old-fashioned Thanksgiving
Our famous ancestors
Pumpkmeaters' pumpkin
Strictly Puritan
Surprise guests
T for turkey
Thankful hearts
Thankless Tate
Thanks to Billy
Thanks to Butter-fingers
Thanks to Sammy Scarecrow
Thanksgiving a la carte
Thanksgiving feast
Thanksgiving is for everybody
Thanksgiving night
Thanksgiving proclamation
Thanksgiving scarecrow
Thanksgiving through the ages
Thanksgiving wishbone
Turkey, anyone?
Turkey for all
Turkey gobblers
Turkey turns the tables
Unexpected guests
What makes Thanksgiving?
What, no venison?
What's in a name

THEATRE

Alfred, dear
Final curtain
Half-hour, please
Hangs over thy head
The idol and his girl
Murder of Shakespeare
Stage entrance

THRILLER

Man at the door

Cupid's post office
Cupies & hearts
Game of hearts
Happy hearts
Happy Valentine's day
Have a heart
Heart throbs
Heart trouble
Hearts, tarts & Valentines
Littlest artist
Message of the hearts
New hearts for old
Pioneer Valentine
Queen of hearts
Queen of Heart's party
Queen with the broken heart
Somebody's Valentine
Stolen heart
To my Valentine
Valentine box
Valentine family
Valentine stardust

VAUDEVILLE

Afterpiece
Comedy sketch
Double blackfarce act
Double Dutch act
Double Irish act
Double wop act
Dramatic sketch
Man & woman act
School act
Straight & the Jew
Two-woman act

VASES

Double exposure

VETERAN'S DAY

Hero's homecoming
Known but to God
Thank you Louise

VETERINARY

Veterinarian in the family
Veterinarian in time

VITAMIN

Vitamin trail
Visit to Vitamin village

VOCABULARY

Mind your P's & Q's

VOCATIONAL

Al the cleaner
Carfare home
Experiment

VOTING

Mr. Bates goes to the polls
Vicky gets the vote
Vote for Uncle Sam

WALES

Birds of a feather
The changeling
Hugh of the Glen & his clogs are all one

WAR

Bury the dead
The island
Old lady shows her medals
Operation Coral
Papa Pepper's bombshell
Silent city

WASHINGTON BIRTHDAY

Attic treasure
Bake a cherry pie
Boy who couldn't tell a lie
Best policy
Corn meal & poetry
Date with Washington
David & the second Lafayette
End of the road
Enter George Washington
Express to Valley Forge
Family matter
February frenzy
Field of honor
General returns
George Washington
George Washington comes to town
George Washington's chair
Guide for George Washington
Handwriting on the wall
In honor of Washington
Jump for George
Letter from George Washington
Lost letter
My honest friend

Needle fights for freedom
New Washington
Sausages & General Washington
Stars & stripes
Washington Shilling
Washington's gold button
Washington's leading lady
Washington's sacrifice
Thanks to George Washington
Valley Forge was never like this
Visitor to Mount Vernon
Winter of our discontent

WASHING

Haunted clothesline

WATCH

Too many hands on a watch

WEALTH

Father hits the jackpot

WEATHER

Hello, Mr. Groundhog
King's weather

WEAVER

Three aunts

WEDDING

Adventure in Paris
All aboard
Berate your mate
Dowry
Forever yours
Golden wedding anniversary
I love you truly
Love honor & obey
Orange blossom
The preview
She laughs last
Silver key
Switch to Mitch
Wedding

WEEK END

Cabin by the lake

WEEPING

Boo-Hoo Princess

WEST

Best of the old West
From Paradise to Butte
Strong & silent

WILL

Dear departed

WIND

North wind & the sun
Useless little wind
Whirlwind comes

WINTER CRUISE

Winter cruise

WISH

Fisherman & his wife
Three wishing bags
Three wishes

WITCH

Cry witch
Broom market day
Frightful forest
Hansel & Grethel
Princess & the pumpkin
Rapunzel
Witch's delight

WOMEN

Amazing Arabella
Danger! Women at work
Many happy returns

WORDS

The test
Who listens to what?

WORKERS

Long fall

WORKHOUSE

Workhouse ward

WORLD

To be alone

WRITERS

Dream lost
Out of this world

SUBJECT INDEX

A

Acting
Actor
Actress
Adaptations
Adolescent
Advertising
Alaska
Alumni
Amateur hour
Americanization
Animals
Anthropology

Antiques
Apartment hunting
Arbor Day
Arithmetic
Armistice Day
Army life
Art
Astronomy
Athletics
Auction
Automobile
Aviation

B

Baby sitter
Ballads
Ballet
Beard
Beauty shop
Baking
Baseball
Bells
Better English
Bible
Bible — New Testament
Bible — Old Testament
Biography
    Louisa M. Alcott
    Johnny Appleseed
    Sir Francis Bacon
    Balboa
    Daniel Boone
    Charlotte Bronte
    Beau Brummel
    Admiral Byrd
    William Jennings Bryan
    Edmund Burke
    Fanny Burney
    Robert Burns
    John Calvin
    George Washington Carver
    Columbus
    Dante
    Edison
    Fabre
    Franklin
    Galileo
    Dr. Goldberger
    Washington Irving

    Thomas Jefferson
    Samuel Johnson
    John Keats
    Francis Scott Keys
    Paul Kruger
    Emma Lazarus
    Lincoln
    Dolly Madison
    Morse
    Mozart
    William Pitt
    Pocahontas
    Rembrandt
    Paul Revere
    Richelieu
    Shakespeare
    Mrs. Siddons
    Stradivari
    Queen Victoria
    Washington
    Benjamin West
    Whittier
    Cardinal Wolsey
Bicycle
Birds
Birthday
Blizzard
Blues
Boarding house
Boarding school
Bobby-soxer
Boomerang
Book week
Books
Bookshop

E

Earring
Easter
Easter basket
Easter bonnets
Easter eggs
Easter flowers
Easter hop
Easter Rabbit
Education

Election day
Electricity
Elevator
Engineering
Epidemic
Essay contests
Ethical
Ex-convict

F

Fable
Fair
Fairy
Family life
Fantasy
Farce
Farm
Fashion show
Father's day
Faust story
Feminism
Feud
Fire prevention
First aid
Fishing

Flag day
Flood
Flowers
Folk tales
Food
Football
Formal dress
Free love
Freedom
Friendship
French Modeste
Fresh air
Funeral
Fur coat

G

Gangsters
Gay nineties
Genius
Geography
Ghost
Girl scouts
Give away show
Glasses
Golf
Good speech

Gossip
Government
Gown shop
Graduation
Grammar
Grave
Gremlins
Guardian angel
Gypsies

H

Habits
Halloween
Harlequinade
Health
High School
Hillbilly
Historical
    Belgium
    France
    Great Britain
    Greece — Ancient
    Holland
    India
    Ireland
    Mexico
    Rome — Ancient

    South Africa
    Stone age
    Tibet
    United States
    World War I
    World War II
Hitch-hiker
Hobby
Holidays
Home
Home work
Horse
Hospital
Hotel
Hygiene
Hypnotism

I

Ideals
Immigration
Income tax
India
Indians
Inferiority complex
Inheritance
In-laws

Insurance
Interdependence
Interior decoration
Inventors
Irish
Italian-Americans
Italy

J

Japan
Jealousy
Jester
Journalism
Junior prom

Junior Red Cross
Jungle
Junk
Juvenile delinquency

K

Kittens

L

Laboratory
Language
Law
Legends
Leaves

Light
Lincoln
London — medieval
Lovelorn
Luck

M

Machines
Magician
Mail
Mankind
Manners
Market day
Marriage
Mathematics
Medicine
Medieval life
Melodrama
Melting pot
Memorial day
Mental health
Merchant marines
Mermaids
Mexico
Mice
Migratory workers
Mine
Mink coat
Minstrel show

Miracle play
Missionary
Mistaken identity
Mob
Mock wedding
Money
Months
Moon
Moral
Morality play
Motel
Mother Goose
Mother's day
Movie
Mummy
Murder
Museum
Music
Mystery
Mystic
Myth

N

Narcotics
Nature
Nazi Germany

Neighbors
New Year
Newspaper

Nonsense
Numbers

Nursery rhymes
Nurses

O

Oil stock
Old age
Old people's home

Opera
Orphanage
Old & young

P

Painting
Pantomime
Paradise
Passover
Pastry
Patriotic
Payments
Peace
Pennies
Penmanship
Pet shop
Pharmacy
Philosophy
Physical education
Picnic
Pierot

Pilgrims
Pioneers
Pixies
Planets
Plastics
Playwright
Poetic
Politics
Pottery
Prairie
Press
Printing
Prison
Problem play
Psychiatrist
Psychic

Q

Quest
Questions & answers

Quiz

R

Rabbit
Race track
Radio
Railroad
Rain
Ranch
Reading
Real estate
Red Cross
Reducing

Refugees
Religious
Religious — anthropology
Religious — church
Religious — world
Reunion
Robots
Romance
Russia

S

Safety
St. Patrick's day
Saints
Sayings
School
Science
Screen play
Sea
Seasons of the year
    Autumn
    Spring
    Summer

    Winter
Seeds
Senses
Sex
Shoes
Short weight
Sin
Singing
Sleep
Social background
Social significance
Social work

Sociology
Soil conservation
Songs
Sorority
South
South Africa
Space travel
Spain
Speech
Spelling
Spiritualism

Spy
Stamp collecting
Stars
Stenographer
Story telling
Submarines
Summer resort
Summer stock
Supernatural
Suspense

T

Tall tale
Teaching
Teen-age
Teeth
Telephone
Television
Temper
Temperance

Thriller
Time
Tolerance
Toys
Transportation
Trees
Twins

U

United Nations

V

Valentine day
Vases
Vaudeville
Veterans day
Veterinary

Vitamin
Vocabulary
Vocational
Voting

W

Wales
War
Washing
Washington's birthday
Watch
Wealth
Weather
Weaver
Wedding
Week end
Weeping
West

Will
Wind
Winter cruise
Wish
Witch
Women
Words
Workers
Workhouse
World
Writers

Y

Youth

Youth & age

Z

Zoo